The Economic Development of the YEMEN ARAB REPUBLIC

RAGAEI EL MALLAKH

CROOM HELM
London • Sydney • Wolfeboro, New Hampshire

© 1986 Ragaei El Mallakh
Croom Helm Ltd, Provident House, Burrell Row,
Beckenham, Kent BR3 1AT
Croom Helm Australia Pty Ltd, Suite 4, 6th Floor,
64-76 Kippax Street, Surry Hills, NSW 2010 Australia

British Library Cataloguing in Publication Data

El Mallakh, Ragaei
　The economic development of the Yemen
　Arab Republic.
　1. Yemen — Economic conditions
　I. Title
　330.953'32053　　　　HC415.34
　ISBN 0-7099-0983-7

Croom Helm, 27 South Main Street,
Wolfeboro, New Hampshire 03894-2069

Library of Congress Cataloging in Publication Data

El Mallakh, Ragaei, 1925–
　The economic development of the Yemen Arab republic.
　1. Yemen—economic conditions. 2. Yemen—economic
policy. I. Title.
HC415.34.E4　　1986　　　338.953'32　　　86-8938
ISBN 0-7099-0983-7

Printed and bound in Great Britain
by Billing & Sons Limited, Worcester.

FOREWORD

The last decade in the economic development of the Yemen Arab Republic (YAR), or North Yemen as it is commonly called, is in stark contrast to the centuries of isolation that had marked the country prior to the 1962 Revolution. When economic planning was instituted in the 1970s, the nation was confronted by the needs of reconstruction, after years of conflict, and of development. With the First Five-Year Plan (1976/77-1980/81), the objectives and means for national development were put forward. North Yemen faced a formidable task in establishing basic infrastructure throughout a country with a widely dispersed population and having an extremely rugged—if beautiful—terrain. The Second Five-Year Plan (1982-1986) is now under way and, despite the worldwide recession in the early 1980s and two natural catastrophes of earthquake (1982) and drought (1983 and 1984), implementation is close to being on schedule. The Third Five-Year Plan (1987-1991), while in the draft stage in early 1986, has set the nation's development priorities to the end of the decade. One-fifth of the total anticipated investment is expected to go to infrastructure, continuing the emphasis of earlier plans. Energy-related investments will garner the lion's share—23 percent—with agriculture and industry earmarked for 15 percent of total investment during the 1987-1991 span. Among other sectors, services (including health and education) and housing and urban-related projects will jointly consume around one-fifth of the Third Plan investment. Over a quarter of the plan's cost must be met by foreign borrowing and grants.

The North Yemeni economy has been characterized by the phenomenon of short-term emigration of upwards of half of its labor force. The YAR has been the largest labor pool from which the Arabian Peninsula countries draw. (Preliminary unpublished figures of the census, concluded in early 1986, indicate the population of North Yemen has reached over 9.27 million.) Although predominantly oil rich, such nations as Saudi Arabia and the United Arab Emirates could not have met their development requirements without the contributions of Yemeni workers. The remittances of North Yemen's emigrant laborers were an important component in capital formation, particularly in the private sector. However, there is a vulnerability in this source of

iii

funds when demand for labor decreases in response to lower oil-generated revenues in the neighboring countries as, in fact, occurred in the early 1980s.

The return of North Yemeni workers need not be viewed as an altogether negative situation. The absence of a large portion of the work force has led to labor scarcity, especially in the critical agricultural sector, and has added to inflationary pressures. A gradual return of Yemenis from neighboring countries would be the optimal solution to North Yemen's labor shortages.

Indeed, gradualism would appear to be the most efficient approach as well to the development of the YAR's varied resources. The country has the largest population base in the Arabian Peninsula; it possesses a long-established agricultural sector, dating back to the ancient times of the Queen of Sheba. The topography and climate allow the cultivation of a myriad of crops. Its copper and other minerals hold potential for industrial development. And, most recently, discoveries of petroleum in substantial quantities provide a promising energy-sector base for domestic consumption and export.

North Yemen's geographical location along the Red Sea, its tradition of maritime trade, and the established links with the Arabian Peninsula and East Africa have combined to make the Yemeni population independent-minded, innovative, and open to contacts with the rest of the world—all of which is reflected in an open economy and a favorable environment for domestic and foreign investment.

In 1983 these attitudes and economic principles were embodied in the National Charter, whereby the individual is guaranteed personal and economic freedom. Government institutions are to be strengthened on both the local and national levels. The concept of a participatory citizenry was also advanced. The charter outlined a number of elements that will have a direct bearing on the nation's development, including: (1) equal opportunity; (2) freedom from poverty through the application of social justice; (3) the guarantee of private ownership; (4) support for free trade; (5) encouragement of cooperatives where appropriate to secure the benefits of greater economies of scale; (6) the upgrading of human and physical resources; and (7) continuing the emphasis on the agricultural sector. Finally, two factors bode well for the orderly development of the Yemen Arab Republic: the role given to free enterprise and the political stability of recent years.

Many people have given invaluable assistance, providing data and information, without which this study could not have been written:

H. E. Abdul Aziz Abdul-Ghani, Prime Minister; H. E. Mohsin A. Alaini, Ambassador of the Yemen Arab Republic to the United States; H. E. Mohamed Basendwah, Ambassador of the Mission of the Yemen Arab Republic to the United Nations; the following ministers and their staffs, Ahmed Al Mohanny (Petroleum and Mineral Resources), Dr. Mohammed Saeed Al Attar (Development), Dr. Abdul Karim Al Iriani (Foreign Affairs), Mohammed Al Khadem Al Wajih (Trade and Supply); Mohammed Anam Ghalib (Dean of the National Institute of Public Administration and President of the Yemeni Economic Association); Dr. Abdelaziz Al Saqqaf (University of Sana'a); Mohammed Sayedi (Director General of Geologic Surveys, Ministry of Petroleum and Mineral Resources); Dr. Hassan Makki (Deputy Prime Minister); Fathy Salim Ali (Deputy Chairman of the Central Planning Organization); former Yemen Arab Republic Ambassador to the United Nations Mohammed Sallam; and my students from North Yemen over many years, including Ameen Nouisser and Sammy Sallam. Acknowledgement also should be made of the valuable support for this study through a grant from The Hoover Institution at Stanford University, which allowed a leave of absence from teaching obligations for a semester.

In preparing the manuscript I have been assisted in research by the International Research Center for Energy and Economic Development staff: Dr. Dorothea H. El Mallakh, Elizabeth Isacke, Saad Khalil, David Koger, Kathleen O'Brien, and Lloyd Quist and by Senior Administrator Glenda Bolin.

Ragaei El Mallakh, Director
International Research Center for
Energy and Economic Development

To the memory of engineer and architect Yousef El Mallakh, whose many projects stand throughout the Middle East.

CONTENTS

Tables and Figures

Abbreviations/Acronyms

1. Introduction and Historical Outline — 1

2. Population and Labor Force — 15

3. Human Resources Development — 28

4. Infrastructure — 70

5. Agriculture — 92

6. Development of Industry — 121

7. International Linkages: Trade and Investment — 152

Selected Bibliography — 187

Index — 190

TABLES AND FIGURES

Tables

2

1	Total Population of the Yemen Arab Republic, 1975 Census and 1981 Census	16
2	Recorded Short-Term Yemeni Migrants in the Gulf States, 1975	17
3	Population Projections to 2000	18
4	Enumerated Population, Labor Force, and Crude Participation Rates for YAR Residents and Short-Term Yemeni Migrants, 1975	20
5	Educational Status of the Recorded Yemeni Population, 1975	21
6	Summary of Labor Force Deployment, 1975	23
7	Public Employment in the Central Administration by Grade, 1977 and 1980	23
8	Distribution of the Yemeni Labor Force by Occupation, 1975	25
9	Distribution of the Yemeni Labor Force by Economic Sector, 1975 and 1981	26

3

10	Breakdown of Student Enrollment Increases by Educational Level, First Five-Year Plan (1976-1981), 1982, 1983	30
11	Targeted Enrollment Increases, Second Five-Year Plan (1981-1986)	31
12	Registered Enrollments and Graduates (Yemeni) at University of Sana'a, 1970/71-1982/83	37
13	Yemeni and Non-Yemeni Teachers Distributed According to Educational Level, 1979/80-1982/83	39
14	Estimates of Recorded YAR Citizens in Selected Countries, February 1975	41
15	Private Transfers and National Disposable Income, 1971/72-1984	44
16	Selected Items in the Balance of Payments, 1973/74-1984	45
17	Changes in Manpower and Employment Structure	

	During the First Five-Year Plan	53
18	Planned Changes in Manpower and Employment Structure During the Second Five-Year Plan (1981-1986)	54
19	Balance of Additional Supply and Demand for Labor, Second Five-Year Plan (1982-1986)	56
20	Employment of Migrants in Saudi Arabia by Selected Years	60
21	Estimate of the Recorded North Yemeni Migrant Population and Labor Force in Saudi Arabia, 1969-1977	61
22	Expatriate Employment Shares by Skill Level in Saudi Arabia, 1974 and 1978	64

4

23	Population by Governorate and Capital City, 1975 and 1981	71
24	Yemen Airways Passenger Load, 1977-1983	80
25	Generation and Consumption of Electricity, 1975-1982	84
26	Investment in the Water and Electricity Sector, 1982-1986	89

5

27	Structure of Gross Domestic Product by Sector, 1971/72-1983	94
28	Value of YAR Agriculture-Based and Edible Exports and Imports, 1978/79-1982	105
29	Actual Agricultural Production and Targets During First Five-Year Plan, 1976/77-1980/81	108
30	Loan Disbursals by the Agricultural Credit Bank in YAR, 1976-1980	110
31	Base Year and Targeted Agricultural Production, 1981 and 1986	112
32	Agricultural Production Targets During the Second Five-Year Plan, 1982-1986	113
33	Allocation of Planned Investment in the Second Five-Year Plan	114
34	Land and Water Resource Development Projects, Second Five-Year Plan	115
35	Growth and Structure of YAR Gross Domestic Product (GDP), 1982-1984	117

6

36	Growth and Composition of Manufacturing Value Added	123
37	Output of Major Manufactured Products, 1978, 1980, 1982, 1983	124
38	Value of Energy Imports, 1979/80-1982	129
39	Projected Petroleum-Product Consumption, 1982-1990	131
40	Energy Consumption by Type of Fuel, 1979	132
41	Changes in Employment by Occupation/Skill Level and Sector, 1975 and 1981	146
42	Wages in Selected Occupations in the Modern Sector, 1980	148

7

43	Composition of Imports, 1973/74-1979/80	155
44	Imports by Groups to Yemen Arab Republic, 1979/80-1982	156
45	Imports by Major Supplying Countries, 1980-1982	160
46	Exports to Selected Countries, 1974/75-1982	164
47	Summary Balance of Payments, 1973/74-1984	168
48	Capital Flows, First Five-Year Plan	170
49	Balance of Payments in the Second Five-Year Plan (1982-1986)	172
50	Target Change in the Composition of Imports During the Second Five-Year Plan	174
51	Government External Loan Drawings by Sector, Three-Year Program (1973/74-1975/76)	178
52	Foreign Loans Position as of March 31, 1984	180
53	Summary of Public Finances, 1976-1984	183

Figures

1

1	Map of the Yemen Arab Republic and Region	2

4

2	Governorates and Population	72
3	Highway Network	75

ABBREVIATIONS/ACRONYMS

API	American Petroleum Institute (gravity for crude)
b/d	barrels per day
BP	British Petroleum
c.i.f.	cost, insurance, and freight
f.o.b.	free on board
hectare (ha)	2.47 acres or 10,000 square meters
GDP	gross domestic product
GNP	gross national product
I.D.A.	International Development Association, an affiliate of the World Bank
km	kilometer
KVA	kilovoltsamperes
KW	kilowatt
kWh	kilowatt-hour
LDA	Local Development Association
liwa	governorate
mm	millimeter
MW	megawatt
P.D.R.Y.	People's Democratic Republic of Yemen (Aden, also called South Yemen)
SITC	standard industrial trade classification
TDA	Tihama Development Authority
YAR	Yemen Arab Republic, also called North Yemen
YGEC	Yemen General Electric Corporation
YIB	Yemen Industrial Bank
YOC	Yemen Oil Company
YOMINCO	Yemen Oil and Minerals Corporation
YR	(North) Yemeni rial. Before February 1973 U.S. $1 = 5.00 YR; February 1973 to February 15, 1984 U.S. $1 = 4.500 YR; after February 15, 1984 devaluation U.S. $1 = 4.719 YR; U.S. $1 = 4.925 YR (March 1984); and U.S. $1 = 6.5 YR (June 1985).

1 INTRODUCTION AND HISTORICAL OUTLINE

The Land and People

The Yemen Arab Republic (YAR, also known as North Yemen) is located on the southwest corner of the Arabian Peninsula, bordered to the north and east by the Kingdom of Saudi Arabia and to the south by the People's Democratic Republic of Yemen. The western edge of the YAR is formed by the Red Sea and runs down from the Asir province of Saudi Arabia to the narrow strait of Bab El Mandeb which stretches 15 miles across to the tip of Ethiopia (figure 1).

North Yemen's topography can be divided into two distinct regions: the coastal plain, or Tihama, and the mountainous central highlands of the interior. This latter rich agricultural region eventually gives way to an expanse of desert that runs into the border with Saudi Arabia. The climate in the highlands is considered the best in all Arabia, similar to that of eastern Africa, with a warm, temperate, and rainy summer and a cool, moderately dry winter that brings occasional frost and some snow to the mountains. YAR's rainfall is dependent on its position on the northern rim of the Indian Ocean monsoon system at two summer maxima, one during April and May, and a second lasting from July through September. Rainfall in any given year is far from certain. As much as 35 inches of rain may fall annually on the higher parts of the interior, with 15 to 20 inches over much of the plateau. The Tihama, on the other hand, is relatively dry, receiving on the average only 5 inches of rainfall annually, often in the form of brief downpours. This situation creates a phenomenon of perennial streams and rivers in the highlands that fail to run their course into the coastal plain, which is exacerbated in the summer months by temperatures in the Tihama that swell into the hundreds, causing rapid evaporation of the surface water. Temperatures in the highlands range from 60° Farenheit to 70° Farenheit during the rainy season to below freezing for some periods in the winter. Temperatures on the coast remain fairly warm throughout the year.

Because of this climatic gradation, from desert to temperate conditions, the Yemen Arab Republic has a similar gradation of crops and

2 *Introduction and Historical Outline*

Figure 1: Map of the Yemen Arab Republic and Region

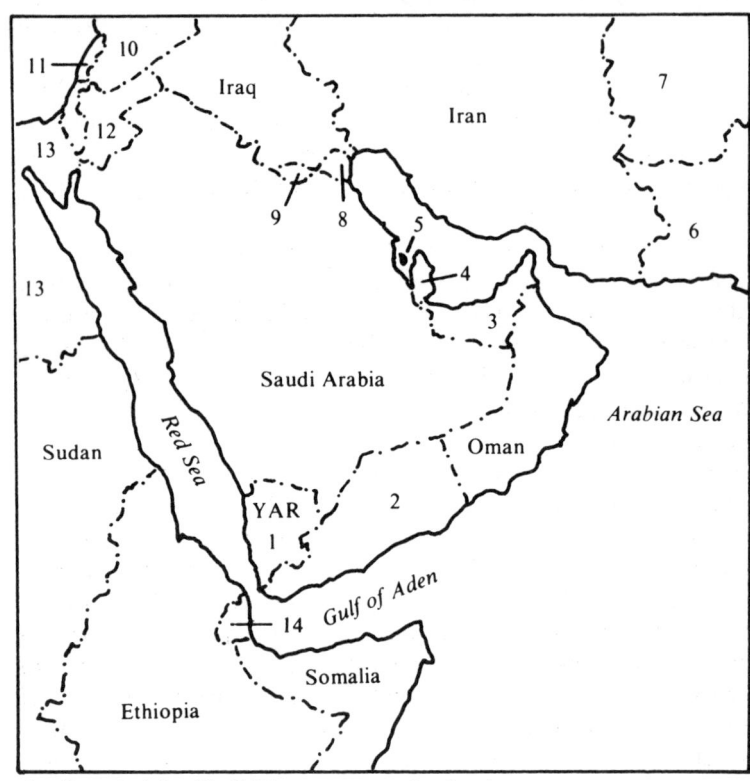

1 — Yemen Arab Republic (YAR)
2 — People's Democratic Republic of Yemen
3 — United Arab Emirates
4 — Qatar
5 — Bahrain
6 — Pakistan
7 — Afghanistan
8 — Kuwait
9 — Neutral Zone (Kuwait/Saudi Arabia)
10 — Syrian Arab Republic
11 — Lebanon
12 — Jordan
13 — Arab Republic of Egypt
14 — Djibouti

Source: Based upon map in World Bank, *Yemen Arab Republic: Development of a Traditional Economy* **(Washington, D.C.: World Bank, 1979).**

vegetation. The highlands are characterized by scattered trees and grassland and support such crops as its world-famous coffee, the exclusive Yemen *qat*, cereals, and certain varieties of vegetables. Lower down, along the plateau, fruit can be produced along with crops like millet. On the coastal plain irrigation water may provide the proper conditions for such diverse items as cotton and bananas. Sorghum and dates are also cultivated here. As a result of these relatively benevolent conditions, North Yemen possesses more arable land than any other country on the peninsula.

Total land area of the Yemen Arab Republic is nearly 75,000 square miles, supporting a population, including expatriate workers and other nationals abroad, of 8.6 million according to the census taken in 1981 and of 9.27 million in the preliminary 1986 census. The state is divided into 11 governorates or *liwas* which are broken down into districts (*kadas*) and subdistricts (*nahayas*). The capital of North Yemen is the ancient and picturesque city of Sana'a, the traditional center of Yemeni government. Sana'a had an estimated population in 1981 of 279,395 and is located in the central highlands at an elevation of approximately 7,300 feet. In but five years, the capital's population is estimated to have increased by almost 70 percent, reaching around 474,000 in 1986. As with other developing countries, the YAR is experiencing a rural-to urban population shift, further quickened by returning expatriate workers. Other principal cities are Taiz in the southern highlands with a population in 1981 of 116,382, and the port city of Hodeidah, a thriving metropolis of nearly 126,427 in the same year.[1] About three-quarters of North Yemen's citizens live in numerous small villages or agricultural communities. The Yemenis are Arabs and adhere to the Islamic faith.

The Yemen Arab Republic is governed by a president who is also supreme commander of the armed forces, a vice president, and a prime minister who oversees a cabinet of ministers.[2] The Yemeni citizens are represented by a 159-member constituent People's Council, 30 members of which are currently nominated by the president and the remaining 129 are elected. Each *liwa* is supervised by a governor, also presidentially appointed. The People's Council passes and amends laws and ratifies treaties by a simple majority and can override a presidential veto by a two-thirds vote. North Yemen's judicial system consists both of civil courts, designed to settle business disputes, and of Islamic courts that handle areas of more traditional concern. Yemen's present constitution was ratified in 1972 and establishes the state as one based on the Islamic Shari'a as the source of all laws.

Ancient History

The modern state of the Yemen Arab Republic possesses a rich cultural and historical heritage that is distinctive among the nations of Arabia. North Yemen derives its name from its geographical location on the peninsula. North Yemen, or Al Yaman in Arabic, means "to the right" as one faces to the east. From that standpoint, North Yemen was "to the right" or "south." Roman, Greek, and medieval Arab sources referred to Al Yaman as "Arabia Felix," "Eudaimon Arabia," and "As Saida," all translated as "fortunate, happy Arabia." It is presumed that this designation resulted from the view that the region, with its prosperous trade centers, precious metals and spices, and fertile valleys, was indeed a happy place compared with the then more foreboding areas of the peninsula. It may have also resulted from linguistic confusion between the Arabic word *yumn* which meant "happy" and *yaman* which meant "right."

Whatever the correct origin of that term may have been, Al Yaman could have been considered fortunate during the period it flourished as a trading center for the empires of Rome and Egypt. A succession of four prosperous and highly developed kingdoms were established there by Semitic peoples who invaded Al Yaman and its indigenous population about 1000 B.C. The first of these was the Minean Kingdom (13th to 7th centuries B.C.) founded by elements of a civilization presumably from the banks of today's Arabian/Persian Gulf. The Mineans gave way around 650 B.C. to the Sabeans. It is Saba, or, as called in various religious texts, Sheba from whence came the fabled Queen who it is popularly assumed visited the court of King Solomon of ancient Israel. Sabean dominion (ca. 9th century to 115 B.C.) is divided into two eras, the first lasting nearly 300 years during which time the famous stone and earthen dam at Marib was constructed. The huge dam was a marvelous technological achievement—evidence of a highly advanced society—and serviced an extensive irrigation system that fed numerous agricultural projects throughout the kingdom.[3] During this period the city of Marib served as the capital of Saba. The second era of Sabean rule began around 550 B.C. and lasted until 115 B.C. This was a period of expansion for Saba as expeditions sent out from the Red Sea ports established a number of colonies in Ethiopia and Eritrea. The Sabean kingdom existed concurrently with the kingdoms of Hadramut and Qataban.

Although the Sabeans were able to subdue the entire region of Al Yaman, the Kings of Himyar or the Himyarites (115 B.C.–525 A.D.)

gradually grew stronger.[4] The Himyarites were converts to Judaism and Al Yaman remained largely Jewish until the final invasion by Ethiopian Christians in 525 A.D. It is during this Himyarite era that the long history of Sana'a as the capital of Yemen began.

When the Ethiopians conquered Yemen, the indigenous Arab tribes called on the Persian Empire to rescue them. This was accomplished in 574 A.D. and North Yemen was then established as a Persian protectorate. It remained so until 628 A.D. when the Persian viceroy accepted the Islamic faith and Yemen thus became part of the new Arabian Empire.

Early Islam

The area of today's North Yemen had accepted the tenets of Islam during the lifetime of the Prophet Mohammed and Yemeni tribesmen played an active role in the establishment of the Islamic faith throughout the Near East and North Africa. At the time of the Prophet's death in 642 A.D., the Muslim community split over the issue of choosing his successor. The majority favored selection by popular consensus while others believed the rightful successor to be the Prophet's son-in-law, 'Ali. His followers eventually became known as the Shi'a 'Ali or "party of 'Ali." While the initial separation was a result of a political controversy, the Shi'a later developed a divergent religious doctrine as well. The majority of Muslims were referred to as the Sunni, following the *sunna* or "the beaten path." The Sunni-Shi'a division remains in the Islamic world and within North Yemen today.

The Shi'a Muslim world eventually became divided within itself as various factions split off from the main line theology over the issue of succession. One of these sects, the Hashemites, established themselves as the rulers of Yemen, creating a dynasty that was to last, with some interruptions, for over 1,000 years beginning in the year 893 A.D. In that year violent intratribal conflict was occurring in the city of Saadah. The leaders of the warring factions eventually recognized the urgent need for a mediator to help them settle their differences and called on a noted Medina jurist to send someone to settle the conflict. They agreed in turn to obey whatever the Imam would prescribe, no matter the cost. The Imam sent his grandson, Al Hadi Yahya Bin Al Husayn. Though establishing initially only governorship over Saadah, Al Hadi's decendents would eventually become the sole rulers of North Yemen until the establishment of the republic in 1962.

The Imamate and Ottoman Occupation

The period between the birth of the Hashemite dynasty and the eventual eviction of suzerain foreign powers from North Yemen in 1918 was marked by both internal and external forces struggling to secure governance over the strategic corner of Arabia. The last of these imperial powers, and by far the one with the most lasting effects, was the Turkish Ottoman Empire. The Ottoman occupation brought North Yemen out of its centuries of relative isolation and into the game of geopolitical chess between the world powers of the day. In the thirteenth century the Rassuli Dynasty (c. 1232–c. 1454) established control over an area that stretched from the present Tihama through Aden to Dhofar. The Rassulis fell in the fifteenth century. It was not until 1545, when the Ottoman Turks entered the region, that the presence of another unifier was felt.

In response to Portuguese threats from positions in the Red Sea and the Indian Ocean, the Mameluke Sultan of Egypt invaded North Yemen in 1514; however, by 1517 the Ottoman Turks invaded Egypt and subsequently captured the port of Aden (South Yemen) in the south in 1538 and Taiz in 1545. Soon thereafter, a Turkish pasha was installed at the North Yemen capital in Sana'a. But the Turks were never able to decisively subjugate the mountains. Upon the Turks' departure in 1636, the Imam came out of the northern mountains, captured Sana'a, and unified the mountains and the plain into a single state.

The Egyptian ruler Mohammad Ali invaded North Yemen in 1849, and in 1871 the Ottomans captured Sana'a in response to threats to the coffee trade in the region. The Turks tried to contain the Zeidi tribes in the north led by Mohammed Bin Yahya of the Hamid Al Din family who was chosen Imam in 1891. Imam Mohammed's son, Imam Yahya, continued the struggle against the Turks. Eventually the Turks had to come to terms with Imam Yahya. Under the Treaty of Da'an, Imam Yahya was recognized as the head of the northern community with the right to collect taxes, appoint administrators and judges, and receive an annual subsidy from the Ottoman court. In effect, this treaty divided Yemen into its northern-southern areas, with the Imam in the mountains and the Turks ruling the southern plain. Ottoman occupation was eventually terminated at the end of World War I when, by treaty, the Turks had to withdraw from North Yemen and Arabia. Imam Yahya was then in a position to reconquer the southern areas and by 1918 united both parts of the area into the unit known today as North Yemen.

The Imamate, 1918-1962

After the unification of 1918, North Yemen was ruled by the Imams until the Revolution of 1962. Imam Yahya (ruled 1904-1948) and Imam Ahmad (ruled 1948-1962) consolidated their position through two policies which eventually led to their collapse. First, the Imams maintained their control by strengthening key social relations under themselves and by excluding, as much as possible, foreign influences that might challenge these relations. Second, the army was divided into a royal corps derived from loyal tribes and a regular army used for less-sensitive activities. Both groups were drawn from the northern tribes, particularly from the Hashed confederation. However, an element of instability was introduced when Iraqis and then Egyptians were brought into North Yemen to train the Yemen army after a 1934 experiment which sent Yemeni officers to Iraq for training. These foreign officers introduced the same nationalist ideas as had the Yemeni officers trained in Iraq.

Under Imam Ahmad the checks and balances in the government structure were arranged to prevent the emergence of any independent authority which could contradict the leadership of the Imam. A capital city was not established. The foreign ministry, a main palace, chief merchants, and the British diplomatic mission were in Taiz, close to their contacts in Aden. The Crown Prince, other ministries, and the Egyptian and Italian delegations were in Sana'a.

North Yemen remained relatively isolated from world politics and economics both because the Imams wanted to keep the world out and because foreign nations had no strong economic or strategic incentive to enter the country.

One of the few exceptions to this trend came in the summer of 1956 when Iman Ahmad allowed his son Crown Prince Muhammad Al Badr to tour the communist countries, establishing diplomatic relations with the Soviet Union and China and signing an agreement with Moscow for the import of Russian arms. In October 1956 the first Soviet freighter arrived at the port of Salif with a cargo of arms and ammunition.[5] By the end of 1958 there were 500 Russian technicians and instructors in North Yemen and another 1,000 Chinese working on the Sana'a-Hodeidah road.[6] The Imam was careful, however, to restrict the activities of these foreigners within the country so that they never managed to establish themselves outside the three major towns of Sana'a, Taiz, and Hodeidah.

Foreign trade reflected this relationship. North Yemen's 1961 exports were estimated to be $8.2 million (out of a gross national product of $300 million), of which coffee was 49 percent and cotton was 19 percent of the total. Total imports were valued at $17 million, of which 29 percent was food, 7 percent tobacco, and 17 percent textiles.[7] North Yemen was exporting primary products in order to import other primary products rather than manufactured goods.

No foreign capital was invested in North Yemen and no foreign control of production was present except through purchases from abroad, which represented only a marginal element in North Yemen's total production. The deficit in its foreign trade was partly filled by remittances from Yemenis abroad, numbering between 80,000 and 100,000 in Aden alone by 1962.[8]

There was also a lack of financial institutions and essential public structures. The only bank that operated in North Yemen before 1962 was the Saudi National Commercial Bank. The only currency was the Maria Theresa Thaler. There was no distinction between the Imam's private purse and the country's treasury since he was both the religious and secular leader. There was also no distinct cabinet or legislative body. The law was based on both the Shari'a and tribal custom.

Traditional opposition in North Yemen is tribal, religious, and dynastic. Imam Ahmad had suppressed the outward signs of opposition but inward resentment increased. Most of Imam Ahmad's dynastic rivals had been disposed of by 1955 but Crown Prince Badr had a rival for succession in the Imam's brother Prince Hassan, who was North Yemen's United Nations representative. Tribally, the Imam's support was strong for he had the loyalty of the two great tribes of the north: Hashed and Bakil.

Among the modern opposition were a few officers and intellectuals who harbored revolutionary principles, a few businessmen, and a large group of more-or-less detribalized townsfolk, especially in Sana'a, Taiz, and Hodeidah. Outside the country there was an organization known as the "Free Yemenis" that advocated a republican regime.

The Republic

Upon Imam Ahmad's death on September 18, 1962, Crown Prince Badr proclaimed himself Imam. However, Colonel Abdullah Al Sallal led a military coup on September 26, 1962 and gave the country the name of the Yemen Arab Republic. Many sectors of the Yemen society responded enthusiastically. The southern merchants, North Yemeni migrant workers in Aden, the Free Yemenis in Cairo and Aden, some northern tribes in the mountains, and the Hashed confederation led by Abdullah Al Ahmar supported the republic.

The Revolution of 1962 introduced modernization of the Yemeni economy. The first actions of the republic were to form a cabinet and to enact a series of reforms. The new government created a new currency, set up the Yemen Reconstruction and Development Bank, and encouraged the return of capital. A number of Egyptian advisers in 1963 and 1964 supervised the replacement of the Imam's government with about two dozen ministries and other government agencies, as well as a number of mixed public-private economic enterprises.

From October 1962 to the summer of 1968 the Imamist forces (or Royalists) and the Republicans were engaged in a civil war; it was transformed into an international affair through the direct or indirect intervention of foreign countries, notably Egypt, Saudi Arabia, the Soviet Union, and the United States.

The Al Sallal regime was replaced by a group under the titular leadership of Qadi Abdul Rahman Al Iryani in November 1967. The evolution of the Yemen policy during this era—restoration of civilian supremacy, the national reconciliation of 1970, the promulgation of an Egyptian-style constitution, and the inauguration of the government at the end of 1972—constituted a progressive reassertion of the traditional loci of social and political power.[9]

The Al Iryani regime made only two attempts at establishing political institutions or entities. One was the creation of an official political party, the National Yemeni Union, in early 1973 with President Al Iryani as leader. The other consisted of the establishment of the Consultative Council. The Permanent Constitution of the Yemen Arab Republic provided for a 159-member, largely elected legislature (National Assembly).[10] The first general election in the Yemen Arab Republic's history was held on March 10, 1971.[11] Important sheikhs were given key consultative, executive, and administrative positions, thus incorporating tribal elements into the government. A United Nations report described the multibased power of the sheikh governors:

> Several Governors remain powerful because of their tribal leadership, maintain almost complete independence from the central administration and report directly to the Republican Council (i.e., to President Al Iryani and two others). Their power and influence not only dominate the life of the people of their tribe, which administratively belongs to a different

province, but also of those in the province over which they have administrative authority.13

Institutions established before the end of the Al Iryani era—among them the Central Bank, the Ministry of Finance, and the Central Planning Organization—increased the capability of the state for economic and financial management and development planning. The Central Bank made possible the creation of a commercial banking system in 1972 and the Ministry of Finance began to subject government expenditures to modern budgetary procedures in 1974. The Central Planning Organization, created in 1972, established itself as the government's locus for the formulation of development policies and as its principal point of contact with foreign aid donors and contractors. By early 1974, the Central Planning Organization completed both the final draft of the Three-Year Program (1973/74-1975/76)—the country's first economic development plan—and most of the preparatory work for the first population census.

A number of important development projects were also initiated by the end of the Al Iryani regime. Improvements in transportation and communications systems were the regime's most important accomplishments. Considerable basic construction—schools, medical facilities, and public buildings—was undertaken in the cities and towns. Of a longer-term nature, the Tihama Development Authority was created and planning began on other agricultural schemes, including the Southern Uplands Rural Development Project.

In June 1974, a ten-member military command council assumed power in a bloodless coup under Colonel Ibrahim Mohammed Al Hamdi and ushered in the "Corrective Movement." The cabinet was formed in 1975. Al Hamdi made a determined effort to unify the country and assert an independent Yemeni foreign policy. On October 11, 1977, Lieutenant Colonel Ahmed Hussein Al Ghashmi, a northerner and a member of the Command Council, took over and presented a continuation of the Corrective Movement following Al Hamdi's death. A new assembly was called in March 1978 and in April the assembly elected Al Ghashmi President for a five-year term. In May of that year the cabinet was reformed under Abdul Aziz Abdul-Ghani, the Prime Minister. However, on June 24, 1978, President Al Ghashmi was assassinated. The presidency was replaced briefly by a four-man command council under former Minister of Finance Abdul Karim Al Arishi, who had been nominated speaker of the assembly. In mid-July 1978, Lieutenant Colonel Ali Abdullah Salih was elected president.

President Salih has been striving to achieve national unity against the backdrop of traditional geographical, religious, and tribal fragmentation. Progress toward national unity has materialized in the context of the National Charter endorsed in August 1982, the reinstatement of the original constitution in that year, the General People's Congress, and the Constituent People's Assembly (parliament). Elections for the Constituent People's Assembly were scheduled for early 1983, but were postponed.

The Salih government has managed to handle a number of difficult conditions while still pressing development goals and providing stability and security. In the economic sphere, the late 1970s and the first year of the 1980s stand as the high water mark for the neighboring oil-exporting nations of the Arabian Peninsula. This was reflected in greater availability of foreign assistance from these countries and high demand for Yemeni expatriate labor which, in turn, led to higher levels of remittances. The 1980s have not been so benevolent to the region, given the long worldwide recession and downward pressure on oil prices. Nonetheless, the Salih administration has been able to meet the critical development targets through careful management and the fact that the targets themselves were realistic.

Under President Salih a number of significant developments have been implemented or initiated. In the agricultural sector, water resources have received a high priority, epitomized by the construction of a new dam at Marib, the site of its ancient predecessor. The planning process has been continued and strengthened; the Second Five-Year Plan is nearing its end in 1986 with creditable results under difficult global economic circumstances and the Third Plan will be inaugurated in 1987. Development has been achieved without incurring the kind of crippling debt burden that now hampers many of the developing nations. Finally, encouragement of foreign participation in exploration for the YAR's natural resources has proven successful, specifically in the petroleum sector. The positive results in 1984 for the first exploration well brought North Yemen into the oil-producer group. With reserves still being assessed and the time lag for commercialization, the Salih government is using a cautious and balanced approach to developing this sector within the overall framework of national growth.

Unification of the Yemen Arab Republic and the People's Democratic Republic of Yemen (South Yemen) was first broached in 1972; progress has been sporadic. A great number of decisions and agreements have been reached pertaining more to the economic aspect than the political aspect of such a merger. A joint transport company has been established which has been operating bus service between the capitals of Aden and Sana'a. The Yemen Tourism Corporation has been charged with the task of attracting more visitors, particularly to the YAR. Numerous commissions have been created to pursue coordination of policies in such areas as economic affairs, planning and mineral resources, and defense and security, among others. The goal is eventual unification or coordination of policy development.

The obstacles to greater cooperation may either individually or collectively provide formidable contention such that a formal merger of the two nations may never be realized. One such hindrance to unity concerns the matter of East-West alignments. The People's Democratic Republic of Yemen (P.D.R.Y.) has a 20-year friendship treaty with the Soviet Union as well as a similar arrangement with other Eastern bloc countries. The Yemen Arab Republic, on the other hand, has adopted a policy of neutrality and hence maintains limited relations with both Western and Eastern bloc countries.[14]

Another point of potential friction in any merger concerns the role of government. Actual unification of the two countries if it were to occur would, by definition, require the downgrading of national autonomy.

Similar to Oman's position on the Strait of Hormouz and on the Gulf of Oman (which could provide an alternate terminal for oil exports of the Arab Gulf states), the YAR's position near the entrance to the Red Sea gives the country added importance because of (a) the increased Soviet involvement in Ethiopia and the P.D.R.Y. and (b) the Red Sea-Suez Canal oil-transit route. Under these circumstances, the government of the YAR has sought to pursue a policy of nonalignment which will prevent the country from being dragged into either regional or superpower rivalries.

While the fact that the Yemen Arab Republic is an active participant in world economic activity may be somewhat obscured, the country indeed is directly and indirectly involved and, in turn, is affected by the international economic environment. Linkages to the world economy exist via Yemenis employed abroad, the country's imports of goods and services from a variety of nations, the exports of its internationally recognized coffee as well as other agricultural products, the inflow of aid monies, its geographical location at the mouth of the Red Sea, and finally, the recent successful oil exploration activities.

The economy of the Yemen Arab Republic has experienced in the past few years a forward momentum propelled by foreign aid receipts and remittances from the large pool of Yemenis employed

Introduction and Historical Outline 13

abroad. During this boom period (1975 to 1980), the government-initiated policies to undertake economic development utilizing the available stock of local productive resources. The three national development plans enacted emphasize this strategy. The premise for this strategy is the realization that the market for their export of labor will eventually dwindle. The following chapters will highlight these strategies and the results so far achieved over the course of the Three-Year Program (1973/74 to 1975/76), the First Five-Year Plan (1976/77 to 1980/81), and the expectations of the Second Five-Year Plan (1982 to 1986). The Third Five-Year Plan (1987-1991), which in early 1986 was moving toward the final draft stage, continues to reflect the critical role of foreign aid despite the petroleum-related activities that may prove decisive to the country as the decade of the eighties closes.

Notes

1. Yemen Arab Republic, The Confederation of Yemeni Development Associations, Central Planning Organization, Statistics Department, *Summary, Final Results of the Cooperative Population Census*, February 1981, p. 9. Although certain figures are given from the 1986 census, throughout this study the primary statistics utilized are from the 1981 census. There have been only preliminary announcements released on overall findings of the 1986 census; the official publication of the complete results, including breakdowns into categories and activities, is expected to be available in 1987.

2. Earlier, there had been two vice presidents for domestic and international affairs, respectively.

3. Gradual silting led to the dam's destruction some 1,400 years ago. Both the *Bible* (I Kings 10:2) and the *Koran* (XXVII:20-24 and XXXIV:15-16) relate the prosperity of Saba based upon trade and agriculture. The bird (a hoopoe) sent by Solomon with an invitation to the Queen of Sheba still is found in the Marib area. Ancient Marib was the largest of the cities along the "incense" trail from South Arabia to Petra in modern Jordan. Archaeological work is continuing to expand the knowledge of the cultures in pre-Islamic South Arabia. See, for example, Thomas J. Abercrombie, "Arabia's Frankincense Trail," *National Geographic*, October 1985, pp. 475-513 and Raymond D. Tindel, "Zafar: Archaeology in the Land of Frankincense and Myrrh," *Archaeology*, March/April 1984, pp. 40-45.

4. The Himyarite rulers frequently used the title King of Saba and Lord of Raydan. Raydan referred to the royal palace at Zafar, the ancient site a few kilometers south of modern Yarim. This period is well described in Raymond D. Tindel, op. cit.

5. David Holden, *Farewell to Arabia* (New York: Walker and Company, 1966), p. 51.

6. Ibid., p. 92.

7. M. Said Al Attar, *Le Sous-develop economique et social du Yemen* (Algiers, 1964), cited in Fred Halliday, *Arabia Without Sultans* (New York: Vintage Books, 1974), p. 102.

8. Fred Halliday, op. cit., p. 41.

9. Robert W. Stookey, "Social Structure and Politics in the Yemen Arab Republic," *The Middle East Journal*, summer 1974, p. 249.

10. "The Permanent Constitution of the Yemen Arab Republic," chapter IV, reprinted in the *The Middle East Journal*, summer 1971, p. 392.

11. Georges Pasteur, "Yemen: Liberation nationale, unification et probleme de classe,"

Cahiers du Communisme, April 1973, p. 98, cited in Patrick Labaune, "Tribal Democracy and the Political System in the Yemen Arab Republic," *Revue Francaise de Science Politique*, August 1981, p. 753 (in French) offers insights on the 1971 election.

12. Fred Halliday, op. cit., p. 126.

13. United Nations Development Program, *Background Paper for a Country Programme for the Yemen Arab Republic* (Sana'a: United Nations Development Program, March 1973), p. 13, mimeo, cited in Robert Burrowes, *Political Construction in the Yemen Arab Republic: An Imperative for the Late 1970s*, prepared for the U. S. Department of State, External Research Program, p. 18.

14. Moreover, a recent survey on North Yemen in *The Financial Times* (London), November 26, 1984, points out that the YAR is basically a free-enterprise economy while South Yemen is "the only genuinely Communist state in the Arab world—though it is not now as radical as it was a few years ago." It should also be noted that in September 1984 the Yemen Arab Republic signed a friendship treaty with the U.S.S.R., in line with its policy of avoiding a single alignment with the West or East only. This agreement was, in fact, a renewal of the 20-year treaty first signed in 1964.

2 POPULATION AND LABOR FORCE

Population

The population census undertaken by North Yemen's Central Planning Organization in 1975 placed the total resident population in the country at 5,258,530. Though this census suffered problems of undernumeration for both technical and social reasons, it marked an important step forward in development planning. The 1975 census, which represented the first attempt to formulate an accurate demographic profile of North Yemen, sought information on population by governorate, age, sex, marital status, education, occupation, and the economic activity sector of employment. As a source of much-needed statistical data, the 1975 census greatly enhanced manpower planning in North Yemen.

A more recent census was undertaken in 1981 by the Confederation of Yemeni Development Associations. This census placed the 1981 resident population at 7,161,851. Both the 1975 Central Planning Organization (CPO) and the 1981 Confederation of Yemeni Development Associations (CYDA) censuses are presented in table 1. The 1975 census remains the major source of demographic information.

The Yemeni population is highly mobile and has an established tradition of emigration. The development of the oil economies of the Arabian Peninsula has enhanced this mobility and has resulted in substantial short-term migration from North Yemen. In 1975, 421,180 Yemeni citizens resided in the neighboring countries of Saudi Arabia, Kuwait, the United Arab Emirates, Bahrain, and Qatar. The majority of these recorded short-term migrants, 97 percent, resided in Saudi Arabia. The distribution of recorded short-term Yemeni migrants is detailed in table 2.

The number of recorded short-term migrants represents only a fraction of the total Yemeni short-term emigration. That is, it represents only those Yemenis who are duly recorded as residing in the host country. Table 2, then, serves not as an accurate measure of the level of short-term emigration but rather as a rough sketch of the deployment of Yemeni migrants on the Arabian Peninsula. What table 2 also reveals is the high degree of interdependence between the economies of Saudi

Population and Labor Force

Table 1: Total Population of the Yemen Arab Republic, 1975 Census and 1981 Census

Category	1975 Census	1981 Census
Recorded population within country	540,230	6,226,921
Population of uncovered areas	294,500	—
Undernumeration for technical reasons	260,000	387,191
Undernumeration for social reasons	163,800	318,471
Recorded migrants within the country	—	229,268
Total resident population	5,258,530	7,161,851
Short-term migrants outside Yemen	740,400	837,073[a]
Long-term migrants outside Yemen	493,600	558,050
Total population	6,492,530	8,556,974
Total population excluding long-term migrants	5,998,930	7,998,924

[a] Assumes the proportion of short-term migrants in the total migrant population has remained constant at the 1975 level of 60 percent.

Sources: Yemen Arab Republic, Central Planning Organization, Statistics Department, *Statistical Year Book, 1979-1980*, p. 39, and World Bank, *Manpower Development in the Yemen Arab Republic* (Washington, D.C.: World Bank, 1981), p. 110.

Arabia and North Yemen. The official estimate of the number of short-term Yemeni migrants is given by the 1975 census as 740,400. If the distribution of recorded Yemeni migrants is taken as a measure of the deployment of all Yemeni short-term migrants, then 717,800 Yemenis can be seen as residing in Saudi Arabia in 1975. Other estimates, based upon imputed sex ratios, remittances, passport entries, and arrival/departure data, put the number of short-term Yemeni migrants as high as 845,000 in 1975. Interviews with Yemeni officials lead to the conclusion that the official estimate of short-term Yemeni migrants in the 1975 census represents an accurate picture of short-term Yemeni emigration. In this sense, the Central Planning Organization's estimate takes into account both the recorded emigration as well as the signifi-

Table 2: Recorded Short-Term Yemeni Migrants in the Gulf States, 1975

Country	Number
Saudi Arabia	409,653
Kuwait	4,683
United Arab Emirates	2,944
Bahrain	2,000
Qatar	1,900
Total	421,180

Source: World Bank, *Manpower Development in the Yemen Arab Republic* (Washington, D.C.: World Bank, 1981), pp. 112-116.

cant level of illegal emigration.

The official estimate of the total population of the Yemen Arab Republic from the 1975 Central Planning Organization census is 6,492,530. If long-term migrants are excluded from total population, this figure is reduced to 5,998,930.

The total population of the Yemen Arab Republic for 1981 given by the Confederation of Yemeni Development Associations census is 8,556,974. This figure, however, includes both short- and long-term migrants. The estimate of long-term emigration in 1981 is unavailable. However, if we assume the ratio of short- and long-term migrants has remained constant at the 1975 level, then the estimate of short-term emigration for 1981 would be 837,073, as shown in table 1. The resulting estimate of the total population of North Yemen, excluding long-term migrants, would be 7,998,924.

The official estimate of North Yemen's population growth rate was 2.5 percent in 1975.[1] This assumes a crude birth rate of 45 births per 1,000 women of child-bearing age and a death rate of 20 per 1,000 people. Population projections through the year 2000 based upon a constant 2.5 percent population growth rate are given in table 3. A World Bank study foresees an increasing population growth rate through the end of the century. Improved health conditions, increased health services, and better infant care are cited as leading to increased

Table 3: Population Projections to 2000

Projection	1981	1986	1990	2000
Total population	7,998,925a	9,050,050	9,989,560	12,787,480
Average annual growth rate (%)		2.5	2.5	2.5

aExcludes long-term migrants.

bThe World Bank assumes a 2.9 percent annual rate of population growth in "Yemen Arab Republic Country Economic Memorandum Current Position and Prospects," Report no. 5621-YAR (Washington, D.C., June 25, 1985), p. 51 (mimeographed), resulting in a projection of 12,326,000 for the year 2000 and using a 1981 base of 7,239,000.

Source: International Research Center for Energy and Economic Development (ICEED) estimates based upon an assumed 2.5 percent average annual growth rate.

life expectancy, reduced infant mortality, and hence a rising population growth rate.[2] To the extent that the population growth rate exceeds 2.5 percent, the figures in table 3 will understate true population growth. Population remains an issue which has yet to be viewed as requiring serious study by and the attention of the YAR government.

The outstanding characteristics of the Yemeni population in 1975 were its relative youth, low educational and skill attainment, and rural agricultural base. In 1975, 80 percent of the population was under age 40, 50 percent was under age 20, and 34 percent was under age 10.[3]

In addition to youth, the Yemeni population was characterized by a relatively low level of educational achievement. Only 1.1 percent of the Yemeni population age 10 or over held an educational certificate for primary or higher educational achievement.[4] In all, 82.6 percent of the recorded population of North Yemen was illiterate.[5] For males age 10 or over, 65 percent were illiterate as were 97.3 percent of the females in the same age group. These statistics reflect the recent introduction of a modern educational system in North Yemen. Both the First and the Second Five-Year Plans have focused on increased educational enrollment and retention through the higher levels of educational achievement.

The resident population can also be characterized as predominantly rural and engaged in the agricultural sector. In 1975 only 7.6 percent of the population lived in the seven major cities with populations of 10,000 or more;[6] an additional 3.5 percent of the resident population lived in towns with populations of 2,000 to 10,000.[7] As noted earlier, the majority of Yemenis are engaged primarily in agriculture, in a production-for-use type of economy. About 70.9 percent of the Yemeni labor force list their occupation as agricultural, while 73.6 percent of Yemeni workers are engaged in the agricultural sector.[8] Nonetheless, the YAR is undergoing rapid urban population growth (8.3 percent between 1970 and 1982, the third highest in the world), a factor that can have major implications for the nation's development.[9] This would translate into the share of the urban population rising from 14 percent in 1982 to around 35 percent in the year 2000.

Labor Force

A breakdown of the 1975 labor force and crude participation rate for the recorded domestic population as well as recorded short-term migrants is presented in table 4. The recorded Yemeni labor force of 1,390,669 is predominantly male, accounting for 90 percent of the recorded labor force. The crude participation rate for resident males age 10 years and over is fairly high: 74.4 percent. On the other hand, the economic participation rate for resident women age 10 years and over is low, only 8.3 percent. The overall economic activity rate for the resident population aged 10 years and over is 38.6 percent. In most traditional developing countries women engaged in agricultural activities are often considered to be helping their husbands or families rather than being formally employed. Hence, the undernumeration of working women skews in a downward direction the economic activity rate of women and the aggregate economic activity rate.

As noted, the Yemeni population has a high percentage of young people; 34 percent of the population is under the age of 10. This fact is reflected in a low economic participation rate of 28.0 percent for the aggregate Yemeni population (both in the Yemen Arab Republic and abroad). The overall economic activity rates for men and women were 50.5 percent and 5.4 percent, respectively. However, the economic activity rate for Yemeni males residing in Saudi Arabia and the Gulf states is very high, 80.4 percent, reflecting the fact that young single

Table 4: Enumerated Population, Labor Force, and Crude Participation Rates for YAR Residents and Short-Term Yemeni Migrants, 1975

Category	Population	Labor Force	Crude Participation Rate (%)
Resident population and labor force			
Male (10 years and older)	1,337,938	995,560	74.4
Female (10 years and older)	1,581,605	132,012	8.3
Total (10 years and older)	2,919,543	1,127,572	38.6
All males	2,163,123	995,560	46.0
All females	2,377,115	132,012	5.5
Total resident population	4,540,238	1,127,572	24.8
Population and labor force of short-term migrants in Gulf states			
Male	323,952	260,700	80.5
Female	97,228	2,327	2.4
Total	421,180	263,027	62.5
Total population and labor force			
Male	2,487,075	1,256,330	50.5
Female	2,474,343	134,339	5.4
Total	4,961,418	1,390,669	28.0

Sources: Yemen Arab Republic, Central Planning Organization, Statistics Department, *Statistical Year Book, 1979-1980*, pp. 47, 60-64, and World Bank, *Manpower Development in the Yemen Arab Republic* (Washington, D.C.: World Bank, 1981), p. 47.

male workers comprise the majority of Yemeni emigrants.[10]. As mentioned earlier, 80 percent of the Yemeni population is under the age of 40; correspondingly, 68 percent of the recorded labor force is under the age of 40.[11]

With respect to the relatively low educational levels of the Yemeni population, 1.1 percent of the resident Yemeni population aged 10 years and over hold an educational certificate. Table 5 provides a break-down of educational status for males and females in 1975. Only

Table 5: Educational Status of the Recorded Yemeni Population, 1975 (*10 years of age and above*)

Educational Status	Male	Female	Total
Not stated	5,956	5,881	11,837
As % of population	(0.4)	(0.4)	(0.4)
University	2,844	268	3,112
As % of population	(0.2)	(0.02)	(0.1)
Secondary	5,193	536	5,729
As % of population	(0.4)	(0.03)	(0.2)
Preparatory	8,267	911	9,178
As % of population	(0.6)	(0.1)	(0.3)
Primary	13,606	2,357	15,963
As % of population	(1.0)	(0.1)	(0.5)
Reading and writing ability	288,546	20,694	309,240
As % of population	(21.6)	(1.3)	(10.6)
Reading only	144,160	11,393	155,553
As % of population	(10.8)	(0.7)	(5.3)
Illiterate	869,366	1,539,603	2,408,969
As % of population	(65.0)	(97.3)	(82.6)

Source: Yemen Arab Republic, Central Planning Organization, Statistics Department, *Statistical Year Book, 1979-1980*, pp. 50-55.

2.2 percent of males aged 10 years and over hold an educational certificate at the primary level or above; 65 percent are illiterate. Almost a quarter of 1 percent of women aged 10 and over hold an educational certificate at the primary level or above; 97.3 percent are illiterate. In 1980 the adult literacy rate was 21 percent.[12] It is the low skill level of the labor force as revealed by these educational statistics which has prompted planners to place education as the highest priority of both the First and Second Five-Year Plans.

Deployment of the Recorded Labor Force: Table 6 provides an overview of the deployment of the recorded Yemeni labor force in 1975. Domestic employment accounted for 75 percent of the Yemeni labor force while employment abroad accounted for an additional 19 percent. In all, 6 percent of the recorded Yemeni labor force was unemployed in 1975. Within the domestic private sector, employment utilizing traditional skills (primarily subsistence agricultural production) accounted for the majority, 69 percent, of private-sector employment. Domestic private-sector employment accounted for 73 percent of the Yemeni labor force. Only 4 percent of private-sector employment was in the modern urban sector. The small-scale modern sector—those enterprises with four or less workers—accounted for 70 percent of modern-sector employment.[13] Breaking down the modern urban-sector further, we find that retail and wholesale trade represented the majority, 50 percent, of private modern-sector employment.[14] Manufacturing and construction were the next most important employers in the modern sector, accounting for 16 percent and 15 percent, respectively.[15] As a note of interpretation, the 1975 Central Planning Organization study defined "modern sector" as all fixed-location establishments.

Sinclair and Socknat estimated that 31,315, workers or 2 percent of the recorded labor force were employed in the public sector in 1975.[16] As in the private sector, the public sector was severely hampered by a lack of skilled administrators, technicians, and professionals. In 1975 the Ministry of Interior employed 11,512 persons, all with only informal training.[17] The majority of these people worked as civilian security personnel. Of the remaining 19,803 employees in central administration, 75 percent were illiterate or had less than primary education, 12 percent had preparatory or secondary education, and only 3.5 percent had attained an undergraduate degree.[18]

While comparative data are not yet available for the evaluation of the success of the First Five-Year Plan in alleviating skill shortage in the public sector, table 7 provides an insight into the trend in composition and growth of employment in that sector. The greatest increases in employment have occurred in high- and middle-level skill ranges; skilled employees accounted for 22 percent of public-sector employment in 1980 as opposed to 18 percent in 1977. In all, 45 percent of new employment in the central administration between 1977 and 1980

Table 6: Summary of Labor Force Deployment, 1975

Area of Employment	Number	Percent of Labor Force
Total labor force	1,403,000	100
Domestic employment	1,060,000	75
Public sector	31,000	2
Private sector	1,029,000	73
(Modern)	(53,000)	(4)
(Traditional)	(976,000)	(69)
Unemployed	80,000	6
Employment abroad	263,000	19

Source: World Bank, *Manpower Development in the Yemen Arab Republic* (Washington, D.C.: World Bank, 1981), p. 19.

Table 7: Public Employment in the Central Administration by Grade, 1977 and 1980

Grade	1977 Number	1977 Percent	1980 Number	1980 Percent	Relative Increase in Employment (%)
Top level	448	2.3	660	3.0	47
Middle management	2,963	5.7	4,211	19.0	42
Support staff	15,499	82.0	17,220	78.0	11
Total	18,910	100.0	22,091	100.0	17

Source: World Bank, *Manpower Development in the Yemen Arab Republic* (Washington, D.C.: World Bank, 1981), p. 27.

occurred at the high- and middle-skill levels. The World Bank estimated an increase in employment for the public sector from 19,800 in 1975 to 28,000 in 1980, exclusive of employees of the Ministry of Interior.[19] This indicates a public-sector growth rate of 7.2 percent per annum.

The majority of Yemeni workers are employed in occupations requiring traditional skills, primarily those in agriculture. As table 8 reveals, 70.9 percent of Yemeni workers were engaged in agriculture, herding, or fishing while only 4.0 percent of Yemeni workers were employed as professional or technical workers. If administrative and managerial personnel are included, less than 5 percent of the Yemeni work force was employed in positions requiring high-level skills. Mid-level clerical, service, and sales skills accounted for 10.6 percent of total domestic occupation employment in 1975, with an additional 12.4 percent of Yemeni workers engaged in production and construction. Overall, in 1975, 83.3 percent of the Yemeni work force was employed in occupations requiring low skill levels, primarily traditional pursuits.

An analysis of the deployment of the labor force by economic activity can be derived from table 9. As expected, employment related to agriculture, fishing, and forestry accounted for 73.6 percent of recorded domestic employment in 1975. Services, wholesale and retail trade, and construction were the next major employers of the domestic labor force in 1975. Manufacturing accounted for only 3.0 percent of recorded domestic employment.

The data for the estimated employment of Yemenis in the various sectors of the economy presented in table 9 provide a preliminary indication of the trend of employment over the course of the First Five-Year Plan. Agriculture remained the predominant employment sector, engaging approximately 69 percent of the domestic labor force. Total recorded employment was estimated to have increased from 1,127,572 in 1975 to 1,201,600 over the course of the First Five-Year Plan, with services, construction, and manufacturing accounting for 85 percent of the increase. Employment in the services sector increased by 48,125 workers between 1975/76 and 1980/81, and the share of services in total domestic employment rose from 7.6 percent to 11.2 percent over the course of the plan period. It is important to note that while services accounted for only 11.2 percent of total domestic employment, the service sector employed approximately 90 percent of the professional and technical personnel, 92 percent of the administrative/managerial personnel, and 82 percent of clerical personnel.[20]

Employment in construction rose by 19,538 workers between

Table 8: Distribution of the Yemeni Labor Force by Occupation, 1975

Occupation	Number	Percent
Professional/technical	45,543	4.0
Administrative/managerial	5,749	0.5
Clerical	12,380	1.1
Sales	53,018	4.7
Services	54,316	4.8
Agriculture/fishing/hunting	799,642	71.0
Production	140,046	12.4
Not stated	16,878	1.5
Total	1,127,572	100.0

Source: Yemen Arab Republic, Central Planning Organization, Statistics Department, *Statistical Year Book, 1979-1980*, p. 68.

1975/76 and 1980/81, and the share of construction in domestic employment rose from 4.7 percent to 6.0 percent. The increase in construction activity was fueled by repatriated emigrant earnings and the popularity of urban housing as the major investment form of these funds.

The manufacturing sector achieved an increase in the share of domestic employment from 3.0 percent to 4.4 percent between 1975/76 and 1980/81. More importantly the increase of nearly 19,000 new workers represented a 56 percent increase in employment within the manufacturing sector over the course of the First Five-Year Plan.

In overall terms, there appears to be a gradual trend away from the traditional agricultural sector toward the urban modern sector. While the domestic population is estimated to have grown at a rate of 2.5 percent over the decade of the 1970s, the urban population is estimated to have grown at a rate of 6 percent over the same period.[21] The key element in this rural-to-urban migration has been the flow of emigrant remittances and relocation of returning expatriates to cities. These funds have allowed for the more rapid development of a cash economy as well as for substantial investment and innovation in the urban sector. It is important to note, however, that agriculture continues to dominate

Table 9: Distribution of the Yemeni Labor Force by Economic Sector, 1975 and 1981

Sector	1975 Number	Percent	1981 Number	Percent
Agriculture/forestry/fishing	830,340	73.6	830,400	69.1
Mining and quarrying	576	0.1	1,300	0.1
Manufacturing	33,920	3.0	52,900	4.4
Electricity and water	1,511	0.1	3,900	0.3
Construction	52,460	4.7	72,000	6.0
Wholesale and retail trade	68,979	6.1	71,100	5.9
Transport and communications	24,709	2.2	31,600	2.6
Finance	1,976	0.2	4,500	0.4
Services	85,775	7.6	133,900	11.2
Not stated	27,326	2.4	—	—
Total	1,127,572	100.0	1,201,600	100.0

Sources: Yemen Arab Republic, Central Planning Organization, Statistics Department, *Statistical Year Book, 1981*, pp. 60-61 and Central Planning Organization, *Second Five-Year Plan (1982-1986)*, March 1982.

the economy and subsistence agricultural production remains the primary occupation of the Yemeni workers. The impact and numbers of Yemenis working outside the YAR will be addressed in greater detail in the next chapter.

Finally, employment in the mining and quarrying sector is likely to see expansion by the end of the 1980s as oil exploration activities continue and even expand and as commercial production starts up. A vigorous oil sector can be expected to have a ripple effect throughout the economy in the demand for support industries and services. The oil sector itself, however, will not become the major direct domestic employer, regardless of the eventual size of Yemeni petroleum reserves, because of the capital-intensive, not labor-intensive, characteristic of the industry. For employment projections, it should be recalled that the most labor-intensive portion of oil-sector activities is in the exploration and energy-related infrastructure stages, that is, the period that is only now beginning.

Population and Labor Force 27

Notes

1. World Bank, *Manpower Development in the Yemen Arab Republic* (Washington, D.C.: World Bank, 1981), p. 11. A more recent estimate is on the order of 2.9 percent annual population growth rate, given in World Bank,"Yemen Arab Republic Country Economic Memorandum Current Position and Prospects," Report no. 5621-YAR (Washington, D.C., June 25, 1985), p. 51 (mimeographed).
2. World Bank, *Manpower Development in the Yemen Arab Republic*, p. 11.
3. Yemen Arab Republic, Central Planning Organization, Statistics Department, *Statistical Year Book, 1979-1980*, pp. 45-46.
4. Ibid., pp. 51-52.
5. Ibid.
6. Yemen Arab Republic, Central Planning Organization, Statistics Department, 1975 final census results cited in World Bank, *Yemen Arab Republic: Urban Sector Report* (Washington, D.C.: World Bank, 1981), p. 3.
7. Ibid.
8. Yemen Arab Republic, Central Planning Organization, Statistics Department, *Statistical Year Book, 1979-1980*, pp. 67.
9. World Bank,"Yemen Arab Republic Country Economic Memorandum Current Position and Prospects," p. 57.
10. Yemen Arab Republic, Central Planning Organization, Statistics Department, *Statistical Year Book, 1979-1980*, p. 68.
11. World Bank, *Manpower Development in the Yemen Arab Republic*, p. 127.
12. World Bank,"Yemen Arab Republic Country Economic Memorandum Current Position and Prospects," p. 43.
13. World Bank, *Yemen Arab Republic: Urban Sector Report*, p. 25.
14. Ibid.
15. Ibid.
16. C. A. Sinclair and J. Socknat, *An Assessment of Manpower Development and Policy and Program Suggestions for YAR*, ILO/UNDP/GOYAR, January 1976 cited in World Bank, *Yemen Arab Republic: Urban Sector Report*, p. 26.
17. World Bank, *Manpower Development in the Yemen Arab Republic*, p. 137.
18. Ibid.
19. Ibid., p. 24.
20. Ibid., p. 21.
21. World Bank, *Yemen Arab Republic: Urban Sector Report*, p. 13.

3 HUMAN RESOURCES DEVELOPMENT

Education

The rudiments of a modern educational system have existed in North Yemen for little more than a decade. This period, however, has been marked by impressive gains toward the eradication of illiteracy and increased overall participation in the formal educational system. There remains, however, a formidable challenge before the Ministry of Education, both in terms of continued expansion of formal education as well as the fulfillment of its role in providing the skilled national labor force requisite for development.

The First Five-Year Plan pursued a strategy of expansion of the educational infrastructure, both in terms of physical capacity and the staff of teachers and administrators. Its success has been a keynote of the last two decades; primary schools alone have risen in number from 900 in 1962/63 to over 2,500 in 1979/80.[1] However, in terms of providing the requisite skilled manpower for development needs, there remains a substantial shortfall. The Second Five-Year Plan, which emphasizes the essential link between the educational system and the skilled manpower requirements of the development process, thus, will continue to focus on the expansion of the educational infrastructure and will address the increased skilled manpower demands.

The substantial gains of the educational system in North Yemen cannot be overstated. North Yemen entered the 1970s with both high illiteracy and low age-group participation rates in the formal educational system. Ministry of Education statistics for this period cite a literacy rate of 10 percent and respective age-group participation rates of 12 percent and 1 percent for primary and secondary education, respectively.[2] The same study reveals that by 1980 the adult literacy rate had doubled to over 20 percent and the respective age-group participation rates had risen to 36 percent and 4 percent for primary and secondary education, respectively.[3]

Since education is a time-consuming process of the "building-block" type, the key is getting a relatively broad-based primary (age 7 to 12) education system in place. The progress has been steady. This can be seen in the enrollment ratio for the first level of education, a ratio derived from the total enrollment of all ages divided by the population of the specific age group which corresponds to the age group of primary schooling—7 to 12 years for the YAR. In 1970 the enrollment ratio for primary education was 12 percent, reflecting 23 percent for males and 2 percent for females. By 1975, the primary enrollment ratio reached 29 percent, representing 59 percent for males and 7 percent for females. Five years later in 1980, the ratio was 47 percent (82 percent for males and 12 percent for females), a fourfold increase in one decade, reaching 59 percent by 1982.[4] Given the youthful skew of the YAR population described in chapter two, human resource development costs in education and for upgrading health will continue to be high for some years to come.

With the stated goal for the educational sector in the First Five-Year Plan of expanding the educational infrastructure, the Education Ministry's share of the state budget rose from 10.9 percent to 14.3 percent over the course of the plan.[5] In terms of expenditures, spending rose from 63.3 million Yemeni rials to 400.9 million Yemeni rials between 1976 and 1980. This increase led to massive construction of new schools and classrooms, the end result of which was a jump in total student enrollment at all levels from 278,595 students in the base year of the plan (1976/77) to 481,615 in the final year of the plan—in all 73 percent increase.[6] Table 10 gives a breakdown of the increases in student enrollment by educational level.

Despite the significant enrollment gains achieved by the First Five-Year Plan, the second plan continues to emphasize education's role in assuaging the overall general shortage of skilled labor and the specific shortage of skilled Yemeni administrators, technicians, and educators. The 1982-1986 plan thus stresses qualitative as well as quantitative improvement in the education system referring to this goal as "the transformation of education into an effective instrument in the realization of economic, social, and cultural development...."[7] The objective is to implement both the expansion of facilities and the implementation of a modernized curriculum compatible with the development of a skilled national work force. Emphasis is placed on vocational and technical training. Table 11 gives the targeted enrollment goals for the educational sector over the period of the Second Five-Year Plan.

Some additional attention should be devoted to the role of technical education within overall educational requirements for economic development. The Arab countries in general often suffer from an imbalance in the labor force, particularly between the upper and middle lev-

Table 10: Breakdown of Student Enrollment Increases by Educational Level, First Five-Year Plan (1976-1981), 1982, 1983

Educational Level	1976	1981	1982	1983
Primary education	252,100	412,573	522,996	602,212
Preparatory education	15,620	25,037	32,566	43,302
Secondary education	6,050	9,895	11,645	11,984
Technical and vocational education	225	1,860	2,958	3,261
Religious education	4,600	32,250	47,831	56,384
Total	278,595	481,615	617,996	717,143

Sources: Yemen Arab Republic, Ministry of Education, working paper, 1982, p. 2, and Central Planning Organization, Statistics Department, *Statistical Year Book, 1981*, p. 212, and *Statistical Year Book, 1983*, pp. 239 and 244.

els or cadres where university degree holders outnumber graduates of technical institutes. Although the YAR does not yet have such a problem of major proportions, its educational planning can continue to press for a balance in skills.

Regionally in the Arab world, it has been pointed out that university engineering students were estimated at 85,000, those at technology and industrial institutes placed at 35,000, and enrollment in secondary industrial schools was 78,000.[8] This should be kept in mind when reviewing studies of optimal manpower utilization, some of which put ideal utilization as the availability of 3 to 4 technicians and 20 to 30 skilled workers for each university graduate. A survey of technical education in Arab states showed about 28 students registered in this educational form for every 100,000 persons in the 1977 population compared with the developing country of Singapore with 515 technical students for each 100,000 inhabitants.[9] Such rates and ratios will not be adequate for real development, an assertion supported by the fact that in advanced economies technicians usually outnumber university-degree-holding professionals and specialists. The major oil-exporting Arab countries suffer most from this imbalance between upper- and middle-level cadres, an imbalance corrected by importing those techni-

Table 11: Targeted Enrollment Increases, Second Five-Year Plan (1981-1986)

Education Type	Year	Total Enrollment	Increase (%)	Classroom Construction
Primary	1981	479,809	—	
	1986	806,528	68.0	11,254
Preparatory	1981	26,989	—	
	1986	60,968	125.0	998
Secondary	1981	10,622	—	
	1986	18,979	78.6	265
Technical				
Commercial secondary	1981	422	—	
	1986	1,081	145.0	
Agricultural secondary	1981	77	—	
	1986	522	57.0	
Industrial secondary	1981	461	—	
	1986	660	43.0	

Source: Yemen Arab Republic, Ministry of Education, working paper, 1982, pp. 5-8.

cal skills in the form of expatriates. The YAR is a major source of unskilled labor for the region, particularly Saudi Arabia. Increasing technical education could serve to fill Yemen's domestic manpower needs and could also offer more skilled expatriates to neighboring countries.

The Second Five-Year Plan seeks continued expansion of the primary stage of education as a further step toward the achievement of universal compulsory primary education. In the six, seven, and eight year-old age group the plan seeks to increase enrollment from 43.3 percent of the male population in 1981 to 62.8 percent in 1986; female enrollment is targeted to rise from 7.3 percent in 1981 to 12.8 percent in

1986.[10] In addition to increased total enrollment, emphasis will be placed on increased female participation, retention of students through the full six-grade cycle, and completion of primary school facilities to provide the infrastructure for the cycle.

The recommendations of a 1981 World Bank study are noteworthy. Three factors regarding primary education were stressed: accessibility, retention, and a basic curriculum.[11] Accessibility was stressed both in terms of the distance traveled by students to attend class and access to schools with a full six-year educational program. Retention was stressed with respect to improved teacher qualifications, an increase in Yemeni national educators, and a curriculum which was both interesting and within the capabilities of the representative age group of students. Finally, the World Bank study strongly stressed the need for a sound basic education including the "three R's" of reading, writing, and arithmetic. Literacy alone, the study maintained, is not sufficient; enhanced trainability and the development of a skilled national labor force require a sound basic education.

Secondary Education: In 1975/76 there were 27 secondary schools with an enrollment of approximately 6,050 students.[12] By 1981/82 enrollment had increased to 10,645 students, including 1,353 female students.[13] The number of secondary school teachers also increased substantially over the same period, rising from 332 to 806 by 1979/80.[14] However, while Yemeni graduates of the College of Education at the University of Sana'a have been entering the teaching profession since 1976/77, the majority of secondary school teachers (94 percent) remain non-Yemeni. And, with graduating classes ranging in size from 123 to 157, there will be only a gradual reduction in the foreign dominance in teaching, particularly at the upper levels.

The goals of the Second Five-Year Plan with regard to secondary education and secondary vocational/technical training reflect the desire to integrate education and development needs. The plan stresses the need to increase enrollment in the sciences as opposed to the arts. Its essential strategy is the diversification of secondary education with the addition of secondary technical/vocational education in the areas of commerce, agriculture, and technical studies. Emphasis is placed on supplying the medium-level technicians and skilled workers required for planned development projects. The 1981 enrollment in these three-year programs was 461 technical students, 442 commerce students, and 77 agricultural students.[15] The Second Five-Year Plan seeks to substantially increase total enrollment in these special programs from 980 students in 1981 to over 2,200 by 1986.[16]

Much of the growth in secondary vocational/technical education is expected to take place in the area of agricultural secondary education, the newest of the special education programs begun in 1980 with 60 students.[17] Expectations are high for these undertakings. Enrollment in the two new agricultural schools, thus, is targeted to exceed 500 students by 1986.[18]

The Sana'a Technical School offers a three-year program with graduates concentrated primarily in the areas of construction, automotive mechanics, and electronics. The school graduates an average of 60 students annually.[19] Secondary technical education has been greatly enhanced by the completion of the new technical secondary school at Taiz. Overall, the level of enrollment in technical secondary studies is targeted to rise from 460 in 1981 to 660 by 1986.[20] The growth of interest in technical secondary education will be facilitated by the Higher Technical Institute in Sana'a which began operation in 1982/83. The institute offers a two-year course of study for graduates of technical secondary schools and will facilitate the provision of technical-studies teachers as well as providing trained medium-level technicians. Total enrollment at the institute is foreseen to be 428 students over the course of the Second Five-Year Plan.[21]

Commercial secondary education is offered at seven secondary schools, graduating an average of 100 students annually in commercial studies. Enrollment in commercial secondary education is anticipated to more than double from a level of 442 students in 1981 to over 1,000 students by 1986.[22] This expansion in large part is a response to the popularity of the Faculty of Commerce at the University of Sana'a, which has maintained the largest enrollment at the University since 1974/75, with 1,404 students enrolled in 1979/80.

Recent studies of education in North Yemen have emphasized two main directions for improvement of secondary education and secondary vocational/technical training which can be summarized in the key words "image" and "flexibility."

With respect to image, the notion of secondary education's opportunity costs must first be discussed. Given the skewed wage scale in North Yemen, there are significant job opportunities and wage incentives for workers with only minimal educational achievements. There are thus strong incentives operating to direct students to become wage earners at an early age and after only minimal educational achievement. The wage attraction therefore operates as a strong disincentive to continuing education. In economic terms, the opportunity cost of secondary education and secondary vocational/technical training is often perceived as being too high in view of the earnings which would have to be foregone to pursue such education.

One method of increasing participation in secondary education and secondary vocational/technical training is to improve the image of such training. Student counselling should stress the job opportunities, wage potential, and benefits of continued education to create an awareness of the skilled manpower needs of North Yemen and the active role the student can play in the country's future development. The image of secondary education, then, can serve to join the opportunities and benefits of continued education for the student with North Yemen's needs and requirements for skilled manpower. In addition, counselling of students can not only increase participation in secondary education but can also direct students toward fields of study which fulfill skilled manpower requirements. In this manner, the sciences can be stressed over the arts, and emphasis placed on careers based upon a sound science background. The addition of the Colleges of Medicine and Engineering to the University of Sana'a should serve as strong incentives for both continued education as well as the acquisition of a viable science education.

In light of the significant pressure to begin earning a wage as soon as possible, the educational system must also show sufficient flexibility. This would include wider recruitment, work-study arrangements, and task-specific course work. Most importantly, the educational system must have sufficient flexibility to allow for breaks in the educational process, so that students may return to the educational system after gaining work experience. Adult recruitment, work-study arrangements, and night classes can all serve to bring the educational system into contact with a wider segment of the Yemeni population. The participation of the adult population can play a critical role in the full utilization of the vocational/technical schools. In this view, a relaxation of educational requirements for adult vocational training would increase overall participation in the educational system.

Finally, recent World Bank studies on education have emphasized in-service training. The integration of education and development planning requires the ability to offer specialized course work to meet anticipated development needs. At the present time, in-service training programs are offered by the Ministries of Communication, of Agriculture, and of Health, the Highway Authority, the National Water and Sewage Authority, and the Yemen General Electricity Corporation. In addition, the National Institute of Public Administration offers in-service training for civil service personnel in finance, management, public administration, and clerical skills.

In the past, in-service training within the YAR and abroad has been aimed at meeting specific project or ministerial needs. Given the scarcity of trained instructors and training facilities, it seems that the overall efficiency of in-service training would benefit greatly from coordinating training programs across government departments. This coordination would have several positive effects. First, and most significant, there would be an increased likelihood that training institutions would be utilized at full capacity (a recent World Bank study estimates that the National Institute of Public Administration operates at only 50 percent of capacity). Second, the coordination of in-service training programs might allow for the creation of in-country training programs where ministerial needs in the past have been met by out-of-country training. The replacement of out-of-country training programs with in-country training eliminates the problem of foreign language proficiency and increases the likelihood of retention of graduates. Moreover, coordination of in-service training can shift its focus from specific ministerial needs to the overall goals of institutional development and improved administrative efficiency.

In 1978 the National Institute of Public Administration (NIPA) initiated a one-year program in the area of public administration specifically for graduate students desiring skills in this field. NIPA also introduced the unified accounting system in the country and launched an in-service training program to acquaint both the public and cooperative sectors' personnel with the system as well as organizing the local administrative and economic seminars and conferences that dealt with the development process. In coordination with the University of Sana'a, NIPA started a two-year post-secondary-school training program in 1982 to prepare personnel in middle-level administrative jobs in various branches of the public and cooperative sectors. The program was introduced simultaneously in NIPA's three branches in Sana'a, Taiz, and Hodeidah. This program provides a unique opportunity for secondary-school graduates to acquire useful skills without enrolling in the university; however, qualified students in the program are eligible to enroll in the University of Sana'a as juniors.

University of Sana'a: The University of Sana'a was established in 1971 with an initial enrollment of 61 students and was comprised of the faculties of Shari'a and Law, Sciences, and Arts.[23] The faculties of Commerce and Education were added in 1973/74, which increased total enrollment at the university to 1,150 students.[24] By the end of the First Five-Year Plan, university enrollment exceeded 4,220 students and faculty/staff numbered 181, including 56 Yemeni nationals.[25] Two years into the Second Five-Year Plan, the number of students enrolled rose to 5,172 and faculty/staff numbered 210, of which 61 were Yemeni. Development of the educational sector at the university level in the Second Five-Year Plan includes the planned establishment of new faculties of engineering, medicine, and agriculture.

Table 12 outlines the growth of Yemeni enrollment at the University of Sana'a. A prominent factor has been the rapid development of the Faculty of Commerce, where enrollment has grown from 239 students in 1973/74 to 1,493 students in 1981/82. Given the overwhelming popularity of commercial education at the secondary education level, continued expansion of enrollment in the Faculty of Commerce through the period of the Second Five-Year Plan is assured. Enrollment in commercial secondary education is targeted to rise from 442 to 1,081 students between 1981 and 1986. This enrollment increase will provide a plentiful base for recruitment and continued expansion for the Faculty of Commerce.

The position of the Faculty of Science is not as clearly promising. Enrollment in that faculty has increased from 5 students in 1970/71 to 476 in 1981/82. However, despite growing enrollment, only 12 graduates were recorded by the Faculty of Science in 1978/79. Several problems confront this faculty. First, there is an inadequacy of science training at the lower levels of the formal educational system. This problem is generated by a lack of teachers highly trained in the sciences, a shortage of laboratories and laboratory materials, and a failure of curriculum at the lower levels to stress the sciences which, in turn, leads to a longer-than-average attendance period for graduation from the Faculty of Science. Also, a recent World Bank study suggests that the overall pass rate for the University of Sana'a is approximately 50 percent.[26] Second, given the job opportunities available to students with any level of university training, particularly in the sciences, a large proportion of students prefer to drop out before graduation. There are several measures incorporated within the Second Five-Year Plan which should improve the position of the Faculty of Science. First, the second plan emphasizes the need to modernize the formal educational system at all levels. Inherent in this program is the need to incorporate adequate training in the basic sciences at the lower educational levels which should greatly aid the position of students entering the Faculty of Science. Further, the planned development of the Faculties of Medicine

Table 12: Registered Enrollments and Graduates (Yemeni) at University of Sana'a, 1970/71-1982/83a

	Literature Enrollment	Literature Graduates	Shari'a & Law Enrollment	Shari'a & Law Graduates	Science Enrollment	Science Graduates
1970/71	12	—	47	—	5	—
1971/72	119	—	123	—	9	—
1972/73	249	—	164	—	21	—
1973/74	468	8	189	—	27	—
1974/75	496	31	219	21	47	3
1975/76	399	46	319	39	70	2
1976/77	463	24	509	64	87	—
1977/78	698	25	686	30	154	10
1978/79	660	36	749	48	170	12
1979/80	837	—	922	—	356	—
1980/81	777	—	1,208	—	265	—
1981/82	1,002	—	1,487	—	476	—
1982/83a	1,267	—	2,608	—	495	—

	Commerce Enrollment	Commerce Graduates	Education Enrollment	Education Graduates	Total Enrollment	Total Graduates
1970/71	—	—	—	—	64	—
1971/72	—	—	—	—	251	—
1972/73	—	—	—	—	434	—
1973/74	239	—	227	—	1,150	8
1974/75	678	—	416	—	1,856	55
1975/76	875	—	680	—	2,343	87
1976/77	1,178	71	906	153	3,143	312
1977/78	1,154	63	830	142	3,522	270
1978/79	1,019	79	707	123	3,305	298
1979/80	1,404	—	682	—	4,191	—
1980/81	1,321	—	948	—	4,519	—
1981/82	1,493	—	714	—	5,172	—
1982/83b	1,783	—	807	—	6,960	—

aFigures show actual attendance rather than registered enrollment.
bIn the 1983/84 academic year, the three colleges of Agriculture, Engineering, and Medicine were added.

Sources: World Bank, *Manpower Development in the Yemen Arab Republic* (Washington, D.C.: World Bank, 1981), pp. 171-172; Yemen Arab Republic, Central Planning Organization, Statistics Department, *Statistical Year Book, 1981*, p. 219, and *Statistical Year Book, 1983*, p. 244.

and Engineering should greatly aid recruitment and retention to graduation of students in the Faculty of Science.

The Faculty of Education was established in 1973/74 with an enrollment of 227 students; total enrollment reached 682 students by 1979/80. However, despite growing enrollments, the Faculty of Education will have only a very small impact on the problem of filling the shortage of Yemeni teachers during the Second Five-Year Plan because the number of graduates from this faculty has remained fairly constant, ranging from 123 to 157 annually. These graduates help meet the country's need for teachers only at the preparatory and secondary levels as well as filling staff positions in the Ministry of Education; the large majority of teachers at the lower educational level will remain non-Yemeni throughout the course of the Second Five-Year Plan.

Table 13 provides the composition of the teaching staff up to the secondary level of education for the years 1979/80 and 1981/82. It is clear from this table that non-Yemeni teachers are overwhelmingly predominant at the higher levels.

Substantial steps are being taken to increase the number of Yemeni teachers at the primary and preparatory levels. For example, the number of teacher-training institutes for primary school teachers has increased from 4 to 12 between 1970/71 and 1979/80. Enrollments in the same period increased from 285 to 907 students. In addition, 10 primary/preparatory teacher training institutes were established between 1968/69 and 1979/80. Enrollment in these institutes reached a level of 675 students in 1979/80.[27]

Despite the gains at all levels of teacher training, however, the shortage of Yemeni teachers will continue throughout the course of the Second Five-Year Plan. Essentially, though there has been growth in teacher-training programs, these programs will be unable to keep pace with the growth of enrollments in the formal educational system at all levels. The Second Five-Year Plan estimates that the demand for teachers will increase from 15,622 (3,371 Yemeni and 12,252 non-Yemeni) in 1981 to 23,043 (4,090 Yemeni and 18,953 non-Yemeni) by 1986.[28] Thus, even though there have been efforts to increase the percentage share of Yemeni teachers in the educational system, the percentage share of non-Yemeni teachers will increase between 1981 and 1986 from 78.8 percent to 82.1 percent.

The realization of an all-Yemeni national teaching staff is a long-term goal, the first step of which has been taken. A dramatic effort has been made to increase the participation of all Yemenis in the educa-

Table 13: Yemeni and Non-Yemeni Teachers Distributed According to Educational Level, 1979/1980-1982/83[a]

Educational Level	Year	Non-Yemeni Teachers	Percent Non-Yemeni	Yemeni Teachers	Percent Yemeni	Total Teachers
Primary						
	1979/80	4,111	61	2,656	39	6,767
	1981/82	10,187	87	1,513	13	11,700
	1982/83	11,149	85	2,016	15	13,165
Preparatory						
	1979/80	942	89	119	11	1,061
	1981/82	1,561	95	79	5	1,640
	1982/83	2,224	93	157	7	2,381
Secondary						
	1979/80	452	94	28	6	480
	1981/82	774	96	32	4	806
	1982/83	988	97	63	6	1,051
Total						
	1979/80	5,505	66	2,803	34	8,308
	1981/82	12,522	89	1,624	11	14,146
	1982/83	14,361	87	2,173	13	16,534

[a]Excludes teacher-training institutes.

Sources: World Bank, *Manpower Development in the Yemen Arab Republic* (Washington, D.C.: World Bank, 1981), pp. 167-170, and Yemen Arab Republic, Central Planning Organization, Statistics Department, *Statistical Year Book, 1983*, pp. 234-235 and 242-243.

tional system. Expatriate teachers must be relied upon for the present to guide this new generation of Yemeni students. However, from this greatly increased body of educated Yemenis will arise the teachers of the future.

The commitment to expanding educational opportunities is financed in part through foreign projects assistance, such as the May 1, 1984 loan from the World Bank's affiliate the International Development Association. This $10-million credit—interest free, with a 10-year grace period before repayment begins, and a 50-year maturity—will meet half the $19.3 million total cost for an education project geared toward upgrading the primary and nonformal education system.

Emigration

Labor migration from North Yemen is not a recent phenomenon. Traditional migration routes have led Yemeni workers to the ports of Aden and Djibouti since the British and the French, respectively, established these ports in the mid-nineteenth century. These ports provided a gateway for Yemeni migration throughout the world. Enclaves of Yemeni workers are established throughout Africa, Asia, Europe, and, more recently, in the United States.

The decade of the 1970s introduced a shift in the migration pattern of Yemeni workers from overseas to intrapeninsula. The reason for this shift lies in the development surges of Saudi Arabia and the oil-rich Gulf states during the 1970s, which created a massive regional demand for emigrant labor. These nations were characterized by labor scarcity which, coupled with substantial manpower requirements for their ambitious development plans, created a regional labor market with relatively high wages and plentiful job opportunities. In 1975, for example, migrant workers made up 82 percent and 85 percent of the total labor force of Qatar and the United Arab Emirates, respectively.[29] By contrast, the domestic labor market in North Yemen was characterized by low per-capita income, low wages for unskilled labor, and minimal job opportunities for the rural unskilled workers. Thus, in the early 1970s there existed a push-pull incentive for intrapeninsula migration of workers from North Yemen as labor scarcity and massive manpower requirements in Saudi Arabia and the Gulf states joined with a Yemeni tradition of migration for an unprecedented regional migration of labor from the YAR.

The deployment of short-term emigrants is given in table 14, where it can be seen that in 1975, 97 percent of Yemeni emigrants resided in Saudi Arabia. The World Bank estimates that emigration grew from 295,730 in 1970 to 444,706 in 1977 in response to increased labor demand for Yemeni expatriates.[30] Recorded estimates tend to understate the true level of emigration in that such estimates take into account only those emigrants recorded as residing in the host countries. Official estimates by the Central Planning Organization of the YAR are substantially higher because they take into account both the recorded

Table 14: Estimates of Recorded YAR Citizens in Selected Countries, February 1975

Country	Males	Females	Total
Saudi Arabia	314,051	95,602	409,653
Kuwait	3,654	1,029	4,683
United Arab Emirates	2,687	257	2,944
Bahrain	1,826	174	2,000
Qatar	1,734	166	1,900
Total	323,952	97,228	421,180

Source: World Bank, *Manpower Development in the Yemen Arab Republic* (Washington, D.C.: World Bank, 1981), pp. 112-116.

and the illegal flow of Yemeni emigrant workers. The 1975 census estimated the level of short-term emigration at 740,000, and in 1981 the Confederation of Yemeni Development Associations' estimates increased to 837,000.[31]

The tremendous surge in intrapeninsula migration of Yemeni workers has had significant effects on the economy of North Yemen. These effects on economic development can be considered in the context of their impact on (a) the domestic labor force, (b) the balance of payments, (c) repatriated skills and innovation, and (d) investment of remittances and concomitant inflation. As the breadth of this structure of analysis suggests, it is often difficult to judge in total whether emigration has furthered or hindered the course of development.

The effects of Yemeni emigration on the domestic labor force have been most significantly felt in the agricultural sector as the typical emigrant is a rural unskilled single male worker. The surge in emigration of this type of worker in the early 1970s created an acute shortage of unskilled labor in agriculture and construction. In the agricultural sector, the absence of the unskilled single male worker led to an increasing reliance on women, children, and the elderly. It was estimated that in 1981 approximately 5,000 Indians and 3,000 Pakistanis were working in the YAR as well as other large groups of unskilled foreign workers.32 In so much as this was insufficient to meet the shortage of unskilled labor, wage rates soared dramatically through the mid-1970s. A study of emigration by Jon Swanson cites an increase in the daily wage rate in the agricultural sector from three to six Yemeni rials between 1972 and 1975.33 Further, sharecroppers who once received one-third share of the crop increasingly operated on a 50/50 basis on generally more productive land.34

In the construction sector both an acute shortage of unskilled labor and a significantly increased demand combined to rapidly increase wages. Overall, a World Bank study notes that the wage rate for general unskilled labor rose from 5 Yemeni rials per day in the early 1970s to between 60 and 80 Yemeni rials per day in 1980.35 The World Bank study assumes that comparable or greater increases have affected the entire skill spectrum.

The rapid increase in wages substantially reduced the differential between wages paid for unskilled labor in Saudi Arabia and North Yemen. Swanson notes that though the wage differential had been reduced, the incentive to migrate remained high. A tradition of emigration has evolved which advocates frugal living and saving abroad while expecting conspicuous consumption and the display of wealth at home. Thus, the early 1970s were typified by the returning emigrants bringing with them the automobiles, refrigerators, and television sets which marked their success. Their acquired tastes and the tradition of conspicuous consumption are readily apparent today in the abundance of automobiles, processed foods, and imported retail items available in North Yemen. It is the unrelenting growth and reliance on imports, particularly consumer goods, which represents the most damaging aspect of emigration for domestic development.

Conspicuous consumption aside, the standard of living in North Yemen has unquestionably improved as a result of emigration and repatriated earnings. As one indicator, per-capita income has risen from 928 Yemeni rials in 1975/76 to 1,081 Yemeni rials in 1979/80 (in constant 1975/76 prices).36 Recent improvements in nutrition, living conditions, and a reduction in child mortality rates are at least partly attributable to the increased income derived from remittances. There is no doubt that remittances have increased income, increased consumption, and provided potential funds for investment. The problem has been one of coordinating the direction of the spending and investment of remittances with the goals of development in North Yemen.

The impact of private transfers on income in North Yemen was substantial throughout the 1970s. From a 1971/72 level of 14 percent of national disposable income, the share of private transfers peaked at 46 percent in 1977/78. As noted in table 15 this inflow of private funds stabilized between 1978 and 1980 while income derived from domestic production continued to increase, reducing the share of private transfers in national disposable income to 34 percent in 1979/80 and to 26 percent in 1982. It is significant to note that private transfers in 1977/78 were nearly three times the total national disposible income in 1971/72.

Private transfers from emigrant workers have come to play a major role in the balance of payments of North Yemen. Table 15 reveals the dramatic rise in the level of private transfers through the early and middle part of the 1970s. From a level of 328 million rials in 1971/72, private transfers rose to a peak level of 6,351 million rials in 1977/78 and then stabilized at an annual average level of approximately 6 billion rials through the end of the decade. The growth of private transfers allowed the Yemen Arab Republic to overcome a persistent balance-of-trade deficit and enjoy a positive balance-of-payments current account through the middle years of the decade.

A number of factors have acted to stabilize and bring a decline in the level of private transfers to North Yemen: the winding down of the construction phase of regional development; the alteration of expatriate labor demand from the oil-rich developing countries including increased competition from such Asian labor pools as Korea, the Philippines, and Thailand; continuing inflation; and the global recession of the early 1980s. The massive construction phase of development in the oil economies of the Arabian Peninsula initiated in the early part of the 1970s began to wind down at the end of the decade. The infrastructural buildup phase gradually gives way to the operations of major industries as initiated projects begin to come on stream and to produce.[37] Expatriate labor demand is altered in two ways: (l) it is quantitatively reduced in some sectors of the economy, particularly the construction sector, and (2) there is a qualitative shift in demand toward emigrant workers with higher skill levels. Both these factors have acted against the unskilled Yemeni emigrant worker. The government of North Yemen also initiated a complusory military service law in 1979 which acted in some measure to restrict the flow of emigrant workers from North Yemen. Continuing inflation and the potential for political tension between the two Yemens served to reduce the flow of private transfers into North Yemen. Increasing quantities of emigrant earnings were invested outside North Yemen or entered the country in the form of consumer durables purchased at cheaper prices outside the country.

Stabilization in the level of remittances in the latter part of the

Table 15: Private Transfers and National Disposable Income, 1971/72-1984
(in million Yemeni rials)

Year	National Disposable Income (NDI)	Private Transfers	Percent Increase Decrease/	As Percentage of NDI
1971/72	2,195	328.0	—	14
1972/73	2,816	564.0	72	20
1973/74	3,499	594.6	5	17
1974/75	5,090	1,013.0	70	20
1975/76	7,584	2,363.3	133	31
1976/77	10,838	4,561.2	93	42
1977/78	13,740	6,350.7	39	46
1978/79	15,600	5,595.0	-12	36
1979/80	17,810	6,118.4	9	34
1980/81	17,575	4,935.8	-19	28
1981	18,312	4,444.2	-10	24
1982	20,508	5,360.6	21	26
1983	21,580	5,600.7	4	26
1984	—	4,417.1	-21	—

Sources: Yemen Arab Republic, Central Planning Organization, Statistics Department, *Statistical Year Book, 1979-1980*, pp. 219 and 349, *Statistical Year Book, 1981*, pp. 184 and 334-335, *Statistical Year Book, 1982*, pp. 186 and 348; Central Bank of Yemen, Research Department, *Financial Statistical Bulletin*, July-September 1984, pp. 23-24; and World Bank, "Yemen Arab Republic Country Economic Memorandum Current Position and Prospects," Report no. 5621-YAR (Washington, D.C., June 25, 1985), pp. 71, 82, and 84.

decade and even a decline in remittances, however, was not coupled with any restraint in the growth of imports until mid-1984, as evident in table 16. Imports continued to grow between 1977/78 and 1979/80 at an annual rate of approximately 30 percent, reaching a level of 6,958 million rials in 1979/80 and 8,620 million rials in calendar year 1980, a level unmatched except in 1982. Stabilized or somewhat lower levels of private transfers, coupled with the continued growth in the value of imports, led to a growing current account deficit which peaked at 3,110.5 million rials in 1980 (table 16).

Table 16: Selected Items in the Balance of Payments, 1973/74-1984 *(in million Yemeni rials)*

Year	Current Account	Balance of Trade	Imports	Private Transfers
1973/74	-83.7	-811.4	873.3	594.6
1974/75	306.7	-1,105.4	1,163.4	1,013.0
1975/76	1,100.4	-1,666.0	1,721.3	2,363.3
1976/77	1,257.4	-3,199.9	3,283.8	4,561.2
1977/78	1,472.7	-4,102.7	4,134.5	6,350.7
1978/79	-621.3	-5,613.2	5,626.4	5,595.0
1979/80	-1,480.4	-6,925.5	6,957.6	6,118.4
1980	-3,110.5	-8,562.0	8,619.5	6,034.1
1981	-2,989.4	-7,820.4	7,867.8	4,444.2
1982	-2,771.3	-8,764.1	8,785.7	5,360.6
1983	-2,556.5	-8,038.0	8,802.0	5,600.7
Jan.-Sept. 1984[a]	-458.4	-4,974.8	4,993.4	4,417.1

[a]Change in 1984 due to policies aimed at "rationalization" of imports, especially government imports.

Sources: Yemen Arab Republic, Central Planning Organization, Statistics Department, *Statistical Year Book, 1979-1980*, pp. 218-219, and Central Bank of Yemen, Research Department, *Financial Statistical Bulletin*, July-September 1984, table 16, pp. 23-24.

In response, the government of North Yemen instituted an austerity program in the spring of 1983 that called for increased tariffs, spending cuts in the budget, a slowdown in the issuing of import licenses along with other measures of import controls that included the halting of certain commodities such as fruit. Table 16 would indicate some degree of success for these measures; for example, imports fell by about 8 percent annually in the two-year span from 1982 to 1984, in large measure attributable to the policy of "rationalizing" imports adopted by the Central Bank. Thus, despite a decline in 1983 of around 63 percent in workers' remittances from the previous year, the YAR managed to reduce its balance-of-payments deficit by 41 percent, traceable to its reduction in imports.[38] In 1984 the North Yemen government continued and even expanded the austerity program. Taxes were raised and the capital budgets slashed by 22 percent.[39]

Swanson, in his study of Yemeni emigration, dismissed acquired skills of Yemeni workers as insignificant, reasoning that the bulk of emigrants are unskilled workers and are employed as such in both North Yemen and Saudi Arabia.[40] However, a World Bank study contradicts this view.[41] Though Yemeni workers tend not to be employed in the large-scale, high-technology development projects, even at the medium contractor level, Yemeni workers are still exposed to a wide variety of skills. Thus, a significant number of Yemeni workers return home to engage in trades such as carpentry, blacksmithing, and electrical work, as well as entering the areas of small-scale retailing and transportation.

Swanson is correct in his dismissal of acquired skills of Yemeni emigrant workers as insignificant in the sense that very few emigrants return to the agricultural sector or develop any skills pertinent to agricultural production. But he tends to ignore the fact that most emigrants return with the skills to become productive members in other sectors of the economy.

In terms of innovation, it seems clear that where opportunity presents itself former expatriates are quick to avail themselves of experience gathered abroad. Returning emigrants have readily responded to the potential in the transportation sector, particularly in the form of taxi services and trucking. In the rural agricultural sector, Swanson cites examples of power grinding mills, tractors, and irrigation equipment while noting that the introduction of such equipment was hampered by the rough terrain. The World Bank study on manpower offers examples of individuals purchasing generators and selling electrical current locally as well as the aforementioned entry of individuals into various retail and skilled labor trades.

It seems clear that the returning emigrant is willing to innovate and exercise acquired skills. The problem is not a lack of enterprise but rather the range of opportunity.

Investment of Emigrant Remittances: Thus far the flow of remittances to North Yemen has not served adequately to fuel the engine of development. Repatriated earnings in the economy of North Yemen are largely observable in the form of cash surplus, imported consumption, and inflationary ventures such as the bidding up of prices for land and housing in real estate transactions. The failure to productively utilize remittances is not due to a lack of enterprise or innovation on the part of returning emigrant workers, but rather in part is a measure of the present limited absorptive capacity for investment in certain sectors, particularly in rural North Yemen.

Rural investment in the YAR is essentially limited to the agricultural sector. Traditional theory suggests that the impact of the flow of remittances to the agricultural sector in less-developed countries will result in increased mechanization and consolidation of land holdings.[42] As the Swanson study shows, such has not been the case in North Yemen. In the first place, the flow of remittances holds a much larger share of domestic income than anticipated by traditional theory. The freedom of mobility and opportunity to migrate has created a cash-surplus situation in the rural sector. Emigration of the majority rather than the minority has eliminated the ups and downs of financial fortune which allow for the transfer and consolidation of land holdings. Essentially, the rural landholder in North Yemen is rarely faced with the necessity of selling his land; instead, the option of emigration is always open.

Thus, given the limited transfer of land and the available cash surplus in the rural sector, the net result of the flow of remittances has been a dramatic increase in land prices. Swanson cites rural prices for average land in the early 1960s as 100 to 200 Yemeni rials per shakla (a unit of land 18.5 feet on a side).[43] According to the same study, comparable land in 1974 was selling for 1,000 Yemeni rials per shakla, and by 1976 this had more than doubled to 2,500 Yemeni rials per shakla.[44]

The other avenue of investment in rural areas is the mechanization of agriculture. The Yemenis' ability to undertake this form of investment, however, is severely constrained by the mountainous terrain which constitutes much of the agricultural land in North Yemen. Where feasible, Swanson has noted the willingness of returning emigrants to invest in tractors and irrigation equipment. Such investment is generally unfeasible, however, on the picturesque, steeply terraced crop lands in the interior, where farmers continue to use hand cultivation or livestock.

An important development toward the increase in absorptive capacity for rural investment in North Yemen has been the rise of the Local Development Association (LDA). There are 191 LDAs organized on a village level which operate under the direction of the Confederation of Yemeni Development Associations.[45] The focus of the LDAs in the recent period has been infrastructural development. Financed largely through local resources, LDAs have engaged in investment in roads, water projects, schools, and health facilities. Specifically, LDAs have been responsible for the construction of 5,567 kilometers of access roads, 881 water projects, 580 schools, and 46 health projects.[46]

Urban investment offers somewhat greater absorptive capacity than the rural sector. Labor scarcity, high wages relative to productivity, skyrocketing land and construction costs have combined to severely constrain the range of viable domestic industry. Urban investment is thus largely limited to the retail trades, transportation, real estate speculation, and housing construction. With imports rising from 5,626 million rials to 8,786 million rials between 1978/79 and 1982 and still at 8,082 million rials in 1983, the retail trades continue to be a popular form of urban investment.[47] In overview, the modern private sector in North Yemen consists largely of small-scale enterprises organized primarily on a family basis. About 70 percent of the businesses in the modern private sector employed four or less workers in 1975.[48] Within the modern private sector, the wholesale and retail trades accounted for 50 percent of total private-sector employment.[49] The very popularity of the retail trades, however, serves to limit their profitability. High profits are primarily earned by the large wholesalers in direct contact with overseas suppliers.

Transportation is a second major area of remittances investment. The number of trucks imported into North Yemen rose from 372 in 1971/72 to 1,964 in 1975/76.[50] This is a logical extension of the increased flow of imports to the country, as enterprising individuals seek to facilitate distribution of goods throughout the countryside. Taxi services are also a popular form of investment, for not only is there a substantial flow of goods in the country, emigration has also enhanced the mobility of the population.

Real estate speculation and housing investment played a dominate role in urban investment throughout the decade of the 1970s. The First Five-Year Plan allocated 13 percent of gross fixed capital formation to urban-based housing.[51] The popularity of investment in the housing sector far exceeded the plan's expectations. In 1975 the housing-sector share in gross fixed capital formation was 37 percent and rose to an unprecedented level of 43.3 percent in 1977/78.[52] These percentages contrast with an industrial investment share ranging from 8 to 14 percent during the same period.[53] This is essentially a reflection of the impact of skyrocketing wage and land prices on the viability of investment in domestic production.

The massive housing demand has led to steeply rising urban land prices. The Swanson emigration study cites prices of 700 Yemeni rials per shakla for an average site outside Taiz in 1974.54 By 1976 such land was estimated to be worth 8,000 Yemeni rials per shakla, and prime land had risen from 1,000 rials in 1974 to approximately 20,000 rials by 1979.55 A World Bank study cites government land prices outside Sana'a rising from 10 to 15 rials per square meter in the early 1970s to 100 or more rials per square meter by mid-decade, with prime land selling at 200 to over 500 rials per square meter.56

The increased demand for housing has affected not only land prices but also rental costs, power and water costs, and, most dramatically, construction costs. The Sana'a general price index reflects the overall impact of labor scarcity and the effects of limited absorptive capacity for urban investment. From a base year level of 100 in 1972 the index rose to 348 in 1977/78 and 470 in 1979/80.57 Rent and water costs increased far more rapidly than the general rate of inflation, rising from 100 in 1972 to 513 in 1977/78 and 811 in 1979/80.58 Even more dramatically, fuel and lighting costs rose from 100 in 1972 to 791 in 1977/78 and 1,036 in 1979/80.59 In the initial years of the 1980s the price index showed slower escalation. With reindexing based on 100 = 1977/78, rent and water in Sana'a were 153, 157, and 151 for 1980, 1981, and 1982, respectively. Fuel and lighting costs in Sana'a on the new index base were 147 (1980), 185 (1981), and 183 (1982).60

Labor scarcity and increased housing demand had the greatest impact on the construction sector. As noted, unskilled labor wages rose from 5 Yemeni rials per day in the early 1970s to 60 to 80 Yemeni rials per day by 1980. In addition to labor costs, materials costs in the construction sector were also steeply rising throughout the decade of the 1970s. Rose limestone, a popular building material, increased from 120 Yemeni rials per truckload in 1974 to 600 rials per truckload in 1977.61 The cost of cement rose less dramatically, increasing by 75 percent over the period 1975 to 1979.62 A World Bank study, however, noted a trend towards moderation and even decline in housing construction costs. The study cited figures showing cut stone prices rising at a modest 6 percent annual rate, cement and gravel prices falling to 1978 levels, and wages rising at a more moderately paced 10-15 percent annual rate in 1980.63 Estimates of the production cost of a typical cut-stone home showed a dramatic rise in the 1970s from 800 Yemeni rials per square meter in 1975 to 3,000 Yemeni rials per square meter in 1978 but showed a decline by late 1980 to 2,500 Yemeni rials per square meter.64 The reasons cited for declining construction costs were the increased capacity of the construction industry and the decline in housing demand associated with the stabilization of private transfers from emigrant workers.

Conclusions: As noted earlier, the breadth of the impact of emigration on the economy and people of North Yemen makes it difficult to assess the overall positive or negative effect of emigration on development. On the one hand, emigration has contributed to rising incomes, increased consumption, increased investment, improved nutrition and health conditions, and acquired skills and innovative concepts derived from the emigrant experience. On the other hand, emigration has contributed to labor scarcity, general inflation, rapidly rising factor costs which limit the viability of domestic production, as well as an increasing dependence on imports and a growing current account deficit, with its threatening implications for growth and development.

The studies of Yemeni emigration have generally concluded that, on the whole, emigration has been beneficial to development in the 1970s. The social and economic benefits of increased incomes, increased consumption, and improved nutrition and health conditions are viewed as outweighing the detrimental effects on agricultural and industrial production.

The negative effects of emigration on development during the First Five-Year Plan are expected to be subtantially abated during the Second Five- Year Plan. Several manpower forecasts predict an easing of the unskilled labor shortage created by emigration during the 1970s. The manpower forecast of the Second Five-Year Plan anticipates a cumulative surplus of unskilled labor of approximately 140,000 during the period 1982 to 1986.[65] The end of the general unskilled labor shortage should have a twofold effect through the availability of such labor and through the expected depressing effect on wages. A closer linkage of wages and productivity during the Second Five-Year Plan would act to increase the viability of domestic productive investment as well as to improve the competitiveness of domestic production with foreign imports.

The problem during the Second Five-Year Plan may not be one of general labor scarcity but rather the financing of continued growth and development should private transfers from emigrant workers decline sharply. Several of the constraints on the supply and demand for Yemeni emigrant labor have been noted earlier as has the trend toward increased purchases and investment of emigrant earnings outside of North Yemen. Also adversely impacting economic development in the Yemen Arab Republic has been the worldwide recession of the early 1980s, the slow economic recovery, and the world oil glut with its depressing effects on economic activity in the Gulf states. The net result of these factors has been a decline in private transfers from 6,118 million rials to 4,444 million rials between 1979/80 and 1981.[66] However, remittances rebounded in 1982 to 5,360.6 million rials and to 5,600.7 million rials in 1983 (table 16), to some extent due to Yemenis returning to the YAR for good and bringing their end-of-stay savings with them. Estimates put 1984 remittances at 5,900 million rials, with a decline to 5,560 million rials in the final year of the second plan (1986).[67]

The Second Five-Year Plan projected stabilization and slight growth in private transfers between 1982 and 1986. Private transfers were expected to increase from 4,450 million rials in 1982 to 4,550 million rials in 1986.[68] Continued growth and development will remain heavily dependent on the flow of private transfers from emigrant workers. Total private transfers during the Second-Five Year Plan were forecast to equal 25,600 million rials, which represents 87.4 percent of total gross fixed capital formation forecast for the plan period.[69]

Manpower Planning

The general objectives of the First Five-Year Plan (1976/77-1980/81) with reference to manpower planning in North Yemen specified increased self-reliance, development of educational infrastructure, and integration of the educational system with development needs. The plan recognized the low level of skill and education of the national labor force. North Yemen entered the 1970s with a literacy rate of 10 percent and age-group participation rates of 12 percent and 1 percent for primary and secondary education, respectively.[70] The plan therefore placed top priority on the development of the educational system and expansion of enrollment.

Efforts made toward the goal of expansion of the educational system by the First Five-Year Plan were highly successful. Expenditures by the Ministry of Education rose from 51.6 million Yemeni rials to an estimated 575.2 million Yemeni rials between 1975/76 and 1980/81.[71] Massive construction of new schools and expansion of associated educational infrastructure led to an increase of enrollment from 277,900 students in 1976 to 457,700 students in 1980.[72] The World Bank estimated that by the end of the decade literacy had doubled to over 20 percent and respective age-group participation rates had risen to 36 percent and 4 percent for primary and secondary education, respectively.[73]

Other primary goals of manpower planning in the First Five-Year Plan included increased employment, increased job opportunity, and filling the skill needs of development objectives. The strategies outlined for achieving these goals included increased participation of women in the national labor force, the development of a medium-level skill cadre through vocational and technical training, and the integration of educational policy and development planning. In terms of long-range planning, the plan recognized the need to decrease the reliance on foreign professionals through education of nationals both at home and abroad.

The First Five-Year Plan was a valuable document in that it represented an attempt to measure the existing national labor force against the manpower requirements of development objectives. Such analysis revealed the requisite dependence on imported labor, the feasibility of projected goals, and the need for a guideline for educational policy. The weakness of the First Five-Year Plan was the lack of institutional infrastructure to carry through such detailed planning and analysis. In this sense, the first plan was successful in achieving its broader objectives but left to the Second Five-Year Plan the detailed linkage of education and training with specific development needs.

The First Five-Year Plan emphasized job creation and expanded job opportunities. During the period of the plan jobs were created for 101,900 new workers, exceeding the target goal of 101,300.[74] This represented an expansion of the domestic labor force, from 1,099,700 in 1975/76 to 1,201,600 in 1980/81, of 9.3 percent.[75] Between 1975/76 and 1980/81 the domestic labor force grew at an annual rate of 1.8 percent.

Table 17 details the changes in the composition of employment over the course of the First Five-Year Plan. The agricultural sector was essentially stagnant, with production growing at an annual rate not exceeding 1 percent between 1975/76 and 1980/81.[76] Given continued expansion in other sectors of the economy, particularly the public sector, manufacturing, and construction, the share of agriculture in total employment fell from 75.4 to 69.1 percent during the first plan period. The prime areas of employment expansion, accounting for 85 percent, were public and private services, construction, and manufacturing.

The Second Five-Year Plan of the Yemen Arab Republic recognizes the manpower constraints facing North Yemen. The period of the first plan was marked by a labor shortage, particularly in terms of skilled professionals in the areas of administration, agriculture, engineering, and industry. The second plan therefore emphasizes the inte-

Table 17: Changes in Manpower and Employment Structure During the First Five-Year Plan *(thousands of workers)*

Economic Activities	Number of Employees 1975/76	1980/81	Employment Structure (%) 1975/76	1980/81
Agriculture, forestry & fisheries	830.4	830.4	75.4	69.1
Mining & quarrying	0.6	1.3	0.1	0.1
Manufacturing & industries	33.9	52.9	3.1	4.4
Electricity & water	1.5	3.9	0.1	0.3
Construction	52.5	72.0	4.8	6.0
Wholesale & retail trade	69.0	71.1	6.3	5.9
Transport & communication	24.7	31.6	2.2	2.6
Financing, insurance, & real estate	2.0	4.5	0.2	0.4
Services	85.8	133.9	7.8	11.2
Total	1,100.4	1,201.5	100.0	100.0

Source: Yemen Arab Republic, Central Planning Organization, *Second Five-Year Plan (1982-1986)*, March 1982, chapter 3, p. 29.

gration of educational policy and development planning. In particular, the plan places high priority on continued development of educational infrastructure, expanded participation in the educational sector, increased utilization of vocational and technical training, and improvement of administrative capabilities. The strategies for linking educational participation and development planning stress the creation of a general awareness of development objectives. The plan emphasizes the importance of popular participation in the development effort; a high priority is therefore placed on improving the image of educational attainment, particularly among young people, by stressing the opportunities afforded by education as well as the aspect of participation in the nation's development.

Table 18: Planned Changes in Manpower and Employment Structure During The Second Five-Year Plan (1981-1986) *(thousands of workers)*

Economic Activity	Base Year 1981		Final Year 1986	
	Number of Employees	Employment Structure (%)	Number of Employees	Employment Structure (%)
Agriculture	830.4	69.1	866.7	63.9
Mining	1.3	0.1	1.9	0.1
Manufacturing	52.9	4.4	81.6	6.0
Electricity & water	3.9	0.3	7.0	0.5
Construction	72.0	6.0	78.0	5.8
Wholesale & retail trade	71.0	5.9	85.9	6.3
Transport & communications	31.6	2.6	38.2	2.8
Finance, insurance, & real estate	4.5	0.4	6.0	0.4
Public adm. & services	133.9	11.2	190.7	14.1
Total	1,201.5	100.0	1,356.0	99.9

Source: Yemen Arab Republic, Central Planning Organization, *Second Five-Year Plan (1982-1986)*, chapter 3, p. 32.

The plan also emphasizes the modernization of the health and education sectors, a key element of which is the linking of educational content with the needs of society and the labor market. The World Bank study points out the need for a sound basic education which promotes the sciences.[77] Overall, the Second Five-Year Plan strives to achieve increased employment opportunities primarily through increased educational opportunities. This strategy rests heavily on increased participation in vocational and technical training programs.

Employment in North Yemen is forecast to grow from 1,201,600 in 1981 to 1,356,000 by 1986.[78] This entails the creation of 154,400 new jobs during the Second Five-Year Plan and an increase in the labor force of 12.9 percent. Table 18 gives the expected shifts in the composition of employment by economic activity sector during the plan, given expected rates of growth in output, worker productivity, job turnover, and replacement of imported laborers.

Agriculture, manufacturing, and services are expected to account for 86 percent of new employment during the second plan period. Services alone will account for 37 percent of new employment, or 56,800 new jobs, largely in the public sector. This employment expansion is the targeted result of the plan's focus on the expansion of education, health, and other services provided by the government.

The contribution of manufacturing industries in domestic output is forecast to grow from 6 to 8.3 percent of gross domestic product during the 1982-1986 period. This is expected to bring about the creation of 28,700 new job opportunities in manufacturing, or 19 percent of all new employment during the Second Five-Year Plan. The forecast is for an increase in the share of manufacturing employment from 4.4 to 6 percent of total domestic employment by 1986.

An easing of the unskilled labor shortage and moderation in the growth of domestic wage rates is expected to allow expansion of employment in the agricultural sector. The Second Five-Year Plan forecasts a 4.8 percent annual rate of increase in real agricultural output and the creation of 36,300 new jobs in the agricultural sector.[79] Despite this increase in employment, agriculture's overall share of total domestic employment is expected to decline from 69.1 to 63.9 percent between 1981 and 1986.

Official estimates anticipate a rate of entry of new workers into the labor force of approximately 57,500 annually between 1981 and 1986.[80] This represents a cumulative increase in the labor supply of about 287,500 during the 1982-1986 span. Demand for manpower during the same period is forecast to increase by 284,136.[81] This total is arrived at through the forecast of the creation of 154,400 new jobs, job turnover of 108,000, and 21,736 jobs resulting from the replacement of expatriate labor.[82]

Strictly on a quantitative basis, the manpower forecast of the Second Five-Year Plan predicts an excess of the supply of additional labor over demand of 3,323 workers. North Yemen's manpower planning problem is not one of scarcity, as is the case with many of the other countries on the Arabian Peninsula, but rather one of upgrading the skill levels of and retaining the domestic labor force.

Table 19 details the manpower forecast for the additional supply and demand for labor during the second plan by professional occupa-

Table 19: Balance of Additional Supply and Demand for Labor, Second Five-Year Plan (1982-1986)

Professional Category		Additional Supply of Labor	Additional Demand for Labor	Surplus (+) or Deficit (−)
A1	Occupations requiring a university degree in the sciences	2,895	3,076	−181
A2	Occupations requiring a university degree in the arts	3,228	9,584	−6,356
B1	Occupations requiring 1 to 3 years post-secondary education in the sciences	1,940	5,069	−3,129
B2	Occupations requiring 1 to 3 years post-secondary education in the arts	2,424	5,729	−3,305
C1	Occupations requiring secondary education	8,102	49,452	−41,350
C2	Occupations requiring intermediate-level education plus vocational training	4,633	17,752	−13,119
D	Occupations requiring intermediate or primary education plus vocational training	4,712	43,709	−38,997
E	Occupations requiring primary education or no education	259,525	119,765	+139,760
Total		287,459	254,136	+33,323

Source: Yemen Arab Republic, Central Planning Organization, *Second Five-Year Plan (1982-1986)*, chapter 3, p. 43.

tion categories. The salient features of the forecast are the emergence of an unskilled labor surplus of 139,760 workers and deficits of manpower demand over supply in all other professional categories.

The additional demand for professionals with a university degree is expected to total 12,660 between 1981 and 1986. This demand is generated primarily by the expected employment growth in public administration and the services sector, mainly in education, health, and other government services. In all, 87 percent of the demand for professionals in table 19 in the A1 and A2 categories is expected to come from the public sector during the Second Five-Year Plan.[83]

The increased demand for professionals with university degrees will be met in part by the expected entrance into the labor force of 3,184 non-Yemenis during the 1982-1986 period.[84] It is important not to be misled by the level of deficits for the A1 and A2 professional classifications shown in table 19. In the A1 category—professionals with a university degree in the sciences—91 percent of the additional supply of labor will be expatriate.[85] This contrasts with the A2 category—professionals with a university degree in the arts—where only 17 percent of the additional labor supply is expected to be expatriate.[86] Thus, while there appears to be a substantial deficit in the A2 category during the Second Five-Year Plan, the point should be made that the majority of the demand is being met by Yemenis. Further, the World Bank forecasts the emergence of a surplus of professionals with arts-based university degrees on the order of 800 to 2,600 by 1985, given stabilized emigration at 1975 levels.[87] But, regardless of variations in the expected growth of public sector demand for professionals with university degrees, it is clear from the long-run perspective there is a need to steer a greater number of Yemeni students towards science-based university degrees.

The outlook for subprofessionals or technicians with one to three years post-secondary training in the arts or sciences is essentially the same as that for university graduates. The 1981 World Bank manpower forecast predicts a deficit of 3,500 to 5,000 for subprofessionals with science-based training and a surplus of 700 to 1,300 for subprofessionals with arts-based training by 1985.[88] This forecast focuses attention on the need to improve student participation in the sciences at all levels, to be achieved through modernization of curriculum, improved science training, and career guidance counselling to promote science-based fields of study.

The manpower forecast of the Second Five-Year Plan predicts deficits in those occupations requiring secondary school training, skilled office labor, and skilled manual and semi-skilled labor, which comprise the professional categories C1, C2, and D in table 19. The overall deficit for these categories during the plan period is 93,466. In contrast, a surplus of 139,760 is expected in category E—general unskilled labor—during the same period. The relative magnitudes of the deficit categories and the surplus of general unskilled labor make it clear why expanded participation in the educational system and increased vocational/technical training are expected to play a major role in upgrading the skill levels of the domestic labor force.

A large portion of the deficit in the C1 professional category (table 19) is due to the expected increase in demand for teachers of the primary school cycle during the Second Five-Year Plan. Primary school enrollment is expected to increase 68 percent during the 1982-1986 span, reaching a level of nearly 805,528 students.[89] Total demand for teachers at all educational levels is expected to increase from 15,622 in 1981 to 23,043 by 1986.[90] The majority of this increase in demand will be for primary school teachers.

Twelve teacher-training institutes for instructors of the primary school cycle were functioning in 1979/80 with an enrollment of 907 students.[91] In addition there were 10 primary/preparatory teacher training institutes in 1979/80 with an enrollment of 675 students.[92] While enrollment in these two programs has increased from 416 in 1970/71 to 1,582 in 1979/80, it is clear that the growth in graduates of these programs cannot keep pace with the forecast growth in primary school enrollment during the Second Five-Year Plan.[93] The shortfall of trained teachers at the primary and higher educational levels will continue to be met by expatriate teachers. It is likely that the general scarcity of trained teachers will continue to be a serious problem through the course of the Second Five-Year Plan.

Professional categories C2 and D (table 19) represent occupations in the areas of skilled office, skilled manual, and semi-skilled labor requiring primary or intermediate education plus vocational training. From the forecast deficits in these two categories it is clear that substantial potential gains exist for the direction and training of the unskilled labor surplus in those requirements of the indicated low- to intermediate-skill occupations. The emphasis in the Second Five-Year Plan is thus not only on primary, intermediate, and secondary education, but also on vocational and technical training.

The training system in the Yemen Arab Republic has two goals: the upgrading of the skill level of the domestic labor force and increased worker productivity within the labor force. The number of trainees is expected to be increased by 36,766 persons during the 1982-1986 period.[94] Of these, 65 percent will be trained in the local vocational/technical training institutes while 35 percent will receive training abroad.[95] Training takes place on the short- and long-term bases, with short-term training not exceeding four months. Of the trainees, 42 percent would receive short-term training and 52 percent would receive long-term training.[96]

In overall terms, the number of persons trained is expected to satisfy 23.8 percent of the demand for labor due to planned growth in the gross domestic product (GDP).[97] In addition, 27,904 students are expected to graduate from primary, intermediate, and secondary schools during the Second Five-Year Plan.[98] Together, training and formal education are expected to satisfy 41.9 percent of demand for labor from planned expansion of the gross domestic product.[99]

The upgrading of the skill levels of the domestic labor force is a long-term development goal and must be viewed as such. In this sense the existence of skilled labor shortages is merely a symptom of the development process. The fact that approximately 64,700 new workers entering the labor force during the 1982-1986 span are expected to have primary, intermediate, secondary, or vocational/technical education is a clear sign that substantial progress is being made.

The Second Five-Year Plan's manpower forecast, as noted earlier, estimates that approximately 260,000 unskilled workers will enter the domestic labor supply between 1981 and 1986, creating a general unskilled labor surplus of almost 140,000. A 1981 World Bank manpower forecast puts the general unskilled labor surplus for the period 1980-1985 in the range of 92,600 to 141,200 under the condition of stabilized emigration of Yemeni workers at 1975 levels.[100] Alternatively, under a scenario of increasing emigration by YAR workers in the 1980-1985 period, the World Bank estimates a shortfall of general unskilled labor in the range of 14,400 to 63,300.[101]

The emergence of a general unskilled labor surplus is thus heavily dependent on a scenario of stabilized emigration from North Yemen. Such a scenario in turn is heavily dependent upon the level of expatriate labor demand of the oil economies of the Arabian Peninsula—particularly Saudi Arabia, which accounts for in excess of 90 percent of recorded Yemeni short-term emigrants.[102]

In the past, labor scarcity has created heavy reliance on expatriate labor in Saudi Arabia. This situation has been accentuated by the reluctance of Saudi nationals to engage in employment in the construction and manufacturing sectors. The growth of nonnational employ-

Table 20: Employment of Migrants in Saudi Arabia By Selected Years

Year	Employment
1962/63	60,000
1966/67	240,400
1975	723,400
1980	1,023,600
1984	1,000,000

Sources: J. S. Birks and C. A. Sinclair, *Arab Manpower: The Crisis of Development* (New York: St. Martin's Press, 1980), chapter 5, cited in *Saudi Arabia: Energy, Developmental Planning, and Industrialization*, eds. Ragaei El Mallakh and Dorothea H. El Mallakh (Lexington, Massachusetts: Lexington Books/D.C. Heath and Company, 1982), p. 164, and *The Financial Times* (London), November 26, 1984.

ment has followed the course of increased oil revenues. Table 20 documents the growth of expatriate labor in Saudi Arabia for selected years. The drop in the estimated number of YAR expatriates in Saudi Arabia in 1984 is traceable to the slowed world economy of the early 1980s, reflected in lower international oil demand and prices, and to increased numbers of workers imported for specific projects from such Asian labor pools as Korea, the Philippines, and Thailand. Moreover, as the basic infrastructure of Saudi Arabia nears completion, less unskilled manual labor is required for massive construction programs.

Over the years, the demand for emigrant workers in Saudi Arabia has been met to a large extent by the Yemenis. Their emigration to Saudi Arabia grew steadily through the early 1970s, with the Yemeni share of the nonnational labor force in the Kingdom peaking at 39 percent in 1975.[103] Table 21 provides a World Bank estimate of the recorded YAR migrant population and labor force residing in Saudi Arabia for the years 1969-1977. The World Bank study presents a very conservative estimate of Yemeni emigration in that it considers only Yemenis *recorded* as residing in Saudi Arabia. However, table 21 is indicative of the responsiveness of Yemeni emigration to labor demands in Saudi Arabia. The recorded Yemeni expatriate labor force increased 63 percent between 1970 and 1975 to meet the increased economic activity caused by the tremendous surge in Saudi Arabian development spending. With the relationship between labor needs in

Table 21: Estimate of the Recorded North Yemeni Migrant Population and Labor Force in Saudi Arabia, 1969-1977

Year	Population	Labor Force
1969	302,066	187,885
1970	295,730	183,944
1971	323,410	201,161
1972	337,933	210,194
1973	383,233	238,371
1974	403,186	250,782
1975	480,794	299,054
1976	469,668	292,133
1977	444,706	276,607

Source: World Bank, *Manpower Development in the Yemen Arab Republic* (Washington, D.C.: World Bank, 1981), p. 161.

Saudi Arabia and migration of Yemeni workers, manpower planning in North Yemen must anticipate the labor requirements of the Third Five-Year Development Plan of Saudi Arabia.

In overall terms, the Saudi Third Five-Year Development Plan anticipates a level of spending on the order of $363,000 million in constant 1980 dollars; this contrasts to a level of spending of $133,000 million at constant 1980 dollars for the Second Five-Year Development Plan.[104] It is estimated that total employment in Saudi Arabia will grow by 4 percent over the course of the Third Five-Year Development Plan, from 2,213,570 to 2,693,900. Within this total employment projection, expatriate employment is forecast to rise by 5.1 percent over the course of the Plan from 1,023,580 to 1,314,370.[105]

Continued rapid growth of employment in manufacturing, utilities, and services in Saudi Arabia has been predicted for the 1980-1985 period. In terms of the construction sector, the main source of jobs for Yemeni workers, employment is seen as stable. The Birks and Sinclair study estimates that the existing work force of 385,390 is sufficient to meet the demands in that sector given planned government expenditures.[106] The essential rationale of zero growth in the construction sector is the transferral of priority from massive infrastructural development to concentration on industrial capacity.

One assessment by Birks and Sinclair of the Third Five-Year Development Plan of Saudi Arabia reinforces the World Bank's "most-likely scenario" forecast of stabilized Yemeni emigration.[107] Several main points can be detailed. First, there has been a clear indication of the desire of the Saudi government to limit expatriate labor growth in Saudi Arabia. However, a suggested constraint of 1 percent per annum on the expatriate labor force growth rate seems untenable in light of planned expenditures on the Third Five-Year Development Plan. But the Birks and Sinclair forecast of a 5.1 percent per annum expatriate labor growth rate represents a significant reduction from the official Saudi estimate of 7.2 percent for 1975 to 1980 and the 1980-1985 expected increase in expatriate employment of 9 percent.[108]

Stabilization of employment in the construction sector will have a substantial impact on Yemeni emigration because the construction sector provides the main source of employment for Yemeni emigrants. There is also a trend toward increased reliance on Asian contractors in the construction sector. This trend works against Yemeni employment in that such contracts specify that the contractor supply the requisite labor from their country of origin.

Most importantly, the stabilization of Yemeni emigration can be traced to a fundamental shift in the focus of development in the oil states. Sirageldin describes the general pattern of development as one of (a) infrastructural buildup, (b) operation of major enterprises, and (c) stabilized growth.[109] The initial stage of infrastructural development is marked by massive construction activity on roads, ports, power systems, and the initiation of industrial development projects. The oil-exporting country, as Sirageldin puts it, is turned into "one large construction site" highly dependent upon large-scale importation of unskilled manual labor.[110]

Such was the scenario in the bulk of the oil states (excluding Bahrain and Kuwait) during the decade of the 1970s. A peninsula-wide concentration on infrastructural development occurred which created and favored a massive demand for low-level skilled or unskilled manual labor. This demand was, to a large extent, met by Yemeni emigrants.

The decade of the 1980s marks the transition to Sirageldin's second stage of development, that of the operation of major enterprises. Infrastructural development is largely complete and initiated industrial projects begin to enter production. Infrastructural development and industrial projects will continue but at a controlled pace. The key implication for Yemeni planners is the gradual shift in the qualitative demand for expatriate labor, shifting from lower-level skilled and unskilled manual labor to medium- and higher-level skilled labor required for the operation of major industries. While the 1970s favored the unskilled emigrant from North Yemen, the 1980s will favor the higher-level skilled emigrants from Arab countries such as Egypt.

This ongoing phenomenon—the qualitative shift in expatriate labor demand—can be seen in table 22. In 1974 low-level skilled expatriate employment accounted for 53 percent of total expatriate employment in Saudi Arabia while high-level skilled expatriates accounted for only 14 percent. These figures are consistent with initial infrastructural and industrial development. By 1978 expatriates employed in high-level skill positions accounted for 56 percent of total expatriate employment in Saudi Arabia; the low-skills share had fallen to 29 percent. And this is consistent with the shift from infrastructural development to industrial operations.

There are two factors operating to reduce the demand for expatriate labor from North Yemen. First, there is the overall reduction in the rate of growth in expatriate labor demand as the oil states shift to industrial operations. Second, there is a qualitative shift in expatriate labor demand which favors the higher-level skills required for the operation of major industry. These two factors reinforce the World Bank's forecast of a growing domestic surplus of Yemeni unskilled labor, possibly reaching 142,000 workers by 1985.

The preceding analysis supports the plausability of a stabilized emigration scenario for North Yemen. The main points of the 1981 World Bank manpower forecast, based upon such a scenario, can now be stated and considered for their implications in North Yemen: (1) an unskilled labor surplus of up to 141,200 Yemeni workers by 1985; (2) substantial shortfalls for the skill categories, i.e., skilled office, skilled manual, and semi-skilled labor; (3) a trend towards a surplus of arts-based professionals and subprofessionals beyond 1985; and (4) a growing shortfall of trained science-based professionals and subprofessionals over the course of the Second Five-Year Plan.[111]

The first two points in the preceding paragraph can be considered in conjunction with one another; a growing unskilled labor surplus coupled with significant shortfalls in the indicated low- to medium-skill categories. It is clear that the greatest gains can be obtained through the direction and training of the unskilled labor surplus toward the requisite skill requirements of the indicated low- to medium-skill occupations. This is very much in line with the emphasis of the Second

Table 22: Expatriate Employment Shares by Skill Level in Saudi Arabia, 1974 and 1978

Skill Level	1974	1978
High (professionals, managers, administrators)	13.8	55.5
Medium (clerical, sales, service)	33.2	15.8
Low (farmers, fishermen, craftsmen, laborers)	53.0	28.7

Source: Naiem A. Sherbiny and Ismail Sirageldin, "Expatriate Labor and Economic Growth: Saudi Demand for Egyptian Labor," in *Rich and Poor States in the Middle East: Egypt & the New Arab Order*, eds. Malcolm H. Kerr and El Sayed Yassin (Boulder, Colorado: Westview Press, 1982), p. 235.

Five-Year Plan on vocational and technical training. Such training should allow sufficient flexibility in course content, length, and recruitment to allow for part-time or evening study as well as greater adult participation. Literacy courses and apprenticeship programs would further augment the transformation of the unskilled labor surplus into the needed low- to medium-skill workers.

The trends toward a surplus of arts-based professionals and subprofessionals in the face of a growing shortage of science-based professionals and subprofessionals can also be considered together. These trends can best be addressed by first introducing a sound math and science foundation at the primary and preparatory levels. Such action will provide a pool of potential candidates with the requisite skills and favorable outlook for the pursuit of careers in scientific occupations. Second, intensive counselling at the collegiate and graduate level should stress the career opportunities and benefits of science-based occupations. In this sense, counselling can serve to provide a more favorable image of scientific education and its long-run career potential.

It is widely accepted that as long as all graduates in any collegiate field are exposed to a sound analytic background in problem solving, then a country would possess a trained work force of sufficient flexibility to adopt to any development needs. In essence, if rigorous analytic training is at the core of all education, regardless of art- or science-based career objectives, then the graduates of such a system will possess the flexibility to adapt to the development requirements of the country.

Having an impact on human resources development is the level of health-related services available to the population. With serious financial constraints, a largely rural population, and the years of isolation prior to the Revolution, North Yemen is confronted with a low base in health services and a burgeoning youthful population. In 1982 the crude birth rate was 48.3 per 1,000 with a crude death rate of 21.8 per 1,000.[112] As with other social infrastructure, the capital requirements are high and the return on investment is not immediate and frequently is not direct. In 1981 recurrent expenditures for health were 103 million rials, which extended to about 15 percent of the population. It has been estimated that by the year 2000, if 50 percent of the population is covered, the recurrent expenditures for health services would reach 1.754 billion rials (in 1981 rials).[113]

In just a little over one decade, the YAR has made significant strides in raising the level of social services, an even more impressive feat when the low initial base is considered. During the period between 1970 and 1982, life expectancy at birth rose from 31.5 to 43.7 years; infant mortality (per thousand) fell from 188 to 163; the crude death rate (per thousand) declined from 26.5 to 21.6; the population per physician dropped more than 50 percent from 24,370 to 11,670; the share of the population with access to safe water rose from 4 percent to as high as 20 percent; the adult literacy rate doubled from 10 percent to 21 percent; and school enrollment as a percent of school-age population rose from 12 percent to 47 percent for the primary grades and from 1 percent to 5 percent for the secondary level.[114] Nonetheless, by the United Nations definition of social indicators for low-income countries, North Yemen remains in that category in the 1980s.[115]

Notes

1. World Bank, *Manpower Development in the Yemen Arab Republic* (Washington, D.C.: World Bank, 1981), p. 67.

2. Ibid., p. 63.

3. Ibid., and World Bank,"Yemen Arab Republic Country Economic Memorandum Current Position and Prospects," Report no. 5621-YAR (Washington, D.C., June 25, 1985), p. 43 (mimeographed).

4. United Nations Educational, Scientific, and Cultural Organization (UNESCO), *Statistical Yearbook 1982* (Paris: UNESCO, 1982), table 3.2; The Arab Planning Institute,"Regional Cooperation in Human Resources Development in the Arab Countries" (Kuwait, October 1983), p. 35 (mimeographed); World Bank,"Yemen Arab Republic Country Economic Memorandum Current Position and Prospects," country data page.

5. Yemen Arab Republic, Ministry of Education, working paper, 1982, p. 2.

6. Yemen Arab Republic, Central Planning Organization, *Second Five-Year Plan (1982-1986)*, March 1982, chapter 1, p. 14.

7. Yemen Arab Republic, Ministry of Education, working paper, 1982, p. 6.

8. The Arab Planning Institute, "Regional Cooperation in Human Resources Development in the Arab Countries," p. 40.

9. Ibid.

10. Yemen Arab Republic, Ministry of Education, working paper, 1982, p. 5.

11. World Bank, *Issues and Priorities in Human Resource Development in the Yemen Arab Republic* (Washington, D.C.: World Bank, 1981), p. 4.

12. World Bank, *Manpower Development in the Yemen Arab Republic*, p. 169, and Yemen Arab Republic, Central Planning Organization, *Second Five-Year Plan (1982-1986)*, chapter 1, p. 15.

13. Ibid.

14. Ibid.

15. Yemen Arab Republic, Ministry of Education, working paper, 1982, p. 8.

16. Ibid.

17. World Bank, *Manpower Development in the Yemen Arab Republic*, p. 176.

18. Yemen Arab Republic, Ministry of Education, working paper, 1982, p. 8.

19. World Bank, *Manpower Development in the Yemen Arab Republic*, p. 69.

20. Yemen Arab Republic, Ministry of Education, working paper, 1982, p. 8.

21. Ibid.

22. Ibid.

23. Mohammed Ahmed Zabarah, *Yemen: Traditionalism Versus Modernity* (New York: Praeger, 1982), p. 121.

24. World Bank, *Manpower Development in the Yemen Arab Republic*, p. 171.

25. Yemen Arab Republic, Central Planning Organization, Statistics Department, *Statistical Year Book, 1979-1980*, p. 248.

26. World Bank, *Manpower Development in the Yemen Arab Republic*, p. 66.

27. Ibid., p. 174.

28. Yemen Arab Republic, Ministry of Education, working paper, 1982, p. 9.

29. The Arab Planning Institute,"Regional Cooperation in Human Resources Development in the Arab Countries," p. 44.

30. World Bank, *Manpower Development in the Yemen Arab Republic*, p. 165.

31. Yemen Arab Republic, Central Planning Organization, Statistics Department, *Statistical Year Book, 1979-1980*, table 2. It is assumed that the ratio of short- to long-term emigration has remained constant since 1975 up to 1981/82 and the impact of the world oil glut on oil revenues of the Gulf states.

32. United States, Department of Commerce, *Foreign Economic Trends and Their Implications for the United States: Yemen Arab Republic* (Washington, D.C.: Government Printing Office, 1981), pp. 4 and 5.

33. Jon Swanson, *Emigration and Economic Development: The Case of the Yemen Arab Republic* (Boulder, Colorado: Westview Press, 1979), p. 75.

34. Ibid., p. 76.

35. World Bank, *Manpower Development in the Yemen Arab Republic*, p. 55.

36. Yemen Arab Republic, Central Planning Organization, Statistics Department, *Statistical Year Book, 1979-1980*, p. 350. Estimates in 1984 put the unofficial per-capita income at around $1,500 with $1,000 accounted for by remittances and $500 the official

per-capita income, *The Financial Times* (London), November 26, 1984.

37. Ismail Sirageldin,"Labor Adaptation in the Oil Exporting Countries," in *Manpower Planning in the Oil Countries*, ed. Naiem A. Sherbiny (Greenwich, Connecticut: JAI Press Inc., 1981), p. 211.

38. World Bank, *Annual Report 1984* (Washington, D.C.: World Bank, 1984), p.110, and Yemen Arab Republic, Central Planning Organization,"Fourth Year Annual Report of the Second Five-Year Plan" (February 1985), p. 12 (mimeographed, in Arabic).

39. Ibid.

40. Jon Swanson, *Emigration and Economic Development: The Case of the Yemen Arab Republic*, p. 64.

41. World Bank, *Manpower Development in the Yemen Arab Republic*, pp. 53-54.

42. Jon Swanson, *Emigration and Economic Development: The Case of the Yemen Arab Republic*, p. 70.

43. Ibid., p. 71.

44. Ibid.

45. World Bank, *Yemen Arab Republic: Urban Sector Report* (Washington, D.C.: World Bank, 1981), p. 23.

46. Ibid.

47. Yemen Arab Republic, Central Planning Organization, Statistics Department, *Statistical Year Book, 1981*, p. 184, and Central Bank of Yemen, Research Department, *Financial Statistical Bulletin*, January-March 1984, table 16 (mimeographed).

48. World Bank, *Yemen Arab Republic: Urban Sector Report*, p. 25.

49. Ibid.

50. Yemen Arab Republic, Central Bank of Yemen, *Annual Report 1976* cited in Jon Swanson, *Emigration and Economic Development: The Case of the Yemen Arab Republic*, p. 85.

51. World Bank, *Yemen Arab Republic: Urban Sector Report*, p. 9.

52. Ibid.

53. Ibid.

54. Jon Swanson, *Emigration and Economic Development: The Case of the Yemen Arab Republic*, p. 82.

55. Ibid.

56. World Bank, *Manpower Development in the Yemen Arab Republic*, p. 55.

57. World Bank, *Yemen Arab Republic: Urban Sector Report*, p. 49.

58. Ibid.

59. Ibid.

60. Yemen Arab Republic, Central Bank of Yemen, Research Department, *Financial Statistical Bulletin*, January-March 1984, table 19.

61. Jon Swanson, *Emigration and Economic Development: The Case of the Yemen Arab Republic*, p. 82.

62. World Bank, *Yemen Arab Republic: Urban Sector Report*, p. 44.

63. Ibid.

64. Ibid.

65. Yemen Arab Republic, Central Planning Organization, *Second Five-Year Plan (1982-1986)*, chapter 3, p. 41.

66. Yemen Arab Republic, Central Planning Organization, Statistics Department, *Statistical Year Book, 1979-1980*, p. 219, and Central Bank of Yemen, Research Department, *Financial Statistical Bulletin*, January-March 1984, table 16.

67. Yemen Arab Republic, Central Planning Organization,"Fourth Year Annual Report of the Second Five-Year Plan," table 7, p. 16.

68. Yemen Arab Republic, Central Planning Organization, *Second Five-Year Plan (1982-1986)*, chapter 3, p. 25.

69. Ibid.

70. World Bank, *Manpower Development in the Yemen Arab Republic*, p. 63.

71. Yemen Arab Republic, Central Planning Organization, Statistics Department, *Statistical Year Book, 1981*, p. 189.
72. Yemen Arab Republic, Central Planning Organization, *Second Five-Year Plan (1982-1986)*, chapter 1, p. 14.
73. World Bank, *Manpower Development in the Yemen Arab Republic*, p. 63.
74. Yemen Arab Republic, Central Planning Organization, *Second Five-Year Plan (1982-1986)*, chapter 1, p. 16.
75. Ibid.
76. Ibid., p. 6.
77. World Bank, *Issues and Priorities in Human Resource Development in the Yemen Arab Republic*, p. 30.
78. Yemen Arab Republic, Central Planning Organization, *Second Five-Year Plan (1982-1986)*, chapter 3, p. 38.
79. Ibid., p. 3.
80. Ibid., p. 33.
81. Ibid., p. 36.
82. Ibid., p. 40.
83. Ibid., p. 38.
84. Ibid., p. 34.
85. Ibid.
86. Ibid.
87. World Bank, *Manpower Development in the Yemen Arab Republic*, p. 196.
88. Ibid.
89. Yemen Arab Republic, Ministry of Education, working paper, 1982, p. 5.
90. Ibid., p. 9.
91. World Bank, *Manpower Development in the Yemen Arab Republic*, p. 174.
92. Ibid.
93. Ibid.
94. Yemen Arab Republic, Central Planning Organization, *Second Five-Year Plan (1982-1986)*, chapter 3, p. 42.
95. Ibid., p. 43.
96. Ibid.
97. Ibid., p. 42.
98. Ibid.
99. Ibid.
100. World Bank, *Manpower Development in the Yemen Arab Republic*, p. 196.
101. Ibid.
102. Ibid., pp.117-118.
103. J. S. Birks and C. A. Sinclair, *International Migration and Development in the Arab Region* (Geneva: International Labor Organization, 1980), table 10, p. 134.
104. C. A. Sinclair and J. S. Birks,"Manpower in Saudi Arabia, 1980-1985," in *Saudi Arabia: Energy, Developmental Planning, and Industrialization*, eds. Ragaei El Mallakh and Dorothea H. El Mallakh (Lexington, Massachusetts: Lexington Books/D. C. Heath and Company, 1982), p. 166.
105. Ibid., p. 173.
106. Ibid.
107. Ibid.
108. Ibid., and Kingdom of Saudi Arabia, Ministry of Planning, *Third Development Plan 1400-1405 A. H. (1980-1985 A. D.)*, pp. 98-99.
109. Ismail Sirageldin,"Labor Adaptation in the Oil Exporting Countries," in *Manpower Planning in the Oil Countries*, p. 211.
110. Ibid., p. 210.
111. World Bank, *Manpower Development in the Yemen Arab Republic*, p. 196.
112. World Bank,"Yemen Arab Republic Country Economic Memorandum Current

Position and Prospects," country data page.
113. Ibid., p. 59.
114. Ibid., p. 43.
115. Ibid., as seen in the following table:

Comparison of YAR Selected Social Indicators with Other Low-Income Countries, 1982

	YAR	Low-Income Countries
Health		
Life expectancy at birth (years)	43.7	males 58/females 60
Infant mortality (per thousand)	163.0	87.0
Crude death rate (per thousand)	21.6	11.0
Population per physician[a]	11,670.0	5,772.0
Access to safe water (% of population)[b]	20.0	Asia/Pacific: 32.9 Africa: 21.8
Education		
Enrollment ratios (% of school-age population)		
Primary	47.0	94.0[c]
Secondary	5.0	34.0[c]
Adult literacy rate (%)	21.0[a]	Asia/Pacific: 53.4 Africa: 44.3[c]

[a]For 1980.
[b]World Bank estimate.
[c]For 1981.

4 INFRASTRUCTURE

Provisions for basic infrastructure have been concentrated in the principal cities. The major urban areas of the Yemen Arab Republic are located in the main agricultural regions of the country, which are in the governorates of Sana'a, Ibb, Taiz, and Hodeidah, which together account for about 80 percent of all agricultural land and almost two-thirds of all residents. The tendency toward overwhelming growth and importance of any one urban center has been constrained by a widely dispersed rural population, the extremely rugged topography, traditions of regional autonomy, and a diversity of economic functions among the major cities.

Sana'a became the official capital of the Yemen Arab Republic after the Revolution and has evolved as the political and administrative center of the country. Construction, commerce, and service activities are also important in Sana'a. Hodeidah is the main port and the principal industrial city. Taiz was the traditional capital of the Imam prior to the Revolution and has a long history as a trading center due to its position on the major trade routes to Aden and Mocha.

Yemen's governorate capital cities have grown rapidly since the early 1970s. Three major determinants for this growth can be identified: (1) the concentration of investment in the urban areas and consequent economic growth; (2) national population growth and the leveling off of short-term emigration; and (3) rural-to-urban migration, particularly as the higher level of prosperity in the urban areas has induced single males to leave their families in the rural regions. Regardless of whether this rural-to-urban migration is short term or long term in nature, it accounts for the bulk of the population growth in the cities.

Despite the perceived rapid increase in the number of people residing in the cities, only about 7.76 percent of the total resident population lives in one of the capital cities—which is normally the largest city in a governorate.[1] The majority of the population still resides in the countryside. Table 23 and figure 2 present the population of the Yemen Arab Republic by governorate and the population by capital city in each governorate.

Under the Three-Year Development Program (1973/74-1975/76), the first investments were made in urban water supply, sewerage, and

Infrastructure 71

Table 23: Population by Governorate and Capital City, 1975 and 1981

	1975		1981	
	Governorate Population	Capital Population	Governorate Population	Capital Population
Sana'a	819,010	135,625	1,396,535	279,395
Taiz	877,777	79,720	1,173,147	116,382
Hodeidah	673,113	2,895	816,319	126,427
Ibb	789,494	17,496	1,018,422	34,174
Dhamar	453,888	19,540	594,132	39,885
Hajjah	394,827	3,294	664,869	25,444
Saadah	158,410	3,806	249,307	9,587
Mahweet	175,509	2,292	223,531	7,186
Beida	159,129	10,419	247,27	512,988
Marib	39,121	2,494	83,760	4,683
Jawf	—	—	62,066	6,251
Total	4,540,278	347,581	6,529,363	662,402

Sources: Yemen Arab Republic, Central Planning Organization, Statistics Department, *Statistical Year Book, 1981*, p. 34; The Confederation of Yemeni Development Associations, Central Planning Organization, Statistics Department, *Summary, Final Results of the Cooperative Population Census*, February 1981, p. 9; and World Bank, *Yemen Arab Republic: Urban Sector Report*, (Washington, D.C.: World Bank, March 1981), pp. 69-71.

electrification, establishing a small foundation for industrial activities. However, the provision and maintenance of this infrastructure in the three major cities of Sana'a, Hodeidah, and Taiz is still inadequate, and creation of infrastructure in the rural regions is starting from an extremely low base. This chapter surveys the country's road, port, civil aviation, communications, electricity, and water and sewerage infrastructure development.

Roads

Until the late 1950s primitive tracks suitable only for four-wheel drive

72 Infrastructure

Figure 2: Governorates and Population

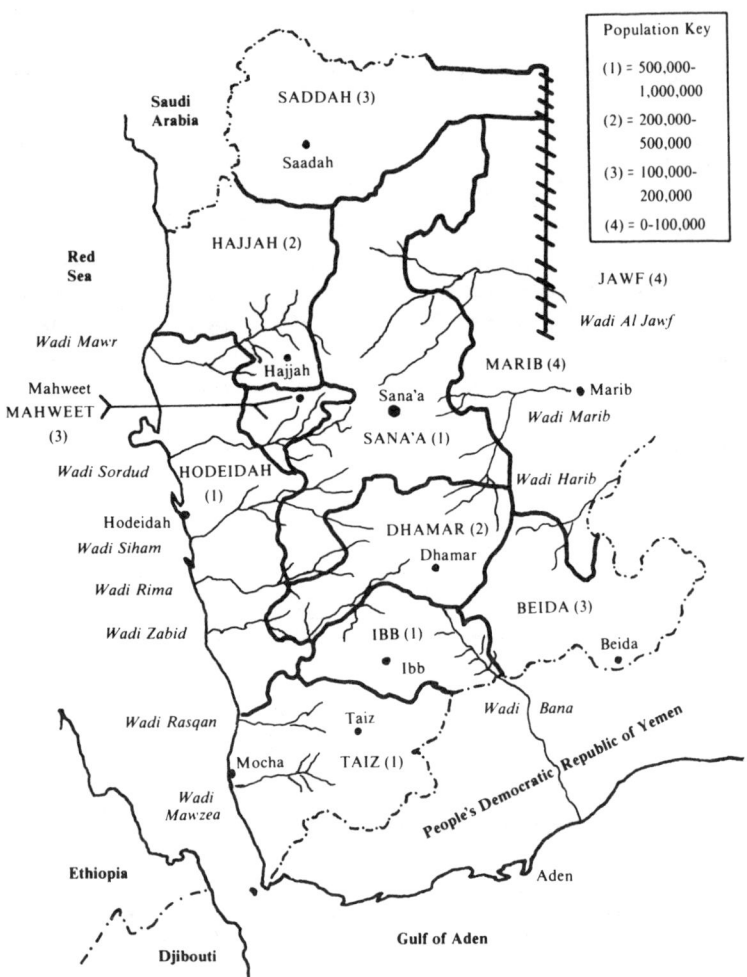

Source: Based upon map in World Bank, *Yemen Arab Republic: Development of a Traditional Economy* (Washington, D.C.: World Bank, 3rd printing, 1983).

vehicles and animal transportion connected major towns and were the only means of land transport. Initial development of modern transportation was on a project-by-project basis, much of which was financed by bilateral assistance. While this development was initiated without any formal national transportation plan, the first investments in transport infrastructure were, nonetheless, directed to the highest-priority projects. In these early years of the development of transportation infrastructure, The People's Republic of China underwrote the costs of a highway from the port of Hodeidah to the capital city of Sana'a which was completed in 1961; the United States financed a road from Taiz to the border with the People's Democratic Republic of Yemen (P.D.R.Y., or South Yemen) and another road to the port of Mocha; and the Soviet Union completed this main road triangle by financing a road down the coast from Hodeidah to an intersection with the Taiz-Mocha highway.

Bilateral aid continued to be a major source of funds for transport infrastructure. The Federal Republic of Germany financed the paving of the Sana'a-Taiz road; China built a paved road from Sana'a north to Saadah; Saudi Arabia financed road construction from Hodeidah north through Zaidya, Azzohrah, Harad, and Madi to connect with a road south from Jizan in Saudi Arabia and financed the Dhamar-Rada-Beida Road.

In addition to bilateral aid, the Yemen Arab Republic has received credits and loans, often for support of infrastructure development, from a number of international development organizations. These include the World Bank affiliate International Development Association, the Kuwait Fund for Arab Economic Development, the Abu Dhabi Fund for Arab Economic Development, and the Arab Fund for Economic and Social Development. Lending from the Abu Dhabi Fund for Arab Economic Development and the Arab Fund for Economic and Social Development helped to finance construction of the Sana'a-Marib and the Taiz-Rahida highways.

Construction of much of the secondary (or feeder) road network has been financed by local authorities and development associations. Construction of certain feeder roads has also been included in the International Development Association-financed Tihama and Southern Uplands projects. A substantial part of the feeder road development has also been carried out by the national Highway Authority.

Within the cities of Sana'a, Hodeidah, and Taiz, only the principal streets are surfaced. Short, intense rainfall and heavy traffic have caused serious damage with repairs lagging. An additional problem in the cities is the lack of project coordination between the municipalities, which are responsible for inner-city roads, and the public utilities projects involving the installation of water supply, sewerage, electricity, and telephone services. And due to the shortage of staff, funds, machinery, and equipment at the municipal level, the municipalities tend to depend on the Highway Authority which also faces a shortage of resources.

The Highway Authority, overseen by the Ministry of Public Works, is responsible for the design, construction, and maintenance of the national highway network, while general planning for highway development and transport planning as a whole are the responsibility of the Ministry of Development and its planning arm, the Central Planning Organization.

The highway network in the Yemen Arab Republic in 1981 consisted of some 1,924 kilometers of asphalt roads and 17,299 kilometers of feeder roads.[2] The main road network is nearly all paved and links the principal urban centers. However, a significant portion of the paved network, much of which traverses some of the world's most rugged terrain, is difficult to keep in good condition due to axle overloading and rapid traffic growth. Public-sector investment under the Second Five-Year Plan, therefore, was expected to total 380 million Yemeni rials for the improvement and maintenance of the Sana'a-Taiz, Sana'a-Hodeidah, and Hodeidah-Taiz roads as well as maintenance of the roads in those cities.[3]

Road construction is still an important priority in the Yemen Arab Republic in order to provide suitable transport links from the agricultural areas to marketing centers. In 1981 work began on a 96-kilometer road between Yarim—which is located approximately at the halfway point on the Sana'a to Taiz road—and Qataba, close to the People's Democratic Republic of Yemen border. The total cost of this three-year construction project was estimated at 320 million Yemeni rials ($70.2 million). The Fourth Highway Project was under way at the beginning of the Second Five-Year Plan period (1982-1986) and involved upgrading the link between Taiz and Mafraq, while the Fifth Highway Project (announced in 1983) added the Udayn to Ibb road (figure 3). Having achieved a national network of paved roads, the emphasis in transportation infrastructure is being transferred to upgrading and maintenance of highways now in place and the development and improvement of feeder-rural roads and urban streets. For example, in 1983 the YAR received a $13 million credit from the International Development Association to help finance a $35.5-million project. This

Infrastructure 75

Figure 3: Highway Network

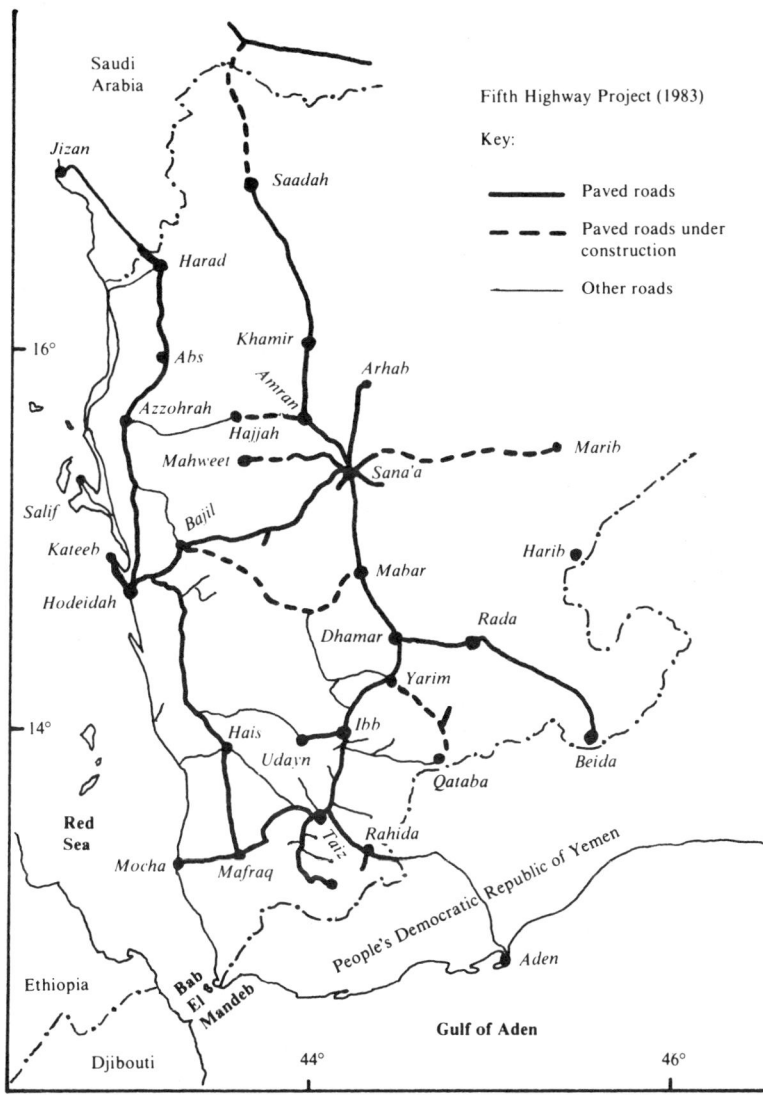

Source: Based upon map in World Bank, *Yemen Arab Republic: Development of a Traditional Economy* (Washington, D.C.: World Bank, 3rd printing, 1983).

project is aimed at improving communications in the more densely populated rural areas and will support the Highway Authority's efforts to upgrade and reconstruct secondary roads, while providing maintenance and training.[4]

Ports

Until 1960 port facilities in the Yemen Arab Republic were limited to the ancient port of Mocha, which was suitable only for lighterage. As a result, prior to the completion of the deep-water port at Hodeidah, much of the import traffic moved through the port of Aden. After the independence of the People's Democratic Republic of Yemen from Great Britain this traffic came to a virtual halt; however, by then the port at Hodeidah had begun operations.

While the port at Hodeidah, the country's busiest, currently requires expansion and modernization of its facilities, the long delays in offloading (often 180 days) experienced in the mid-1970s have been alleviated, with delays running an average of only two days in early 1981 and virtually eliminated by 1984. The severe congestion problems of the mid-1970s were a consequence of the lack of basic infrastructure—warehouse space, handling equipment, and paved and leveled storage areas—and various administrative problems which reduced the efficiency of port operations. Temporary measures to ease traffic flow included the use of a helium-filled balloon named the Queen of Sheba to lift cargo from ships and barges. Also, a temporary floating jetty was commissioned at Ras Al Kateeb near Hodeidah's outer harbor, and a 14-kilometer gravel road was built to link the city of Hodeidah to the new facility.

In 1974 the Hodeidah Port Authority secured technical assistance, materials, and equipment from the Soviet Union for construction of a fourth and later a fifth general cargo berth. Under the provisions of a $6 million credit from the International Development Agency approved in May 1977, a sixth berth was built. The Kuwait Fund for Arab Economic Development provided an $8 million loan for the Hodeidah port expansion project which included deepening the approach channel and the basin of the port, constructing a new dry dock, and the installation of equipment.[5] This project was designed to meet the needs of the Yemen Arab Republic's port facilities up to 1985. The construction manager for Hodeidah's $73-million port improvement scheme was the United Kingdom's Sir Alexander Gibb & Partners; Japan's Mitsubishi

Corporation won the 143 million Yemeni rials ($31.4 million) construction contract. Studies and designs for the undertaking were carried out by the United States' Louis Berger International. Port supply contracts worth about $42 million were offered for a crane, roll-on roll-off tractors, a floating crane, and a container crane. The Overseas Economic Cooperation Fund of Japan is to help finance the construction of a seventh berth as well as a second 300-meter container berth and other support services.

In the mid-1970s certain vessels and cargoes (such as roll-on roll-off) were directed to the port of Salif—which had virtually no equipment for unloading—to reduce the bottleneck at Hodeidah. The Salif port facility, utilizing one of the best natural harbors on the Red Sea, can berth two freighters at a time, but its lack of infrastructure necessitated trucking cargo 60 miles south to Hodeidah. As a result, an expansion program was initiated to enable Salif to handle trucks, grain storage, petroleum import and storage, and general cargo handling.

The port of Mocha lies to the south of Hodeidah and west of the city of Taiz to which it is connected by a paved road. The facilities at the port were constructed in 1955, and only vessels of up to seven-foot draught could enter. The government initiated a major improvement program for the Mocha port with the construction of a 750-meter-long breakwater, the dredging of an access channel including a turning basin and berthing pockets, and the strengthening and enlargement of the pier. This project enables the port to accommodate vessels of up to 15,000 deadweight tons. Sir William Halcrow and Partners of the United Kingdom designed the expansion project and supervised construction by the Dutch company Dirk Verstoep. The design for improvement project costing $50 million for expansion of Mocha port by up to 10 berths was undertaken by the same firm of Sir William Halcrow and Partners in 1981.

Civil Aviation

Air transportation facilities are one of the infrastructural areas where greatest progress was made during the 1970s. Three major airports located at Sana'a, Hodeidah, and Taiz service domestic and international travel, and airstrips at Saadah and Berat provide for domestic service in the north. There are also a number of other rudimentary air strips in the country, some of which can handle DC-3s.

The Sana'a International Airport was originally built through assistance from the Soviet Union; in 1973 it was reequipped and modernized by a project conducted in cooperation with the Federal Republic of Germany. The runway, which is 3,250 meters long, was strengthened and can now accommodate planes of the Boeing 707 class.

Work began in 1982 on further improvements of the Sana'a airport which will enable it to handle more and larger aircraft with maximum safety precautions. The main aircraft apron will be expanded to 84,168 square meters in order to accommodate 10 Boeing 707s simultaneously. At a later stage, the apron will have the capacity to hold 17 such aircraft at one time, and the cargo apron will be widened to 27,500 square meters to handle three Boeing 747 jumbo jets. The project will improve the airport's electricity source and a new lighting system for the taxiways will improve the safety of take-offs and landings. Other improvements include a main storage building to shelter emergency vehicles and other airport equipment; a hanger for air cargo to expand cargo capacity; and a central maintenance building containing workshops for electricity, carpentry, machinery, communications, sheet metal, drafting, printing, and testing and measuring materials. Additional air traffic control equipment was installed in early 1984.

The new Hodeidah airport, with a runway length of 915 meters, began receiving international flights in late 1979. In 1977 the two U.K. firms of Constain International and Amey Roadstone Construction, won the $33.1 million contract for construction of this new facility, which included taxiways, service roads, a control tower, technical buildings, a generating station, and a fire station. The Hodeidah airport project was financed by the Yemen Arab Republic government and a $15 million loan from the Iraqi Fund for External Development. Supervision of the project was undertaken by the French consultants Sofreavia and the Geneva-based International Civil Aviation Organization, which extended a loan of $2.7 million. Additional buildings and an international terminal were included in 1981 as part of the continuing plan to upgrade the airport for which a second credit of $15 million was secured from the Iraqi Fund for External Development.[6]

The Taiz airport, with a runway 2,400 meters long, can handle two-engine and smaller three-engine jets. This airport is essentially for domestic use.

Saudi Arabia has granted Saudi rials (SR) 400 million (about $120 million) to the Yemen Arab Republic for modernization of its airports within the framework of the Saudi-Yemeni Coordination Council. About SR 180 million ($54 million) of this grant was allocated for the establishment of wireless and telecommunication contact stations, and another SR 10 million ($3 million) for the maintenance and operation of observatory instruments. Additionally, Saudi financing was involved in the construction of three observatories in Sana'a, Taiz, and Hodeidah, as well as a weather forecast center and a satellite receiver station at a cost of SR 89 million ($26.7 million).[7]

The SR 134 million ($40.6 million) Sana'a airport expansion project is also being implemented through the Saudi-Yemeni Coordination Council, and contracts for the work were signed between the Yemeni Civil Aviation and Meteorology Authority and two Saudi Arabian companies. The United Nations Development Program has provided electrical equipment for the Sana'a, Taiz, and Hodeidah airports and technical assistance in airline operations, airport management, radio engineering, and civil aviation.

Air traffic has increased tremendously in recent years. In 1976 there were about 5,892 arrivals and departures at the Sana'a International Airport, with about 108,496 arriving passengers and 139,616 departing passengers. The airport also unloaded 897,176 kilograms of cargo and luggage and loaded 154,130 kilograms in that year. In 1981 there were about 13,406 airplane arrivals and departures with about 204,656 passenger arrivals and 234,834 passenger departures. By 1982, flights decreased to 12,422 but passenger load increased to 220,402 arrivals and 238,236 departures. The amount of cargo and luggage unloaded in that year was 8,073,073 kilograms while 3,289,423 kilograms was loaded. Better port facilities by 1982 helped reduce the volume of goods arriving by air. In 1982 the amount of freight and luggage unloaded was 6,111,746 kilograms and the amount loaded was 3,219,897. The amount of imported goods arriving by sea increased from 1,893,850 tons in 1981 to 2,670,888 tons in 1982. The amount of goods exported from the four major ports rose from 43,493 tons to 99,069 tons in the respective years.[8]

Yemen Airways (also known as Yemenia), the national airline, has a fleet that includes Boeing 737s and 727s and McDonnell Douglas DC-3s and DC-6s. The airline offers internal as well as international flights (to the Gulf states, Aden, Djibouti, Asmara, Damascus, Amman, London, New Delhi, Frankfurt, Nicosia and between Athens and Paris), and passenger traffic has increased markedly for the domestic service, as shown in table 24. International flights are also run by Air France, Lufthansa, KLM, British Airways, Saudia Airlines, Egypt Air, Kuwait Airways, Ethiopia Air, and Sudan Airways.

Yemen Airways agreed to establish a joint-venture with Saudia Airlines on May 21, 1977 with capitalization of $30 million, of which

Table 24: Yemen Airways Passenger Load, 1977-1983

Year	Internal Flights Departing	Arriving	International Flights Departing	Arriving
1977	17,256	17,811	80,038	79,850
1978	19,917	26,139	137,705	111,247
1979	24,471	28,520	92,465	106,045
1980	27,789	42,318	83,652	86,146
1981	50,313	38,433	98,172	78,698
1982	42,480	40,998	98,901	88,203
1983	42,177	43,981	100,732	94,184

Sources: Yemen Arab Republic, Central Planning Organization, Statistics Department, *Statistical Year Book, 1981*, p. 123 and *Statistical Year Book, 1983*, p. 139.

51 percent was subscribed by the Yemen Arab Republic government and 49 percent was subscribed by Saudi Arabia. The agreement became official on July 15, 1978, and in 1980 Yemen Airways' capital was increased with a $10 million injection by Saudi Arabia.[9]

Communications

The government of the Yemen Arab Republic has made considerable progress in recent years in the field of telecommunications. Sana'a has a Standard A earth satellite station built by Cable and Wireless of the United Kingdom, and direct international telephone dialing is available. There is also an earth station (grade B) for international connections.

France's CIT-Alcatel won a contract in 1977 for work totaling $63.8 million under a bilateral economic and technical cooperation agreement, including training and exchange of technology. In September 1982, CIT-Alcatel was awarded the contract to build a new switching center in Sana'a to supplement its earlier installation, which is now used only for international lines. The French firm has also built switching centers in Hodeidah and Taiz. By 1985 the digital switchgear—the all-electronic E-10 system—is to provide 130,000 to 140,000 lines.

A project linking Saudi Arabia, the Yemen Arab Republic, the People's Democratic Republic of Yemen, Djibouti, and Somalia through a microwave network cost an estimated $29.3 million.[10] Under an agreement signed on July 27, 1981 the Arab Fund for Economic and Social Development extended a loan of $4.94 million to the Yemen Arab Republic to help finance the Yemeni section of the project which was scheduled for completion in mid-1985. The network, designed to improve communications throughout the southern part of the Arabian Peninsula and East Africa, will introduce direct international dialing with other countries through Saudi Arabia and provide direct television relay among the participating nations through a special channel. Consultant for the project is a consortium of the United Kingdom's Preece Cardew and Rider (PCR) and Swedtel of Sweden with France's Thomson-CSF as the main contractor. Telettra of Italy subcontracted for the 240-kilometer link between the Jebel Aris mountains in the Yemen Arab Republic and the Deloncle peak in Djibouti. The network will include 30 to 40 transmission stations, many of which will be entirely solar powered. International switching centers with up to 200 connections each will be built in Aden and Djibouti.

Better international and regional telecommunications will result from utilization of the Arabsat. This telecommunication satellite was launched into orbit through a cooperative arrangement between France and the League of Arab States in early 1985. As a member of the Arab League, the YAR is involved in Arabsat.

In intracountry communications, the Yemen Arab Republic is actively seeking to introduce telephone services to the rural areas. The Ministry of Communications has installed nine wireless basic stations, each of which provides 30 telephone regions with direct automatic access to the main telephone system. Thus, 308 villages have been brought in touch with the main switchboards.

While advances are being made in telecommunications, the Yemen Arab Republic's postal system still cannot serve adequately the entire population. Not only does the majority of the populace reside outside larger cities, but the topography of the YAR leads to the isolation of smaller villages and farms. Scattered over an area of 195,000 square kilometers are 130 postal establishments, operating with a total of 1,500 postal officials.[11] Thus, the Yemen Arab Republic's postal service does not yet meet the objectives set by the Universal Postal Union—between 3,000 and 6,000 inhabitants per post office and one post office covering 20 to 40 square kilometers—and falls short of facilities considered representative of developed countries—one post office per 24,000 inhabitants and covering 1,000 square kilometers. The Yemen Arab Republic is found to have a postal concentration of one post office per 15,000 square kilometers, serving 49,780 people.

The Yemen postal authorities are currently making efforts to improve the level of services. They have obtained from the Bern-based Universal Postal Union a number of short-term consultant's missions as well as training fellowships for their officials. Moreover, the Universal Postal Union has suggested large-scale technical assistance be provided in two phases corresponding to two five-year planning cycles. The union has proposed to grant this assistance in the form of a United Nations Development Program-financed project consisting of experts, missions, fellowships, and equipment, implementation of which will extend over the second 1982-1986 plan.[12]

Electricity

The long-term goals of the Yemen Arab Republic with respect to electricity generation and supply parallel the aspirations of other developing countries. The overall goals consist of strong and centralized planning in order to meet the energy needs of development projects (in particular, agriculture and industry) and the general needs of the urban and rural areas for electricity. The program for the electricity sector may be divided into three major concerns. First is the linking together of electrical power stations in the country to form a single grid for the transmission of power to main centers of consumption by way of transformer stations, which will integrate and convert the high-tension lines linking Sana'a-Hodeidah-Ibb-Taiz to 33 KV (kilovolts) and thus allow networks to rural areas. Second is the linkage of the main electricity grids of the two parts of Yemen so as to make it possible to exchange the transmission of electrical power. The final objective is the electrification of the countryside to link it with the unified electricity grid in order to narrow the discrepancy between rural and urban areas and to supply power to modernize agriculture, for the extension of agro-industry to the regions producing agricultural raw materials, and for mineral extraction projects.

The first electrical service in North Yeman was offered by a private company (Sana'a Electric Company) in 1959 and was restricted to lighting in Sana'a and its suburbs. Private companies also introduced electricity services to other major cities but the fuel costs were high (especially after the 1973-1974 oil price increases), distribution severely limited, and the small private firms were constrained by lack of capital to expand service to meet demand. Subscriptions were limited because of low generating capacity, leading to such high rates that only a proportion of city dwellers could afford the service. In response, the government established the Yemen General Electric Corporation (YGEC) in 1975, a semi-autonomous public utility under the auspices of the Ministry of Electricity and Water, which absorbed the private electric companies. The budget of YGEC rose from 30 million rials in 1975 to 1,789.5 million rials in 1982.[13] By 1981 YGEC employed 1,609 persons of whom 46 percent worked in Sana'a facilities, 21 percent in each of the cities of Taiz and Hodeidah, with the remaining 12 percent elsewhere throughout the country. This employment distribution reflects the fact that urban centers have been the first and largest recipients of electricity services, although there is an active policy to extend electricity to the majority of the population that still lives in the rural areas. The statistics are encouraging.

In 1975 the 20,300 subscribers in Sana'a represented 56 percent of total electricity subscribers in North Yemen. By 1982, the 55,000 Sana'a subscribers accounted for 40 percent of the total. Similarly, while the number of subscribers in Taiz and Hodeidah rose from 8,500 in 1975 to 24,250 in 1982 and from 7,400 in 1975 to 17,700 in 1982, respectively, their shares fell from about 24 percent to 18 percent (Taiz) and from 20 percent to 13 percent (Hodeidah) of total subscribers over the same 1975-1982 span.[14] Table 25 shows the generation and consumption of electricity from 1975 to 1982, including a breakdown of the major urban consumers. In the eight years given in table 25, consumption of electricity increased over 600 percent. Nonetheless, demand for electrical service exceeds supply. More than one-half (57 percent) of the urban population now receives regular electrical service; it is the rural areas that provide the major challenges.

It should be noted that electricity generation in the YAR requires imported fuel oil and diesel. Fuel consumption by YGEC has risen steadily since 1975, from 11.6 thousand tons to 64.11 thousand tons in 1982. Increasingly, heavy fuel oil has been used for power generation, somewhat replacing diesel oil. Consumption of heavy fuel oil rose from 11,000 tons in 1980/81 to 225,000 tons in 1982 as a result of YGEC's expanded activities and demand from the Bajil and Amran cement facilities. The announcement of oil discoveries in commerical quantities by Hunt Oil Company and the increased interest in concessions in North Yemen by such firms as Exxon and British Petroleum should have an impact on the electricity program of the country, albeit in the

Table 25: Generation and Consumption of Electricity, 1975-1982

Year	Generated Energy (1,000 kWh)[a]	Trans-formers	Generator	Generator Power (KVA)[a]	Sales (1,000 kWh)[a]
1975	—	81	—	14,040	31,884
1976	62,910	86	26	13,390	49,298
1977	69,209	88	36	23,004	50,907
1978	102,672	—	36	32,460	71,468
1979	133,571	12	49	49,090	95,058
1980	170,056	95	44	57,309	120,191
1981	212,628	296	47	99,320	161,100
1982	263,697	308	45	90,940	203,820
1981 of which					161,100
Sana'a	119,748	185	16	43,890	84,600
Taiz	29,940	34	9	22,220	20,400
Hodeidah	7,749	54	10	28,070	33,700
Ibb	6,119	5	4	—	4,800
Dhamar	356	16	3	2,930	4,600
Hajjah	2,716	2	5	2,210	2,000
Other	—	—	—	—	11,000
1982 of which					203,820
Sana'a	146,840	195	15	44,000	109,000
Taiz	35,516	34	5	17,200	24,650
Hodeidah	64,219	64	11	24,950	41,900
Ibb	7,000	—	6	—	5,620
Dhamar	7,069	13	3	2,930	5,740
Hajjah	3,053	2	5	1,860	2,490
Other	—	—	—	—	14,420

[a] kWh = kilowatt-hours; KVA = kilovoltsamperes.

Sources: Yemen Arab Republic, Central Planning Organization, Statistics Department, *Statistical Year Book, 1981*, p. 101, *Statistical Year Book, 1982*, p. 109, and Ministry of Electricity and Water, *Report of Yemen General Electric Corporation Activities, 1975-1982*, p. 10, table 9.

future. Well beyond the Second Five-Year Plan period (1982-1986), the YAR will still depend upon imports of petroleum products for electricity generation.

The unreliable and irregular current, typical of many developing countries, has led industrial enterprises in the Yemen Arab Republic to generate their own power with small diesel generators. Where electrical connections are either very expensive or unavailable, the population continues to rely on kerosene for lighting and butane and wood for cooking. The four electricity consuming sectors are (a) households and shops, (b) factories and workshops, (c) the government, and (d) embassies and councils. The first sector (households and shops) accounted for 70 percent of electricity consumption in 1982, the government sector used just under 17 percent of total 1982 electrical services, and embassies and councils consumed about 7 percent of electricity sold in 1982. Factories and workshops, which in 1979 accounted for over 13 percent of total electricity sales, represented only 5.7 percent of the total in 1982, reflecting the move of some facilities to city suburbs. Projections of electricity sales for the Second Five-Year Plan envisage 80 percent of sales in 1986 (that is, 406,200,000 kilowatt-hours) to the domestic-usage sector.[15]

The Yemen Arab Republic has begun implementation of an 18-year national electrification project to achieve a 5-million-megawatt capacity which will eventually extend publicly supplied electricity throughout the country.[16] The total estimated capital expenditures are 16.6 billion rials ($3.7 billion). The first phase (1981-1983) consisted of the rehabilitation and expansion of the electrical distribution network to 17 smaller urban centers and the three principal farmers' markets at Sana'a, Taiz, and Hodeidah. Toward this end, a power-generating station was constructed in Hodeidah. High-tension lines then connected Hodeidah to Sana'a, Sana'a to Taiz, Sana'a to Amran, and Amran to Saadah. Another distribution network will connect Hodeidah to Ras Al Kateeb, Bajil, Dhamar, and Amran.

A second power station, which started operation in September 1983, was constructed at Ras Al Kateeb (located half way between Hodcidah and Salif). Its five generators have a total capacity of 150 MW (megawatts). This installation is a major hydro facility that utilizes tidal motion for generation with relative low unit-production costs.

The Dhamar-Taiz power transmission project has been designed to distribute surplus electricity from the Ras Al Kateeb power station to Dhamar where a substation then distributes part of it to Ibb and Taiz as well as to villages in the vicinity. There are two 132-KV high-voltage transmission lines equipped with wires of 400-millimeter diameter and a voltage of 115 MW in order to minimize energy loss. From Dhamar the power supply is carried by a double line of pylons 30-meters high, erected, as far as possible, next to the Dhamar-Taiz road. Substations constructed at Ibb and Taiz convert the power to 33 KV and the Dhamar substation has been upgraded. The project cost, included within the Second Five-Year Plan, was 82 million rials ($18.2 million). In December 1982 the Dhamar area suffered a severe earthquake, resulting in sizable infrastructure damage. Thus, the electrification projects in this region have had to be of both a reconstruction and a development nature.

The third stage of the Mocha central station project was completed with a second hydro plant in 1983 at a cost of 1,575 million rials ($350 million). Similiar to the Ras Al Kateeb facility, the Mocha hydro station has four generators with a 160-MW capacity that will contribute substantially to meeting the needs in the southern part of the Yemen Arab Republic. In particular the project will expand the electricity distribution network in four rural areas with about 125,000 inhabitants: Baadan, Misrakh, Marawiah, and Hushaysh. The project also involves 930 kilometers of medium- and low-voltage lines, 33 substations, and 300 distribution transformers.

With the overall electrification program, the targets of the Second Five-Year Plan are substantial and it would appear those goals are being met. Using 1981 as the base year, 236,708,000 kWh of elctricity were produced (that is, 67 perceant of capacity) of which 177,453,000 kWh were sold, the difference being 10,825,000 kWh used internally and 48,430,000 kWh lost in the grid. By 1986, electrical output should be on the order of 677,000,000 kWh, with sales of 507,750,000 kWh—an increase of 186 percent over 1981 or an annual growth rate of 23.4 percent. Moreover, the value of electrical output and related services are projected to rise from 215.864 million rials in 1981 to 579.525 million rials in 1986.[17]

Water and Sewerage

Until recently piped water systems reached only about 50 percent of the combined population of Sana'a, Hodeidah, and Taiz. The water system in Taiz serves about 90 percent of the city's households but on an intermittent basis. Hodeidah has the least adequate water supply system of the three principal cities. Water shortages occur because groundwater levels—the principal source of drinking water—are lowered through excessive pumping for domestic and agricultural uses. Moreover, many wells used for urban drinking water are contaminated as a result of sewage seepage.

Water availability is becoming a pressing problem, even a potential constraint, in and around Sana'a where the water table is falling by five to six meters annually and perhaps only one-third of the water extracted is being replenished. Urban consumption in the capital remains moderate (92 liters per day per person compared to the 95 to 245 liters per day in cities of the Eastern Mediterranean); irrigation is primarily responsible for the plummeting water table in the Sana'a basin. Industrial usage of water is increasing but it still is not a major consumer. The uncontrolled pumping of groundwater for agriculture has been expanding rapidly, from 115 liters per second in 1972 to 1,000 liters per second in 1982. This should be placed in the context of the sales in Sana'a of the National Water Supply Authority of 190 liters per second in 1983.[18] The drought in 1983 and 1984 has added further pressure on the water supplies.

Between 1976 and 1981 there were 385 projects executed for drinking water and improvement of water supplies in the 11 governorates. Sana'a alone benefitted from 175 projects, with the number in the other governorates as follows: Jawf, 24; Mahweet, 7; Marib, 30; Hajjah, 4; Taiz, 24; Hodeidah, 18; Ibb, 35; Dhamar, 29; Saadah, 5; and Beida, 34.[19] Overall, by 1982 upwards of one-fifth of the YAR population had access to potable water.

In 1981 the productive capacity of the water system was 7.2 million cubic meters, and the system was operating at full capacity. The government of the Yemen Arab Republic is expecting a net increase of 145,756,800 cubic meters by the end of the Second Five-Year Plan, yielding a 1986 output of 37,065,000 cubic meters.[20]

The Rural Water Department, a branch of the Ministry of Public Works, is responsible for the supply of potable domestic water to rural areas, either by drilling deep wells or by the improvement of existing water resources, springs and streams, and contributions toward the construction of dams and cisterns. During the First Five-Year Plan (1976-1981), 816 projects were executed at a total cost of 286.8 million Yemeni rials to serve a population of 767,000. And during that period the Rural Water Department drilled 477 wells and installed 511 pumps.

Sewerage systems are under construction or expansion in the three major cities of Sana'a, Hodeidah, and Taiz as well as in Ibb and Dhamar. However, most urban areas have been dependent on septic tanks, cesspools, and soakage pits. Groundwater, therefore, could be polluted in the cities, and there has been an associated incidence of diseases such as typhoid, bacillary dysentery, and infectious hepatitis in lower-income areas. Government efforts in recent years have moved to correct these conditions.

The planning, execution, and operation of the water supply and sewerage facilities in the major urban centers is the responsibility of the National Water and Sewage Authority which was established in 1973 and is under the auspices of the Ministry of Electricity and Water. The National Water and Sewage Authority has secured financing from several international agencies for improvements in Yemen's water supply and sewage services. The Sana'a and Hodeidah projects are partially funded by three International Development Association credits, while a fourth credit was extended for improvements in Ibb and Dhamar. The United States Agency for International Development has also provided loans to improve water and sewage services in Taiz.

Water and sewerage development was constrained in earlier years not only by lack of capital but due to the shortage of skilled engineers and technicians to prepare projects and operate facilities as well as a shortage of skilled laborers to maintain existing systems. Planned investment for the 1982-1986 period is offered in table 26.

The National Water and Sewage Authority is planning investments in water-borne sewerage systems in the main cities. Piped sewerage systems are being implemented because of the volume of waste water generated by the water systems, the problems of narrow streets in old town areas, and unfavorable soil conditions. Where conditions permit, less-expensive sanitation facilities such as septic tanks and composting latrines should be considered as sanitation systems are extended to less dense lower-income areas.

As part of the Second Five-Year Development Plan, water and sewerage projects are currently under way in Sana'a, Taiz, Ibb, Dhamar, and Hodeidah; by 1986, 65,000 sewer connections will be in place in these five cities.[21] The second stage of the Sana'a water project and the first stage of its sewerage project have received financing from international sources, including $28 million from the Saudi Development Fund and $10 million from the International Development Association. The project work includes the construction and installation of about 10 wells, transmission pipelines, a booster pump, a 10,000-cubic-meter reservoir, the laying of distribution pipes and about 18,000 water connections, plus laboratory equipment and consultancy. The water and sewerage schemes in Ibb and Dhamar are supervised by a joint venture between Dorsch and Gitec. However, Kreditanstalt fuer Wiederaufbau will finance the entire $80 million Ibb scheme.[22]

Hazen and Sawyer of New York is the consultant for the $55-

Table 26: **Investment in the Water and Electricity Sector, 1982-1986** (in thousands of Yemeni rials)

Activity	Local	Foreign	Total	Percentage
Water and sewerage	391,834[a]	727,6947[b]	1,119,528	48
Electricity	176,024[c]	1,044,448[d]	1,220,472	52
Total	567,858	1,772,142	2,340,000	100

[a]Private-sector local investment accounts for 7 million rials of this amount.

[b]Private-sector foreign investment accounts for 13 million rials of this amount.

[c]Private-sector local investment accounts for 2 million rials of this amount.

[d]Private-sector foreign investment accounts for 18 million rials of this amount.

Source: Yemen Arab Republic, Ministry of Electricity and Water, working paper, 1982, pp. 16-18.

million Taiz water supply and sewerage project which has received funding from Saudi Arabia, the Abu Dhabi Fund for Arab Economic Development, the United States Agency for International Development, and the government of the Yemen Arab Republic. This program, which began operations in 1982, was designed to provide purified water and sewerage services for up to 180,000 people by 1990. Prime contractor for the $44-million mechanical, electrical, and civil engineering contracts and for the supply of mechanical and electrical equipment was Hanab Stevin Pipelines Middle East, an affiliate of Volker Stevin Pipelines of the Netherlands.[23] The Taiz water supply project involved building five pumping stations, 21 wells and well houses, a central chlorination plant, and six water storage tanks, as well as laying about 170 kilometers of pipe. For the sewerage portion of the project, more than 100 kilometers of pipe was to be laid, and treatment plants and 19 public lavatories are to be built. Power is supplied from a central power plant with three 300-KW generators via 30 kilometers of overhead transmission lines.

The Dhamar water and sewerage project should meet the

demands of the city until 1995. Again, this project started with the basics: drilling and equipping wells; supplying and laying water transmission mains; constructing distribution and sewerage systems; and building a sewerage treatment plant and power generation plants. Funding for this project was supplied by the government of the Yemen Arab Republic, the International Development Association, the government of the Netherlands, and the Arab Fund for Economic and Social Development.

The seriousness of the water problem confronting North Yemen is very real and has led to the formation, in 1982, of the High Council for Water Resources, which is chaired by the Prime Minister. Because private-sector usage, particularly in agriculture and to a lesser extent in industry, has been a major cause for the increasing scarcity of water, the government has not been able to move rapidly to implement recommendations. Eventually such measures as pump taxes may be put in place and enforced and/or certain areas with restricted-extraction designations could be expanded, especially in the Sana'a basin.

Notes

1. Yemen Arab Republic, The Confederation of Yemeni Development Associations, Central Planning Organization, Statistics Department, *Summary, Final Results of the Cooperative Population Census*, February 1981, p. 11.

2. Yemen Arab Republic, Central Planning Organization, *The Second Five-Year Plan (1982-1986)*, March 1982, chapter 1, p. 14.

3. Yemen Arab Republic, Ministry of Public Works, working paper, March 1982, section 1, p. 3 (mimeographed).

4. World Bank, *Annual Report 1984* (Washington, D.C.: World Bank, 1984), p. 135.

5. Kuwait Fund for Arab Economic Development, *Annual Report 1977-1978*, p. 15.

6. *Middle East Economic Digest*, October 7, 1977, p. 40 and August 10, 1979, p. 78, and *Middle East Economic Survey*, December 7, 1981, p. II.

7. *Arab News* (Jeddah), December 6, 1981, p. 2 and August 27, 1982, p. 2.

8. Yemen Arab Republic, Central Planning Organization, Statistics Department, *Statistical Year Book, 1981*, pp. 122 and 124, and *Statistical Year Book, 1982*, pp. 128 and 130.

9. *Middle East Economic Digest*, January 6, 1978, p. 34 and July 21, 1978, p. 39, and *Middle East Economic Survey*, September 29, 1980, p. I.

10. *Middle East Economic Digest*, January 28, 1983, p. 36, and *Middle East Economic Survey*, August 24, 1981, p. V.

11. Universal Postal Union (UPU), International Bureau, *Yemen Arab Republic: Situation of Postal Services and Technical Assistance Needs* (Bern: UPU, 1981), p. 1 (in French).

12. Ibid., p. 2.

13. Direct communication from the Yemen General Electric Company as cited in Ameen Nouisser, "Economics of Energy in the Yemen Arab Republic," paper for the seminar in the economics of energy and development, Department of Economics,

University of Colorado, Boulder, April 26, 1984, p. 8.

14. Ibid., p. 12.

15. Yemen Arab Republic, Ministry of Electricity and Water, working paper, 1982, p. 8, table 2.

16. The State Electricity Organization, under the supervision of the Ministry of Electricity and Water, is the agency charged with implementation of projects relating to the electricity sector.

17. Yemen Arab Republic, Ministry of Electricity and Water, working paper, 1982, pp. 5-8.

18. World Bank, "Yemen Arab Republic Country Economic Memorandum Current Position and Prospects," Report no. 5621-YAR (Washington, D.C., June 25, 1985), pp. 46-47 (mimeographed).

19. Yemen Arab Republic, Central Planning Organization, Statistics Department, *Statistical Year Book, 1981*, p. 100.

20. Yemen Arab Republic, Ministry of Electricity and Water, working paper, 1982, p. 13.

21. Ibid., p. 14.

22. *Middle East Economic Digest*, January 14, 1977, p. 31, July 15, 1977, p. 34, February 26, 1982, p. 70, and December 17, 1982, p. 86.

23. Ibid., January 2, 1981, p. 44.

5 AGRICULTURE

The year 1984 was designated by the Yemen Arab Republic as the year of agricultural development. The political leadership has concentrated on strengthening the foundation of the agricultural sector by a two-pronged objective and approach: (1) more efficient utilization of land and (2) achieving a level of foodstuffs output adequate for domestic consumption.

In the agricultural development year (1984), a number of steps were initiated or under way that indicate the government's commitment to and concern for that sector of the national economy. The construction of a dam in Marib—actually reconstruction of the ancient and famous dam that made the eastern portions of North Yemen bountiful for centuries—will, when completed, provide thousands of additional hectares for cultivation. Another measure was the prohibition of the import of fruit to protect domestic production. Historically, North Yemen and Oman have been the Arabian Peninsula's large fruit producers. In the area of upgrading skills and technology for the agricultural sector, the College of Agriculture within the University of Sana'a was created and the Center for Scientific Agricultural Research was established. The seriousness of agricultural development is underlined when one considers that only 11 percent of North Yemen's land is cultivated while estimates of the arable land range from 25 percent to 50 percent.[1]

Indeed, the economic future of North Yemen ultimately may be determined by two sectors: agriculture and extractive industries. Of the two, agriculture is renewable and of longer term; it is also the most important in employment opportunities. With the return of thousands of expatriate Yemeni workers and with many of these having attained some level in management skills, rural North Yemen will be drastically changed. Moreover, given the wide range of climatic conditions in the YAR, a similarly wide range of agricultural products is possible, from tropical fruits to grains and temperate-weather crops. Although such important crops as coffee and cotton witnessed a decline in the latter part of the 1970s, a revival and expansion in their production is most likely to occur. Agriculture was the basis for the major civilization of ancient Yemen; it remains a valid basis and critical for the balance of payments of the modern Yemen Arab Republic as well.

The purpose of this chapter is to bring the spectrum of agriculture in the Yemen Arab Republic under scrutiny based upon three considerations. The first concern of the discussion will be the extent of agricultural activities in North Yemen in terms of crops, animal husbandry, fisheries, and forestry. The second consideration will be the role of agriculture in development planning as it relates to the Three-Year Program (1973/74 to 1975/76), the First Five-Year Plan (1976/77 to 1980/81), and the Second Five-Year Plan (1982 to 1986). Third, this chapter will explore the fundamental problems which hamper the potential of agricultural output, namely, (a) the traditional procedures employed in agricultural production and (b) bottlenecks deriving from labor and capital scarcity in the agricultural sector.

Agriculture in the Yemen Arab Republic

Although the agricultural share of the gross domestic product (GDP) decreased during the 1970s, agriculture is still the dominant sector of the economy and accounts for over one-fifth of the GDP in the Yemen Arab Republic (table 27). Roughly 90 percent of the population resides in the countryside, and approximately three-quarters of the YAR's labor force is engaged in agriculture.[2]

Land holdings in the Yemen Arab Republic are relatively small, although the average size of holdings varies from region to region. In the mountains, where extensive terracing is carried out, the size of land holdings does not exceed three acres. In the coastal Tihama and in the highlands cultivators own larger plots; however, very few land holdings exceed several thousand acres. Most farming in North Yemen is organized on an extended family basis with production for use. In the provinces of Dhamar, Ibb, Hodeidah, Hajjah, Mahweet, and Taiz, a total of 76 percent of the holdings are individually owned and only 4.9 percent are shared cropped.[3] An additional 4 percent of land in these governorates is rented either from Waqf (the Islamic religious trust) or from individuals.[4] Government ownership of farmland in the YAR is negligible.

It appears that land tenure patterns are unlikely to change in the short term. As the 1980s opened, "reform had not become an issue, nor had any attempt been made to change ownership patterns."[5] Agronomic conditions are exceptional in the Yemen Arab Republic when compared to the rest of the Arabian Peninsula. The high mountains attract clouds and make rainfall more abundant in the YAR than else-

94 Agriculture

Table 27: Structure of Gross Domestic Product by Sector, 1971/72-1983
(percentage at current prices)

Economic Activity	1971/1972	1972/1973	1973/1974	1974/1975	1975/1976	1976/1977
Agriculture, forestry, and fishing	47.0	45.8	42.2	43.6	40.8	35.7
Mining and quarrying	0.9	0.7	1.0	0.7	0.6	0.8
Manufacturing	4.8	5.2	6.1	5.6	5.2	4.6
Electricity, gas, and water	0.3	0.3	0.4	0.3	0.3	0.3
Construction	5.9	5.7	5.8	4.7	5.7	7.4
Wholesale and retail sales	15.3	15.7	17.8	17.9	19.2	18.3
Restaurants and hotels	1.2	1.2	1.3	1.3	1.3	1.1
Transport and communication	3.8	3.4	3.8	3.6	3.0	3.3
Financial institutions	1.4	1.8	2.0	2.5	2.9	4.5
Real estate and business services	5.0	4.5	4.5	4.4	4.2	4.0
Community, social, and personal services	0.9	0.9	1.0	0.9	0.9	0.8
Less imputed bank services charges	-1.5	-1.7	-1.9	-2.3	-2.7	-4.1
Producers of government services	10.2	11.1	10.2	10.6	10.3	8.7
Producers of private, nonprofit services	0.4	0.4	0.3	0.3	0.3	0.3
Import duties	4.4	5.0	5.5	5.9	8.0	14.3
Total[a]	100.0	100.0	100.0	100.0	100.0	100.0

[a]Figures may not total due to rounding.

(continued)

Table 27 (continued): Structure of Gross Domestic Product by Sector, 1971/72-1983 *(percentage at current prices)*

Economic Activity	1977/ 1978	1978/ 1979	1979/ 1980	1980/ 1981	1981	1982	1983
Agriculture, forestry, and fishing	29.3	30.0	29.0	28.3	27.8	23.8	21.2
Mining and quarrying	1.2	1.3	1.3	1.2	1.2	1.1	1.1
Manufacturing	4.6	5.0	5.5	5.8	6.5	6.5	7.4
Electricity, gas and water	0.3	0.4	0.6	0.6	0.9	0.9	1.0
Construction	9.7	10.3	8.4	8.6	8.2	7.6	7.4
Wholesale and retail sales	17.6	16.6	17.3	16.8	15.6	13.8	13.6
Restaurants and hotels	1.0	1.0	1.1	1.1	1.1	1.0	1.0
Transport and communication	3.8	3.6	3.6	3.6	3.6	3.8	4.1
Financial institutions	6.2	7.0	7.3	7.8	7.6	3.8	4.2
Real estate and business services	4.3	4.6	4.8	4.4	4.3	4.3	4.4
Community, social, and personal services	1.0	1.0	1.0	1.0	1.0	1.0	1.0
Less imputed bank services charges	-5.5	-6.4	-6.7	-6.8	-5.4	-1.6	-1.5
Producers of government services	10.4	11.8	12.6	13.9	15.0	22.3	21.6
Producers of private, nonprofit services	0.2	0.2	0.2	0.2	0.2	0.2	0.2
Import duties	15.9	13.6	14.0	13.5	12.4	11.5	13.3
Total[a]	100.0	100.0	100.0	100.0	100.0	100.0	100.0

[a]Figures may not total due to rounding.

Sources: Yemen Arab Republic, Central Planning Organization, Statistics Department, *Statistical Year Books, 1981*, pp. 322-323, *1982*, pp. 330-331, and *1983*, p. 395.

where on the peninsula. As a result, the most fertile soil of the peninsula is in North Yemen. However, it is important to note that of a total land area of 20 million hectares, only 1.5 million hectares are permanently cultivated, 2 million hectares of marginal land are cultivated in periods of high rainfall, and another 1.6 million hectares are covered with shrubs.[6]

Cropping Strategy: Cropping techniques in North Yemen are essentially traditional. Most agricultural work continues to be done by hand or with livestock. Mechanization and modern irrigation is spreading, although the mountainous terrain in many areas serves as a physical constraint to the introduction of new agricultural techniques. Where the more innovative agricultural techniques have been employed in the YAR the results have not always been satisfactory. This problem highlights the need for coordination and cooperation between the government and private sectors in meeting the development goal of raising the level of agricultural productivity.

Rainfall is perhaps the single most important factor determining the level of agricultural output in the YAR and yet it is the one factor least amenable to planning due to its variable and unpredictable nature. North Yemen has established 22 meteorological stations to monitor climatic conditions and aid agricultural planning; however, the effectiveness of these stations is hampered by a lack of skilled personnel to interpret data.[7]

Agriculture in North Yemen, as mentioned, is highly dependent on rainfall. Of the arable land, 83 percent is irrigated by rainfall, 8 percent is irrigated by spate (flood) flow, 5 percent is irrigated by perennial streams or springs, and 4 percent is irrigated using wells.[8] In all, approximately 1.3 million hectares of land in the YAR is dependent on rainfall for irrigation and only one-half of this area receives an average of 600 millimeters (mm) or more of rain annually.[9] The heaviest rainfall (500-1,000 mm) occurs in the central highlands and intermediate plains regions.[10]

The traditional technique of land terracing is the best example of the Yemeni farmers' *savoir-faire*. The farmlands are shaped as terraces all along the highlands and midlands. These terraces are intensively cultivated and this ingenious style of landscaping has two important functions—to absorb precipitation and to prevent soil erosion. Other than rainfall, traditional modes of irrigation consist of shallow wells, perennial springs, stream flows, and spate flows. In aggregate, these irrigation techniques reach approximately 17 percent of the arable land.11

Patterns of land holding and water rights are relatively structured as a result of years of use. Instituting water projects on a regional or national scale must be done in as nondisruptive a manner as possible. For example, the Tihama Development Authority has been involved in a decade-long water improvement program utilizing small dams, channels, and permanent diversions on two of the seven *wadis* (streambed valleys) in the Tihama coastal plains. In 1984 capital expenditure on the Wadi Mawr project was projected at 400 million rials.12

Compared to other countries, the relative use of chemical fertilizers is low in the YAR, though importation of these fertilizers is increasing tremendously in absolute terms. For example, the value of these fertilizer imports tripled between 1975/76 and 1979/80, reaching 20.9 million rials in the latter year, rising still higher in 1981 to 45.4 million rials, then dropping to 21.2 million rials in 1982.13 Use of chemical fertilizers, nonetheless, is still limited. A study of the six agricultural provinces of Dhamar, Hodeidah, Hajjah, Ibb, Mahweet, and Taiz indicated that chemical fertilizers have been used on 16.5 percent of the cultivated area, while natural fertilizer usage reached 33.5 percent. The use of pesticides is even more limited reaching only 3 percent of cultivated arable land.14

The shortage and high cost of labor, as well as the growth in expatriate remittances available for investment, has increased the demand for tractors. In most cases these tractors are used along with draft animals to work the land. In the six representative provinces, 85.9 percent of the land was plowed by draft animals, while tractors were used to plow 28.4 percent of the holdings.15 As noted previously, the size of holdings, mountainous terrain, and terracing in many regions seriously constrains the degree to which mechanization of agriculture is possible in North Yemen.

Agricultural Products: Traditional agricultural efforts in the YAR produce cereal crops, as well as animal, fishery, and forest products. North Yemen's varied climate allows the cultivation of a diversity of tropical and temperate crops. In addition to cereal crops, fruits and vegetables are cultivated and their production increased substantially during the First Five-Year Plan (1976/77-1980/81).

A number of distinct agricultural zones exist in the YAR and they can be classified according to temperature and amount of rainfall. It will be helpful to describe these regions in order to understand North Yemen's agricultural potential.

The eastern part of the country (Marib and Jawf governorates) is covered by the desert of the Rub Al Khali, known as the Empty Quarter. Agricultural activity has not been very profitable in this area due to high temperatures and lack of appreciable rainfall. Still, a few subsistence farms exist.

The rather gloomy agricultural outlook for this zone should change dramatically with the Marib dam and irrigation scheme, a $75-million project for which financing was secured from the United Arab Emirates in 1984. (However, completion of the dam and the commencement of related activities—including an experimental farm and technical/demonstration services for farmers—is not expected until 1990, providing there are no major setbacks or postponements.) Moreover, the Hunt Oil Company discovery of commercial quantities of oil in the Marib-Jawf basin could bolster the agricultural redevelopment of the ancient Marib region, which in turn could facilitate and support increased petroleum exploration.

The Tihama is located in the western coastal portion of North Yemen, between the rugged mountainous area and the Red Sea. The climate is hot and arid and agriculture is dependent on the amount of rainfall received. This zone is divided into two regions: the pasture areas on the shore of the Red Sea, which get very little rainfall, and the cultivated areas near the mountains, which are well irrigated. The water sources are *wadis* (rivers running during the rainy periods), and underground water. Parts of the Tihama are heavily terraced and the area possesses a mixture of desert and fertile soil. On the near-subsistence farms sorghum, millet, sesame, corn, and dates are produced as cash crops. The Tihama zone has the potential to expand its cultivated areas.

The Highlands zone is in the central part of the country and it is steeply terraced. The Ibb governorate in the southern part of the zone receives the heaviest rainfall; altitudes there range from 4,000 to 6,000 feet. Crops grown include sorghum, barley, millet, alfalfa, corn, wheat, potatoes, and some fruits and vegetables.

The Midlands is a mountainous zone and includes the Taiz governorate. The elevation varies between 2,000 and 6,000 feet and rainfall is abundant. This area is the most important agriculturally and it is densely populated. Cereals, qat, fruits, potatoes, and coffee are among the more important agricultural products of the Midlands.

Sana'a and Saadah are to the north of Ibb on the intermediate plains. The altitude varies between 6,000 and 9,000 feet and the soil is of marginal quality. Crops grown in this zone include sorghum, barley, and wheat, and animals are raised extensively as well.

The western slope consists of high mountainous areas with intensive cultivation of crops, including cereals and coffee. Both the pasturage and cultivated lands are used to full capacity and it seems that there is limited potential to increase the acreage available for cultivation. At the foot of the mountains the soil favors the cultivation of corn, sorghum, alfalfa, bananas, and papaya.

As noted earlier, cereals are the most important crop grown in North Yemen—notably sorghum, millet, barley, and maize. These cereals are cultivated on 90 percent of all agricultural land. Other than cereals, agricultural products include cotton, coffee, qat, vegetables, and fruits.

Agricultural development in North Yemen is limited by the use of traditional modes of production and sporadic rainfall. As a result, agricultural practices are based on the following. (a) Cattle are the means of production in Yemeni agriculture. They have limited pasturage and thus handfeeding is required. So it is imperative that a crop to feed both cattle and humans be raised; maize and sorghum can do both. (b) Drought resistent crops are favored. For example, sorghum is highly resistant to drought whereas maize, its rival, needs frequent watering. (c) Cultivation of a crop that provides more grain is preferred. Barley produces more grain than sorghum but it cannot replace sorghum because it is not used for livestock feeding. Maize also has more grain than sorghum and, considering the amount of grain produced, millet ranks below sorghum. As a result, sorghum and millet are the major crops; maize and wheat are significant crops, while the production of barley is becoming less common.

The agricultural sector in North Yemen produces a limited number of cash crops. Qat is the most prevalent and lucrative of the cash crops due to its high return and minimal input requirements. Other cash crops include coffee, cotton, fruits, and vegetables, though production of these crops is constrained by labor scarcity, water requirements, and the lack of adequate marketing and pricing systems to provide incentives for increased production.

Qat is a popular cash crop because it is highly drought resistant and requires minimal irrigation. Labor requirements for qat production are also low. *Catha eduli* (qat) is an evergreen shrub introduced to the Arabian Peninsula from Ethiopia during the fourteenth century. Historically, qat has been used to brew an extract with stimulative properties, while chewing of the stem tips and leaves creates a similar effect. The consumption of qat is widespread in North Yemen and has come to play an important role in social life. It is considered by some to be a distinct economic problem. Demand for qat has kept pace with rising incomes, allowing the price of qat to incorporate rising labor costs more readily than other domestic crops; moreover, qat does not suffer from foreign competition. In 1979 the government issued a decree restricting imports of qat, particularly from Ethiopia. The net result is that qat has consistently enjoyed a higher return than other cash crops. Interestingly, qat is a highly perishable crop that requires a well-developed marketing system. The efficiency of the distribution system for qat in North Yemen points to the responsiveness of the private market when adequate price incentives are present.

Since qat and coffee can be cultivated under similar soil and weather conditions, it has been argued that qat production is being expanded at the expense of coffee output. But the financial return for qat cultivation is much higher than that for coffee. The rewards for labor in coffee and qat production are estimated to be 39 and 161 Yemeni rials per man-day, respectively. Furthermore, in the second year of qat production the return to labor may exceed 700 rials per man-day.[16] Coffee output in the 1930s was on the order of 12,000 tons annually; it declined in the 1970s to 3,000-4,000 tons annually.[17] But not all experts agree that the decline in coffee production has been a result of competition from qat. Some argue that changes in market conditions and distribution patterns have adversely affected coffee cultivation in North Yemen.[18] In addition, qat can be grown successfully under poorer soil conditions and with less rainfall than for many other crops. However, the government of North Yemen has attempted to limit the expansion of qat production through a 30 percent sales tax on qat that was imposed in 1975.[19] Another step to discourage expansion of or switching to qat production is the exclusion of the qat crop from any credit. Finally, the government is expanding its support to various research centers that are involved in evaluating the health effects of qat usage.

It has been argued that in many instances cultivation of qat finances other agricultural development, such as the drilling of wells and installation of pumps, but that it hinders the cultivation of less lucrative but essential crops, such as cereals. Also to be considered is the enormous recycling effect of qat revenues from the cities to the villages.[20]

Cotton crops have suffered from disease, drought, labor scarcity, and marketing difficulties during the 1970s. Cotton output, as a result, declined from 27,000 tons in 1974/75 to 2,800 tons in 1979/80. A slight recovery in cotton production was recorded in 1981, with output reaching 5,000 tons.[21] Substantial recovery in cotton production is forecast for the Second Five-Year Plan, with a target output of 20,800 tons set for 1986.[22] Increased cotton production is expected to derive from an easing of labor scarcity, improved marketing and credit services, and expansion of research and extension services.

While cereal production has suffered due to labor scarcity and a low rate of return as a result of foreign competition, fruit and vegetable production has grown dramatically during the 1970s. The demand for fruit and vegetables has shown itself to be highly income elastic, with fruit and vegetable consumption rising in parallel with increasing incomes in North Yemen. Growing demand has in turn maintained a high return to fruit and vegetable producers, providing a monetary incentive to which the private sector has responded by dramatically increasing domestic output.

A wide range of vegetables are grown in the YAR, among the most important are legumes, potatoes, tomatoes, onions, leeks, and radishes. Vegetable production, excluding potatoes, increased from 259,000 tons prior to the First Five-Year Plan to 371,000 tons in 1981. The production of potatoes over the same period nearly doubled, rising from 76,000 tons to 138,000 tons.[23] In all, approximately 11 percent of the land devoted to agriculture is committed to the cultivation of vegetables.

Due to the wide diversity of climatic conditions, almost the entire spectrum of fruit may be grown in the Yemen Arab Republic. This includes tropical fruits, such as mangoes, papayas, and bananas, subtropical deciduous fruits, and temperate zone fruits such as figs, grapes, peaches, pears, apples, apricots, and a variety of nuts. Approximately 3.6 percent of agricultural land is devoted to fruit production. As with vegetables, fruit consumption has increased with rising incomes in North Yemen. This has resulted in both increased domestic production and rapidly escalating fruit imports. The domestic fruit growers have received a boost with the government's 1983 decision to halt fruit imports.

It is estimated that domestic fruit consumption doubled between 1975/76 and 1981, reaching a level of approximately 290,000 tons in the latter year. Domestic production rose from 65,000 tons in 1975/76 to 80,700 tons in 1981. Increased fruit consumption contributed to the balance-of-trade deficit, with fruit imports reaching a level of 7 percent of total imports in 1979/80.[24] Further expansion of fruit production is desirable to decrease the level of imports and for export potential. However, exports of Yemeni fruits could be constrained by importers because of pest and disease control standards, by the lack of horticulture specialists, and by the scarcity of sufficient water for irrigation in many regions. A recent study indicates that grapes are the only fruit crop with a high export potential, projecting that exports of grapes could reach 10,400 tons by 1990 and 62,500 tons by 2000. The study also placed the potential level of self-sufficiency in other fruit crops at approximately 40 percent of domestic consumption for the next 20 years.[25]

Forests in North Yemen are scarce and are becoming more scarce as the trees are used for fuel. Due to the limited forests, the price of wood is high. Recently, as a result of high wood prices, farmers have been planting their own trees. This not only makes the wood available to them at lower prices but helps to retain the soil and provides a wind break for the irrigated fields.

Animal Husbandry: Domestic animals in the Yemen Arab Republic play a significant role, directly and indirectly, in agricultural output. Priority is given to cattle, used for plowing the land and for the provision of meat. Cows are raised for their milk which is used as an intermediate good for the production of various dairy products; milk itself is not widely consumed. The next important group of animals includes sheep and goats, which provide wool and meat. However, lack of veterinary care and lack of adequate grazing land are responsible for the decline in the number of sheep and goats. In addition, population migration has resulted in instances of insufficient manpower to care for flocks. Donkeys are used for riding and packing. Finally, poultry have had limited value in the YAR's agricultural production until recently. However, in 1981 a contract was signed with a U. S. company, Strickland & Davis, to expand a poultry broiler plant. The expansion is expected to increase broiler production from 3.5 million to 7.3 million a year and double the amount of processed poultry feed imported from the industrialized nations.[26]

The livestock population is not increasing. For instance, in 1974 the livestock population consisted of 900,000 cattle, 10 million goats and sheep, and 6,000 donkeys.[27] The present data show approximately the same figures. As noted elsewhere, this stationary situation is due to labor migration, limited pasturage, and lack of veterinary care. The Second Five-Year Plan seeks to improve the situation. However, solving these problems will require risk taking on the part of the Yemeni farmer, who receives overall high marks. For example,

> . . . Foreign experts working in the agricultural sector are full of praise for the adaptability, skill and enthusiasm of Yemeni farmers. One of the

main hinderances to increased efficiency is the fierce independence of these men and the obsession with land and its water rights.[28]

Finally, like most other activities in the agricultural sector, fishing is carried out by traditional methods and almost all the catch is consumed locally. The portion of fish sold beyond the local market is salted and dried. The most abundant finds of seafood are mackerel, tuna, black cobia, large jacks, sharks, barracuda, lobster, and shrimp.

Agricultural Development Policies and the Role of Government

The development paths followed by less-developed countries in the past 20 years have been diverse. Some nations, such as Iran in the 1960s and 1970s, neglected the agricultural sector and concentrated the attention of their development program on industrialization. The rationale of this approach toward development through rapid industrialization has ranged from the argument that more-developed countries have achieved the status because of their industrial sectors, to the argument that external benefits are captured through the process of industrialization (i.e., skills development, linkages between industries, and market expansion through rising industrial incomes). Recent development theory has begun to reemphasize balanced growth and development which recognizes the interdependence of the agricultural and industrial sectors.

In this respect, the agricultural sector represents a market for industrial products, both consumer goods and agricultural inputs, and provides a source of raw materials for industry. For example, the emergence of the processed-food industry is a major step in North Yemen's industrial development. Rather than enter into the debate between balanced and unbalanced growth, it seems sufficient to note that real economic development cannot take place without a development process which constantly makes reference to all the factors and resource endowments of the country. It is clear that, given the YAR's resource endowments, the agricultural sector can play a major role in the development of the country. With a rising standard of living that accompanies development and the purchasing power created by remittances from the YAR's expatriate workers, consumption of foodstuffs will rise, including some of the products considered to be luxuries. Frequently, such foodstuffs are imported. Thus, imports of agricultural products can be expected to increase and can become a major negative element in the balance of trade if such increased imports occur along the broad range of agricultural products—not just specialty or luxury items. Self-sufficiency in basic foodstuffs can thus be a "saver" of foreign exchange and a vital factor in a country's balance of payments. Table 28 offers some indication of how this economic phenomenon may be applicable to the Yemen Arab Republic in the early part of the 1980s.

The government of North Yemen has developed a framework of medium- and long-term objectives which have been incorporated into development plans. Each of the three plans to date have had specific objectives for the planning period as well as an integrated approach to the achievement of long-term goals of the development process.

From the start of economic planning, agriculture has had a high priority, with attention focused on the development of institutions, infrastructure, and services in that sector. Progress in agricultural development has been slow, primarily due to the low initial level of institutions and infrastructure, the scarcity of data for the planning process, and extensive short-term emigration which has created widespread labor scarcity during the 1970s. Initial progress has been limited to the evaluation of resources, research in the area of improved crop yields, and the implementation of a few large-scale projects. It is important to note that the information gained in this initial phase can pay substantial long-term dividends if the information is translated into a policy that is implemented with adequate support services. The evidence is clear that Yemeni's are willing to innovate but that government and private sector coordination is necessary to overcome the bottlenecks and constraints to development and modernization of agriculture in North Yemen.

The Three-Year Program (1973/74-1975/76): Agriculture was allotted 15 percent of planned expenditures in the Three-Year Program or 138 million rials.[29] Actual expenditures amounted to 73 million rials or an implementation rate of 53 percent of planned expenditures.[30] The majority of expenditures in the agricultural sector were financed through foreign aid or low-interest credits and loans. Priorities in the agricultural sector were placed upon institutional development, evaluation of land and water resources, and the establishment of research stations.

The period was marked by the reorganization of the Ministry of Agriculture, which included a clear delineation of the duties and responsibilities of both the overall ministry and the individual departments within the ministry. Institutional development in the agricultural

Table 28: Value of YAR Agriculture-Based and Edible Exports and Imports, 1978/79-1982 *(in thousand rials)*

	1978/79	1979/80	1980	1981	1982
Exports	15,956	30,305	29,370	34,591	93,801
Live animals	—	80	656	18	—
Fish	22	718	1,704	128	—
Biscuit (cereals)	8,460	12,705	18,755	28,812	37,283
Potatoes	—	—	300	1,270	1,154
Fruits	92	110	761	146	3,016
Coffee	2,196	4,363	879	1,899	2,796
Qat	—	—	—	—	59
Hides/skins	4,736	6,300	6,237	2,107	6,708
Cotton	—	—	—	—	11,465
Cotton yarn	312	—	56	204	57
Cotton fabric	—	5,992	—	—	31,232
Cotton sheet	138	—	—	—	—
Salt	—	37	22	7	31
Imports	1,480,495	2,018,127	2,331,917	2,994,363	2,164,681
Live animals	24,368	40,842	60,569	89,006	102,020
Meat product	177,371	222,827	208,099	359,830	259,511
Dairy products/ eggs	196,061	341,721	473,971	289,390	254,235
Fish/fish products	25,448	30,691	36,352	20,527	26,993
Cereals/cereal products	220,194	400,388	395,788	567,218	570,142
Vegetables/ fruits	370,401	504,034	538,457	482,446	452,119
Sugar/sugar products/ honey	245,378	235,189	363,002	920,239	228,843
Coffee/tea/ spices	55,788	73,202	59,663	64,154	59,306
Animal feed	4,697	13,745	36,128	39,336	46,178
Miscellaneous foodstuffs	48,168	31,995	40,534	41,161	33,710
Hides/skins	—	68	78	250	412
Oil seeds	2,132	8,791	15,186	16,422	9,213
Cotton yarn	—	34	487	512	1,490
Beverages	20,697	65,810	7,018	12,645	8,558
Tobacco	89,792	48,790	96,585	91,227	111,951

Source: Yemen Arab Republic, Central Bank of Yemen, Research Department, *Financial Statistical Bulletin*, January-March 1984, tables 24 and 27.

sector was led by the creation of financial institutions; initially the Agricultural Credit Fund, followed by the the Agricultural Credit Bank. Research and development were furthered by the establishment of agricultural training institutes at Ibb and Zabid and research stations in Taiz, Ibb, and Hodeidah.

A second focus of the Three-Year Program was on resource evaluation and research in the agricultural sector. Water and land surveys were undertaken in Wadi Mawr, Wadi Siham, and the Montane Plains.[31] An important development of this period was the establishment of the Tihama Development Project, financed by the International Development Association and the Kuwait Fund for Arab Economic Development. The project initially involved modernization of irrigation road and canal construction and the extension of agricultural services in Wadi Zabid as well as a study of the irrigation potential in Wadi Mawr.

Research studies completed during this period centered on hybrid seeds, fertilizers, and pesticides. Improved varieties of sorghum, millet, maize, wheat, barley, sesame, and sunflowers were identified.[32] In addition, specific studies were undertaken with respect to cotton, coffee, and fruit trees. In the veterinary field, a laboratory was established in Sana'a to study the spread of animal diseases. Finally, a Directorate for Fisheries was established and an evaluation of coastal fishery potential completed.

First Five-Year Plan (1976/77-1980/81): The First Five-Year Plan continued the design implemented in the Three-Year Program. Emphasis was again placed on institutional and infrastructural development, manpower training, resource evaluation, and research into improved crop yields. Specifically, the first plan set forth the following objectives with respect to the agricultural sector: (1) self-sufficiency in food production within economic limits; (2) integration with industrialization and increased production of agricultural raw materials; (3) improvement of the balance of payments through import substitution and increased exports of agricultural products; (4) improved quality of agricultural products; and (5) increased assistance to small producers.

These objectives were to be realized through emphasis on the following strategies:[33] (a) continued institutional development primarily in the areas of credit and extension services; (b) extensive manpower training to increase skill levels in the agricultural sector; (c) continued development of infrastructure, particularly with respect to roads and water projects; (d) research into higher-yielding varieties of crops; (e) assistance in the formation of farmers cooperatives to facilitate modern production techniques and improve marketing; and (f) conduct studies on marketing, pricing, and taxation to assist in policy formation.[34]

As with the Three-Year Program, the First Five-Year Plan represented a buildup phase for the agricultural sector. During this stage, gains made in institutional and infrastructural development, manpower training, and generation of research data assume a greater importance than short-term changes in agricultural output. However, the virtual stagnation of the agricultural sector during the First Five-Year Plan must be considered disappointing. The agricultural sector had been targeted to realize an annual average increase in output of 5.5 percent; actual annual increases in production averaged less than 1 percent. The Ministry of Agriculture identified a number of factors as contributing to this low growth rate of output in the agricultural sector. First was the dependency of 75 percent of agricultural lands upon rainfall and periods of lower than average rainfall during the plan period. Second was the small and fragmented land holdings which are not economically viable and which present an obstacle to the modernization of agriculture. In all, 80 percent of land holdings are fragmented into more than one piece and 66 percent are less than one hectare in size. Continued emigration was a third factor that created labor scarcity and reduced competitiveness with imports due to rapidly rising agricultural wages. Fourth was the lack of trained manpower to implement planned projects particularly at the local level. The requisite gestation period for the types of projects implemented during the plan was a fifth element, meaning that for some undertakings there was no direct or immediate production. Still another factor was the lack of financial capital to implement planned projects on schedule and the channeling of the greater part of investment into infrastructural development.[35]

Table 29 presents both the actual crop production for 1981 as well as the base year (1975/76) and crop production targets for 1980/81 set forth in the First Five-Year Plan. Before assessing the actual achievements of the first plan it is appropriate to note the final evaluation of the 1980/81 production targets made by the Ministry of Agriculture.

> There was an essential weakness of statistical information especially before and during the preparation of the First Five-Year Plan. This led to overly optimistic estimates of agricultural production for the period, as well as to overly ambitious production goals.[36]

Table 29: Actual Agricultural Production and Targets During the First Five-Year Plan, 1976/77-1980/81 *(in thousand tons)*

Item	1975/76 (Base Year)	1980/81 (Target)	1981 (Actual)	Percent of Target
1. Crop Production				
Cereal crops	1,058.0	1,363.0	865.1	63.5
Sorghum, millet	859.0	1,042.0	635.0	60.9
Maize	72.0	110.0	53.2	48.4
Barley	75.0	83.0	54.1	65.2
Wheat	52.0	128.0	69.6	54.4
Cotton	13.0	32.0	5.0	15.6
Oil crops	5.5	10.8	5.2	15.6
Dry beans	76.0	105.0	79.6	75.8
Tobacco	5.6	9.6	6.3	65.6
Vegetables	183.0	605.0	291.4	48.2
Coffee	3.0	4.0	3.5	87.5
Fruits	112.4	142.0	209.3	147.4
2. Animal Production				
Milk products	331.0	367.0	n.a.	n.a.
Eggs (millions)	210.0	230.0	126.0	54.8
Meat (tons)	39,738.0	46,840.0	44,603.0	95.2
Skins (tons)	7,230.0	7,953.0	4,048.0	50.9
Fish (tons)	11,525.0	17,288.0	17,000.0	98.3

Sources: World Bank, *Yemen Arab Republic: Development of a Traditional Economy* (Washington, D.C.: World Bank, 1979), p. 268, and Yemen Arab Republic, Central Planning Organization, Statistics Department, *Statistical Year Book, 1981*, p. 98.

Cereal cultivation, which early in the decade produced a marketable surplus, has declined below subsistence levels because of a low rate of return, rising incomes, and changing tastes which have favored imported wheat. In particular, domestic production of the traditional staple crops of sorghum and millet has declined substantially while the production of wheat has shown significant growth which is expected to continue.

As noted previously, vegetable and fruit production has benefited from high income elasticity of demand which has maintained a high rate of return for these crops and spurred domestic production. While vegetable production achieved only 48 percent of targeted output for the First Five-Year Plan this is more a reflection of an unrealistic target than deficient expansion. In actuality, vegetable production achieved a respectable growth rate of approximately 10 percent annually during the plan. Fruit production was the only area which exceeded planned expectations, increasing at an annual rate of 13 percent. A recent agricultural study notes that nearly all new land put into agricultural production is devoted to vegetable cultivation. This response is due in large part to improved water management and the willingness of Yemeni farmers to invest in well construction.[37]

The traditional cash crops of coffee and cotton have suffered due to a low rate of return, labor scarcity, and unfavorable marketing conditions. Annual coffee production has remained essentially constant, in the 3,000-4,000 ton range, depending on weather conditions. Cotton production, on the other hand, has declined dramatically. Some recovery of cotton production levels can be expected with the easing of the unskilled labor shortage.

The major achievements of the First Five-Year Plan noted by the Ministry of Agriculture include small dam construction, integrated rural development projects, basic agricultural research, agricultural extension services, expanded agricultural credit facilities, and the establishment of the basic foundation of institutions needed in the agricultural sector. One of the key aspects of institutional development has been the operation of the Agricultural Credit Bank, which was capitalized at 100 million rials in 1976 and began lending operations in July of that year. Capitalization was doubled to 200 million rials in 1981. Loans are predominantly medium-term and are extended at a subsidized interest rate of 8 to 9 percent.[38] Table 30 provides a breakdown of lending operations. In January 1982 the Agricultural Credit Bank was merged with the Cooperative Credit Bank, under the new name of the Cooperative Agricultural Credit Bank, with capital of 300 million rials.

Second Five-Year Plan (1982-1986): The second plan emphasizes integrated development objectives across the various sectors of the economy. As one of the overall objectives, the plan stresses the modernization of agriculture as a means of achieving a reasonable level of food security. The plan is careful to note that the objective is not simply increased investment in agriculture, per se, but rather an inte-

Table 30: Loan Disbursals by the Agricultural Credit Bank in YAR, 1976-1980 *(in million rials)*

Purpose	Amount	Percentage
Agricultural machinery	29.0	21.7
Water development	33.7	25.2
Poultry development	7.8	5.8
Poultry production (seasonal)	8.8	6.6
Tree planting	3.7	2.8
Livestock development	8.2	6.1
Cotton production (seasonal)	8.8	6.6
General production (inputs)	15.5	11.6
Fisheries development	1.5	1.1
Transportation	0.3	0.2
On-farm development	16.5	12.3
Total	133.8	100.0

Source: Consortium for International Development, *Agriculture Sector Analysis, Yemen Arab Republic* (Sana'a: Consortium for International Development, 1981), p. 55.

grated investment effort that seeks to achieve both increased productivity and an improvement in the quality of rural life. Overall strategies for the agricultural sector within the plan include: (1) an emphasis on integrated rural development as a means of increasing productivity and improving the living conditions of the rural population; (2) the promotion of agricultural cooperatives to spur modernization of production and an improvement in marketing; (3) continued development of infrastructure and the creation of strategic buffer stocks of the basic staple crops; (4) the adoption of a price policy which would encourage domestic production and lead to rationalization of consumption; (5) increased attention to the production of livestock, poultry, and fish; and (6) increased access to credit and marketing services for the small farmer.[39]

The specific sectoral objectives for agriculture remain essentially the same as those outlined in the first plan. Emphasis is placed upon the maximization of production given the existing resources of Yemeni agriculture. This, in turn, will serve to provide food security, to provide the necessary inputs for industry, and to help to alleviate balance-of-payments deficits. Diversification of production is stressed, particularly increased production of cotton and coffee, and the slowing of the growth of qat output is encouraged. Soil and water projects continue to have a high priority within the plan, particularly with reference to the expansion of irrigation as a means of increasing fruit and vegetable production. Infrastructural and institutional development will continue during the Second Five-Year Plan; however, emphasis will be placed on increased participation of the private sector in agricultural investment. The plan seeks to assist in the formation and expansion of farmers cooperatives as a means of increasing investment, modernizing production inputs and techniques, and improving the marketing of agricultural output.

The Second Five-Year Plan has targeted an annual growth rate of 4.2 percent in the value of agricultural output, representing an increase in the value of agricultural production from 4,860 million rials in 1981 to 6,386 million rials in 1986.[40] Expected increases in crop, animal, and fish production are presented in table 31. The first statistics available indicate that the growth ratio in the agricultural sector in the period 1981-1984 did not exceed a 1 percent average, per annum, compared to the annual targeted rate of 4.2 percent during the second plan.[41] The drought of 1983 and 1984 coupled with the disastrous earthquake in the Dhamar region were unforeseen elements which had a widespread negative impact on agricultural output and expansion.

In terms of the total increment in agricultural production in the Second Five-Year Plan, about 73 percent of the increase is expected to come from crop output while 22 percent and 5.5 percent of the increase will come from animal and fish production, respectively. (Table 32 provides a breakdown of the expected increases in crop production.) The largest gains in production—60 percent increases or more—are expected for sorghum, vegetables, and cotton. Maize production should benefit from higher yielding varieties, while vegetables and cotton should benefit from expanded irrigation and reduced labor scarcity, respectively. The lowest rates of growth are expected for barley and dry beans. This is primarily due to a lower rate of return, particularly for traditional cereal crops where costs of production make domestic products uncompetitive with cereal imports. Wheat production is expected to continue to increase due to rising incomes and changing tastes which favor consumption of wheat over traditional cereals. The share of domestic wheat production in total consumption of that grain is expected

Table 31: Base Year and Targeted Agricultural Production, 1981 and 1986
(in million rials at constant 1981 prices)

Item	1981 Base Year Production	1986 Production	Increase from Base Year
Plant production	3,435.2	4,543.3	1,108.3
Animal production	1,152.7	1,487.0	334.3
Fish production	144.5	227.5	83.0
Forest production	128.0	128.0	—
Total	4,860.4	6,385.8	1,525.6

Source: Yemen Arab Republic, Ministry of Agriculture, working paper on the agricultural sector, 1982, p. 4.

to increase from 20 percent to 23 percent during the 1982-1986 span. The plan seeks self-sufficiency in sorghum, millet, and barley by 1986. The area planted in these crops is expected to continue to decline but output should rise due to increases in yields of 15 to 20 percent.

The largest increase in planted hectares is expected for cotton—252 percent. The positive expectations of cotton production derive from improved market conditions and an easing of labor scarcity. For crops other than cereals and cotton, the area planted is expected to increase by 10 to 20 percent. Overall, the plan expects an annual rate of increase of 3.8 percent in the extensive margin of arable land. This is in addition to 10,000 hectares of land which will be supplied with irrigation water during the 1982-1986 period.[42]

During the Second Five-Year Plan, 68 development projects are scheduled for the agricultural sector, calling for a total budget of 4.4 billion rials.[43] This amounts to 15.8 percent of total allocations of the budget in the second plan.[44] The domestic share of planned investment is 41.6 percent, while external financial assistance is expected to provide 58.4 percent. This represents an increase in the domestic share of agricultural investment, from 33 percent in the first plan to 41.6 percent in the second plan.[45] Breakdowns of investment for the Second Five-Year Plan are given in tables 33 and 34. The public sector is expected to contribute 58.2 percent of planned investment.[46] Public-sector in-

Table 32: Agricultural Production Targets During the Second Five-Year Plan, 1982-1986 *(in thousand tons)*

	Production 1981 (Base Year)	Production 1986 (Target)	Percentage Increase
Cereal crops	771.4	950.0	23.1
Millet	577.9	687.4	18.9
Sorghum	39.0	44.5	14.1
Maize	49.0	79.8	62.9
Barley	42.5	47.3	11.3
Wheat	63.0	91.0	44.4
Cotton	5.0	20.8	316.0
Dry beans	74.0	81.4	10.0
Tobacco	6.7	8.7	29.9
Sesame	4.3	5.5	27.9
Vegetables	292.0	467.5	60.0
Potatoes	129.0	180.0	50.0
Fruits	153.2	176.0	14.9
Coffee	3.8	4.6	21.0

Source: Yemen Arab Republic, Ministry of Agriculture, working paper on the agricultural sector, 1982, p. 5.

vestment will concentrate on rural development projects, irrigation projects, and on projects overseen by the Tihama Development Authority (TDA) as shown in table 34. The Tihama Development Authority has been allocated 1 billion rials or 22 percent of planned investment in the agricultural sector. Projects to be implemented by the TDA include, among others, Wadi Rima, Wadi Siham, and Wadi Rasqan.[47] The objectives within these projects include irrigation works, experimental research, studies of social constraints to agricultural production, water resource evaluation, credit and technical assistance, health and nutrition studies, and canal and road construction.

The government of North Yemen has been able to secure sources of external financing because of its record in efficient use of funds and careful project preparation and presentation. The YAR, as noted

Table 33: Allocation of Planned Investment in the Second Five-Year Plan
(in thousand rials)

	Number of Projects	Planned Investment YAR Govt.	Planned Investment External	Total	% of Total by Area
Crops	11	251,894	61,271	313,165	7.1
Forestry	1	17,070	21,111	38,181	0.9
Research	2	75,384	137,614	212,998	4.7
Extension	2	15,157	1,500	16,657	0.4
Livestock	12	303,303	315,272	618,575	14.1
Irrigation	15	181,000	543,000	724,000	16.4
Marketing	1	27,005	29,125	56,130	1.3
Construction	3	76,712	22,580	99,292	2.3
Planning and statistics	1	55,502	1,891	57,393	1.3
Integrated rural development	7	409,654	438,834	848,488	19.3
Tihama Development Authority	8	486,175	480,544	966,719	21.9
Fisheries	5	323,740	131,257	454,997	10.3
Total	68	2,222,596	2,183,999	4,406,595	100.0

Source: Consortium for International Development, *Agriculture Sector Analysis, Yemen Arab Republic* (Sana'a: Consortium for International Development, 1981), table IV.1.

elsewhere, frequently arranges loans from several sources for specific projects. For example, the first phase of the Central Highlands agricultural development program was funded with an $8-million credit from the International Development Association in 1984; cofinancing is anticipated from the International Fund for Agricultural Development ($4 million) and the United Kingdom's Overseas Development Administration ($1 million). This program—the total cost of which will be $20 million—will benefit approximately 45,000 YAR citizens through the establishment of extension services, the construction of ru-

Table 34: **Land and Water Resource Development Projects, Second Five-Year Plan** *(in thousand rials)*

	Expenditures to December 31, 1981	Planned Expenditures 1982-1986	Total Estimated Cost
Ongoing projects	244,897	1,235,153	1,479,997
Tihama Dev. Authority	192,197	682,153	874,347
Wadi Zabid	148,278	19,674	167,952
Wadi Rima	37,830	187,478	225,308
Wadi Mawr	500	347,266	347,766
Wadi Siham	4,451	40,655	45,106a
Wadi Rasqan	1,138	87,080	88,215
Wadi Al Jawf	36,750	178,000	214,750
Small weirs construction	6,300	250,000	256,300
Groundwater development	7,000	90,000	97,000
Wadi Bana	2,650	35,000	37,600
Proposed new projects	—	520,000	520,000
Marib dam	—	300,000	300,000
Wadi La'a irrigation	—	220,000	220,000
Water assessment projects	250	81,000	81,250
Agromet stations	250	5,000	5,250
Water resources survey	—	40,000	40,000
New irrigation methods	—	3,000	3,000
Sana'a basin study	—	32,000	32,000
Sewage water reuse study	—	1,000	1,000
Related land projects	2,600	27,000	29,600
Land ownership registration	—	5,000	5,000
Land classification	—	8,000	8,000
Terrace maintenance	2,600	14,000	16,600
Total	247,747	1,863,153	2,110,847

aAdditional expenditure of approximately 120 million rials required after Second Five-Year Plan.

Source: Consortium for International Development, *Agriculture Sector Analysis, Yemen Arab Republic* (Sana'a: Consortium for International Development, 1981), table IV. 5.

ral water-supply schemes, and the provision of technical assistance.[48]

The crop production targets outlined for the Second Five-Year Plan represent a substantially more realistic appraisal of agricultural potential in North Yemen than those goals set forth in the first plan. However, a 1981 study of the agricultural sector states that the 1982-1986 targets are still on the "optimistic" side, with perhaps the exception of vegetable production.[49] The share of agriculture in the GDP (in 1981 constant prices) was 3,685 million rials, rising in 1982 to 3,845 million rials, and falling somewhat in 1983 to 3,418 million rials; estimates for 1984 are for 3,786 million rials, evidencing a modest rebound tempered by the drought. The projected share of agriculture in GDP in 1985 is 3,900 million rials, a targeted increase of 3 percent for that year. If the 1985 goal is met, the growth ratio in the agricultural sector would rise from 0.9 percent to 1.4 percent.[50] (See table 35.)

A major element in the ability of the YAR to meet its production goals turns upon the question of the changing level of Yemeni emigration. There is no doubt that large-scale emigration of unskilled rural workers seriously constrained agricultural production during the 1970s by creating labor scarcity and consequently, rapidly rising agricultural wage rates. This effect, to a certain extent, was mitigated by rising incomes and the increased consumption of crops with a high income elasticity of demand, particularly fruit and vegetables. However, labor scarcity and rising wages seriously affected cereal production—the backbone of Yemen agriculture—and cotton output, a major cash crop.

Currently, the emigration picture is changing. Workers remittances have leveled off in the early 1980s and have, at various times, even declined. This is due both to the impact of the worldwide recession and oil glut on the economies of the oil states and a general lessening in demand for unskilled workers in those countries. By 1986 it is predicted that the situation will have turned around such that a general surplus of unskilled labor will exist.

A lessening of the level of Yemeni emigration will have the positive effect of providing downward pressure on agricultural wages, thereby increasing the return and improving the competitiveness of domestic production, particularly of cereals. The question remains, however, of how rapidly such an improvement will impact on agricultural output.

First, the transition from a situation of labor scarcity to labor surplus will be a gradual process. Second, both cereal and cotton production have experienced very low rates of return for a prolonged period, and the willingness of farmers to expand output rapidly in these

Table 35: Growth and Structure of YAR Gross Domestic Product (GDP), 1982-1984a *(in percent, based on data in constant 1981 prices)*

	Rate of Growth			Structure	
	1982	1983	1984	1975/76	1984
Agriculture	4.7	-11.3	5.0	37.4	23.2
Manufacturing	20.4	23.2	6.0	4.7	8.3
Construction	6.3	-0.7	7.0	6.5	8.0
Trade	4.6	-2.1	3.0	18.2	14.0
Other sectors	14.6	9.6	5.2	11.8	17.0
Government services	12.0	0.0	2.0	12.1	16.3
Import duties	12.1	17.8	-5.4	9.3	13.2
GDP at market prices	9.3	1.9	3.0	100.0	100.0

aFor 1983, figures provisional; for 1984, figures are estimated.

Source: World Bank, "Yemen Arab Republic Country Economic Memorandum Current Position and Prospects," Report no. 5621-YAR (Washington D.C., June 25, 1985), p. 7.

areas will be much less than for crops that have experienced high returns.

On the other side of the coin is the effect of declining emigration on incomes in North Yemen; the fall in the level of workers' remittances to the YAR causes a corresponding decline in the rate of domestic income growth. This, in turn, will reduce the level of demand for and consumption of agricultural products, particularly those crops with a high income elasticity of demand.

In summary, the decline in the level of emigration and easing of domestic labor shortages during the Second Five-Year Plan will have a positive effect on agricultural production through downward pressure on wages. However, to some extent, this will be mitigated by the fall in workers' remittances which will reduce the growth in demand for certain agricultural products. Furthermore, very low rates of return have been experienced for prolonged periods in certain crops. Recovery of output levels in these products can be expected to be gradual. Given the experience of the 1970s, and the forecast conditions for the period of the second plan, it seems likely that recovery of high rates of growth in agricultural production will be a slow process. The important point to note, however, is that the foundations for sustained growth of agricultural production—namely, research, irrigation projects, infrastructural development, and institutional development—have been established. This is the significant achievement of development planning in the agriculture sector in North Yemen.

A final word should be given on the impact of the prolonged drought in 1983 and 1984, similar to that which devastated Africa during those years. Output in 1983 declined from 1982 levels for such major crops as maize (a drop of 49 percent), sorghum and millet (-54 percent), wheat (- 49 percent), barley (- 43 percent), and dry legumes (-48 percent).[51] This decline in agricultural production is reflected in the share of that sector in the GDP, as seen in tables 27 and 35 of this chapter.

Notes

1. Abdullah El Mugahed, "Accomplishments of the Agricultural Year in Yemen," *Asharq Al-Awsat* (London), February 10, 1985, p. 4 (in Arabic), and World Bank, *Yemen Arab Republic: Development of a Traditional Economy* (Washington, D.C.: World Bank, 1979), p. 91.

2. World Bank, *Yemen Arab Republic: Development of a Traditional Economy*, p. iii.

3. Yemen Arab Republic, Ministry of Agriculture, *Summary of the Final Results of the Agricultural Census in Six Provinces* (1981), p. 26.

4. Ibid.

5. Richard F. Nyrop et al., *Area Handbook for the Yemens* (Washington, D.C.: United States Government Printing Office, 1977), p. 120.

6. World Bank, *Yemen Arab Republic: Development of a Traditional Economy*, p. 91. One hectare (ha) is equal to 10,000 square meters or approximately 2.47 acres.

7. Consortium for International Development, *Agriculture Sector Analysis, Yemen Arab Republic* (Sana'a: Consortium for International Development, 1981), p. 50.

8. Ibid.

9. World Bank, *Yemen Arab Republic: Development of a Traditional Economy*, p. 93.

10. Consortium for International Development, *Agriculture Sector Analysis, Yemen Arab Republic*, p. 50.

11. Ibid., table III.11.

12. *The Financial Times* (London), November 26, 1984.

13. Consortium for International Development, *Agriculture Sector Analysis, Yemen Arab Republic*, table II.12, and Yemen Arab Republic, Central Bank of Yemen, Research Department, *Financial Statistical Bulletin*, January-March 1984, table 26.

14. Consortium for International Development, *Agriculture Sector Analysis, Yemen Arab Republic*, table III.17.

15. Yemen Arab Republic, Ministry of Agriculture, *Summary of the Final Results of the Agricultural Census in Six Provinces*, p. 29.

16. Consortium for International Development, *Agriculture Sector Analysis, Yemen Arab Republic*, table III.19.

17. John M. Cohen and David B. Lewis, *Rural Development in the Yemen Arab Republic* (Cambridge, Massachusetts: Harvard Institute for International Development, 1979), p. 15.

18. Thomas Gerholm, *Market, Mosque, and Mofraj: Social Inequality in a Yemeni Town* (Stockholm: University of Stockholm, 1977).

19. John M. Cohen and David B. Lewis, *Rural Development in the Yemen Arab Republic*, p. 41. A recent study by John G. Kennedy, James Teague, and Lynn Fairbanks, "Qat Use in North Yemen and the Problem of Addiction: A Study in Medical Anthropology," *Culture, Medicine, and Psychiatry*, December 1980, pp. 311-344, offers estimates on the level of personal expenditures on qat.

20. *The Financial Times*, November 26, 1984.

21. Yemen Arab Republic, Central Planning Organization, Statistics Department, *Statistical Year Book*, 1981, table IV.2.

22. Consortium for International Development, *Agriculture Sector Analysis, Yemen Arab Republic*, table IV.2.

23. Yemen Arab Republic, Central Planning Organization, Statistics Department, *Statistical Yearbook, 1981*, p. 86.

24. United States, Agency for International Development and Consortium for International Development, *Horticulture Improvement and Training: Agriculture Development Support—Yemen* (Sana'a: U. S. Agency for International Development, 1982), pp. 7, 8, and 15.

25. Ibid., p. 15.

26. J. E. Peterson, *Yemen: The Search for a Modern State* (London: Croom Helm, Ltd., 1982), p. 53.

27. Yemen Arab Republic, Central Planning Organization, Statistics Department, *Statistical Yearbook, 1979-1980*, p. 92.

28. *The Financial Times*, November 26, 1984.

29. World Bank, *Yemen Arab Republic: Development of a Traditional Economy*, p. 104.

30. Ibid.

31. Ibid., p. 105.

32. John M. Cohen and David B. Lewis, *Rural Development in the Yemen Arab Republic*, p. 23.

33. Yemen Arab Republic, Central Planning Organization, *First Five-Year Plan (1976/77-1980/81)*, p. 157.

34. Ibid.

35. Yemen Arab Republic, Ministry of Agriculture, working paper on the agricultural sector, 1982, p. 2.

36. Ibid.

37. Consortium for International Development, *Agriculture Sector Analysis, Yemen Arab Republic*, p. 72.

38. Ibid., p. 55.

39. Yemen Arab Republic, Central Planning Organization, *Second Five-Year Plan (1982-1986)*, 1982, p. 15.

40. Yemen Arab Republic, Ministry of Agriculture, working paper on the agricultural sector, 1982, p. 3.

41. Yemen Arab Republic, Central Planning Organization, "Fourth Year Annual Report of the Second Five-Year Plan," (February 1985) (mimeographed, in Arabic).

42. Ibid.

43. Consortium for International Development, *Agriculture Sector Analysis, Yemen*

Arab Republic, table IV.1.

44. Yemen Arab Republic, Ministry of Agriculture, working paper on the agricultural sector, 1982.

45. Ibid.

46. Ibid.

47. Yemen Arab Republic, Ministry of Agriculture, *Tihama Development Authority, A Record of Achievements*, 1982.

48. World Bank, *Annual Report 1984* (Washington, D.C.: World Bank, 1984), p. 124.

49. Consortium for International Development, *Agriculture Sector Analysis, Yemen Arab Republic*, revised chapter 4, p. 46.

50. Yemen Arab Republic, Central Planning Organization, "Fourth Year Annual Report of the Second Five-Year Plan."

51. World Bank, "Yemen Arab Republic Country Economic Memorandum Current Position and Prospects," Report no. 5621-YAR (Washington, D.C., June 25, 1985), p. 9 (mimeographed).

6 DEVELOPMENT OF INDUSTRY

Introduction

One of the most important long-term objectives of the Second Five-Year Plan (1982-1986) is to induce a structural change in the Yemen Arab Republic's economy in favor of the goods-producing sectors. This goal is to reduce the level of consumer-goods imports and to channel those foreign-exchange funds toward the importation of intermediate and capital goods.

Indeed, a structural transformation of output has already occurred on a limited scale as reflected in the contributions of the various economic sectors to the gross domestic product (GDP). The services sector, fueled by the propensity to import consumer goods and reinforced by the decline in agricultural output, now dominates economic activity (see table 27, chapter five). The contribution of the services sector in 1980/81 was 44.6 percent of GDP whereas in 1970/71 it was estimated at 39.4 percent. In contrast, the contribution of the agricultural sector to GDP had declined to 36.9 percent of GDP in 1980/81 from approximately 50 percent in 1970/71. The share of the industrial sector had slowly risen over the years to 18.5 percent of GDP in 1980/81 from an estimated 10.6 percent of GDP in 1970/71.[1] By the end of the Second Five-Year Plan in 1986, industry's contribution to the GDP is expected to reach 8.6 percent, a target considered attainable and one which may be exceeded.[2]

An initial look into the performance of the YAR's economy during the first three years of the Second Five-Year Plan, i.e., 1982-1984, reveals several trends. The gross domestic product has grown by an average rate of 6 percent annually (based on 1981 prices). Bearing in mind that the targeted growth rate was 7 percent per annum and that North Yemen has suffered from a two-year drought and a devastating earthquake, the pace of growth is impressive. A breakdown by sectors does indicate the areas of strength and weakness in economic performance. For example, the agricultural GDP registered a 0.9 percent growth rate, well below the target of 4.2 percent, although there have been extenuating circumstances noted earlier. The wholesale and retail sales sector grew at an annual rate of 1.7 percent compared to the plan goal of 0.6 percent per annum. On the other hand, some sectors have surpassed the target rates by as much as 100 percent. The housing and real estate sector, for instance, grew by an annual rate of 11.4 percent whereas the planned rate was 6 percent annually. Similarly, the manufacturing and the electricity, gas, and water sectors witnessed an annual growth of 18 percent and 30.2 percent, respectively, against the plan targets for these two sectors of 13.5 percent, and 25 percent, respectively.[3]

Industry in the Yemen Arab Republic is typified by small, light manufacturing enterprises producing primarily consumer goods and building materials. Industrial establishments are heavily dependent on the primary sector and on import goods for their inputs. Nearly 98 percent of industrial organizations employed fewer than five workers in 1975.[4] Estimates of the size of the manufacturing work force in 1975 vary from 23,000 workers[5] to 33,900 workers.[6] Employment in manufacturing by 1981 was estimated to have reached 52,900 workers, representing 4.4 percent of the total labor force.[7]

As in most newly developing countries, the structure of manufacturing output is dominated by the food-processing and beverages subsector which in 1979/80 accounted for 45 percent of the value added in the sector (see table 36). The chemical industries (covering products such as plastic footwear, paints, plastic utensils, and polyvinyl chloride—PVC—pipes), starting from a low base, were the fastest growing subsector during the 1975/76 to 1979/80 span. Food processing experienced the second highest growth rate during the period, despite its very large initial base. Major expansion of output in soft drinks, confectionery, and edible oils was the main source of growth in this subsector. The textiles subsector experienced a substantial decline in output, arising from interruptions in the operation of the country's only major integrated textile plant in Sana'a. The relatively weak performance of the nonmetallic construction materials industries might appear surprising given the strong performance of the construction sector. However, stone, the most important indigenous construction material, is included in the mining sector—and its value added increased at an average annual rate of nearly 25 percent during the 1975/76 to 1979/80 period.[8]

Table 37 highlights the evolution and composition of the major products of the Yemen Arab Republic's manufacturing industry. As can be observed, many new products have been introduced between 1978 and 1980 and production has rapidly increased in two subsectors,

Table 36: Growth and Composition of Manufacturing Value Added *(in percent)*

Manufacturing Sector	Annual Growth Rate[a] 1975/76-1979/80	Share in Value Added[b] 1975/76	1979/80
Food processing	19.1	41.1	45.0
Textiles	-4.2	17.9	8.2
Chemicals	38.3	3.2	10.7
Nonmetallic construction materials	6.3	11.0	10.3
Metal and light engineering	13.1	8.6	8.6
Wood products	16.1	7.8	10.7
Others	2.7	10.4	6.5
Total		100.0	100.0

[a]In constant 1975/76 market prices.
[b]Based on current prices.

Source: Yemen Arab Republic, Central Planning Organization cited in World Bank, *Yemen Arab Republic—Manufacturing Industries: Performance, Policies, and Prospects* (Washington, D.C.: World Bank, October 30, 1981), p. 7.

notably food processing and chemicals. It is readily apparent from this brief inventory of domestically produced items that the manufacturing sector concentrates on production for final consumption rather than on production of intermediate goods to be used as inputs for other industries. Also noticeable from the table is that production is currently oriented toward fulfilling import-substitution goals and that some Yemen-produced goods enjoy a natural protection from imported goods by virtue of the fact that they are bulky (e.g., tins, boxes) and have an associated high transportation cost.

Food-Processing Industries

The structure of manufacturing output is dominated by the food-pro-

Table 37: Output of Major Manufactured Products, 1978, 1980, 1982, 1983a

Product (Unit)	1978	1980	1982	1983
Food, beverage, and tobacco				
Food industries				
Biscuits and confectionary ('000 tons)	13	20	25	32
Biscuits and confectionary ('000 cartons)	177	258	n.a.	n.a.
Biscuits and confectionary (tins)	—	1,000	n.a.	n.a.
Ghee and edible oils (tons)	4,926	13,188	16,000	21,000
Biscuit butter (tons)	600	—	n.a.	n.a.
Soft drinks ('000 boxes)	4,817	12,410	13,693	58,796
Mineral water ('000 cartons)	—	1,482	n.a.	15,138
Vimto drink ('000 carton)	—	2,300	8,280	9,591
Ice ('000 kilograms)	—	10,726	19,600	34,500
Milk ('000 liters)	—	570	n.a.	10,307
Iced products ('000 liters)	—	31,000	n.a.	15,831
Ice cream (tons)	—	365	n.a.	622
Tobacco				
Cigarettes ('000 cartons)	10	17	21	39
Chemicals				
Plastic footwear ('000 dozens)	30	339	344	342
Sponges (tons)	2,000	1,667	1,931	2,006
Household utensils ('000 tons)	89	157	508	543
Buckets ('000 units)	38	385	3,998	3,571
Water tubes ('000 meters)	n.a.	960	1,782	3,036
Plastic sheets ('000 kilograms)	300	364	1,004	1,630
Beverage boxes ('000 boxes)	300	277	328	188
Plastic tubes ('000 tubes)	—	223	n.a.	n.a.
Plastic tubes (tons)	1,000	3,161	3,324	3,508
Polythene bags (tons)	—	200	n.a.	n.a.
Covers and strings ('000 kilograms)	—	72	15	28
Cardboard (tons)	900	1,000	1,769	4,778
Paint ('000 gallons)	312	504	n.a.	1,127
Decorations (cubic meters)	—	6,163	4,927	3,557
Soap and detergents (tons)	—	900	3,706	5,071
Perfumes ('000 ounces)	—	563	448	341
Oxygen gas (cylinders)	—	4,432	9,625	11,200
Carbon dioxide ('000 kilograms)	180	755	368	n.a.

(continued)

Table 37 (continued): Output of Major Manufactured Products, 1978, 1980, 1982, 1983[a]

Product (Unit)	1978	1980	1982	1983
Spinning and weaving				
Spinning and weaving ('000 yards)	2,094	5,410	6,989	6,459
Underwear ('000 dozen)	—	—	148	169
Woolen pullovers ('000 pieces)	—	—	42	98
Metallic				
House utensils ('000 kilograms)	585	708	1,851	1,407
Metallic rubbers ('000 bags)	16	18	56	68
Barrels ('000 barrels)	17	115	107	110
Tins ('000 tins)	1,683	459	143	102
Doors and windows (square meters)	—	6,000	4,578	18,855
Metal bags ('000 bags)	—	—	33	34
Beds ('000 beds)	—	—	19	8
Nonmetallic				
Cement ('000 tons)	66	81	224	623
Red bricks ('000 units)	—	4,800	1,266	6,104
Cement bricks ('000 units)	—	1,290	3,599	2,863
Tiles ('000 units)	—	—	6,749	6,174
Cement blocks and tiles ('000 cubic meters)	—	22	32	81
Pottery ('000 units)	—	—	20	30
Extracting				
Salt extracting ('000 tons)	58	154	70	151
Rock quarrying ('000 cubic meters)	19	76	529	540
Gypsum extracting (tons)	—	—	4,509	23,138
Leather				
Tanning ('000 skins)	306	299	—	—
Wood industries				
Industrial limbs (pieces)	100	300	765	2,295

[a]Some of the data in this table are substantially different from those obtained by the World Bank during plant visits; for example, World Bank figures for sponge production are 1,500 tons in 1978, 1,960 tons in 1979, and 1,675 tons in 1980.

Sources: Yemen Arab Republic, Central Planning Organization, Statistics Department, *Statistical Year Book, 1979-1980*, pp. 98-99, *Statistical Year Book, 1983*, pp. 104-107; and World Bank, *Yemen Arab Republic—Manufacturing Industries: Performance, Policies, and Prospects*, pp. 9 and 36.

cessing subsector with production concentrated in soft drinks and other nonalcoholic beverages (including mineral water), flour, bread, biscuits (crackers and cookies), confectionary, vegetable oils, cooking fats (ghee), ice, dairy products (ice cream, reconstituted milk, yogurt), cigarettes, and tobacco. Vegetable canning, particularly of beans and highly perishable tomatoes, has recently begun.

Most food-processing industries operate at 30 to 75 percent of capacity, largely because they face strong competition from foreign products through unrecorded trade and in some cases because they have not yet penetrated the market. Another problem is high sales prices, determined by high production costs, which in turn render the products uncompetitive even with legally imported similar goods. Soft drink and mineral-water bottling plants are working at full capacity or at reasonable levels of capacity utilization since they do not face serious competition from recorded or unrecorded imports of similar products. However, there is a tendency for duplication of activities by some entrepreneurs—successful ventures are appealing. The Ministry of Planning is considering the problem of excessive duplication and may adopt a policy of withdrawing incentives once a local source of supply is in place. The government's price controls also need close scrutiny to respond to changes so that local production of agro-industries can remain profitable and competitive.

The development of the food-processing industry is constrained by the lack or inadequacy of local raw materials. Thus, a viable long-term development strategy for this branch of industrial activity must focus on agricultural research and programs aimed at the production of crops for which the country has the suitable ecological conditions.

Two agro-industries have substantial potential for growth with the expansion of domestic raw-material inputs. First would be the utilization of Mocha coffee for blending with cheaper imported beans from East Africa. Such a program would maximize the centuries-old and worldwide reputation of Yemen's coffee and result in a product of some allure and luxury status in Western markets. Domestic blending, packaging, marketing, and distribution would provide employment opportunities and foster an industry with foreign-exchange-earning capacity. Second would be an expansion of the textiles industry, based primarily on cotton, that would not only meet domestic demand but allow for some exports. Should cotton production fail to increase sufficiently too meet the industry's demand, cotton could be imported from Egypt and Sudan.

Textiles

Cotton is grown on the Tihama coastal plain, is the principal raw material in the textile industry and the cotton seed oil processing plant, and is an export commodity. The quantity of raw cotton produced in the Yemen Arab Republic reached a record level of 27,238 tons in 1974-1975.[9] Since then production registered a 63 percent decline between 1975/76 and 1980/81, from 13,500 tons to about 5,000 tons,[10] while 1979/80 witnessed production of only 2,100 tons and no exports.[11] The decline in cotton production has been the consequence of a number of factors working in tandem. The amount of land devoted to cotton cultivation—which declined from approximately 39,000 hectares in the early 1970s to 13,233 hectares in 1976/77, and to 5,300 in 1980/81—is associated with competition from other crops, rapidly rising labor costs, and inadequate government procurement prices in relation to rising costs and low international prices.[12]

The Yemen Weaving and Textile Corporation was established in 1973 to operate the Sana'a textile mill and a mill in Bajil. The Sana'a mill has its own ginnery, a spinning, weaving, and finishing plant, a power plant, water-supply system, and workshops, (including a small foundry and pattern-making shop) and has the distinction of being the only major integrated textile factory in the Yemen Arab Republic.

The Chinese-built Sana'a textile mill began production in 1967 but in 1975 its output began to decline and by the late 1970s output was about one-half of the mill's rated capacity of some 10 million linear meters per year of 100 percent cotton fabric—a capacity which could meet 24 percent of domestic demand. Aside from the diminished availability of raw materials, the Sana'a textile mill has experienced labor shortages. The mill was unable to remain competitive with the rising wage rates in the Arabian Peninsula and in the Yemen Arab Republic itself; subsequently, its labor force declined from 1,700 to 1,581 workers.[13] Associated with this reduction in the labor force was the loss of skilled personnel and management.

Renovation of the Sana'a mill will reequip the spinning unit and improve the weaving stage. Eventually the mill will be able to process polyester, in addition to cotton, and produce cotton-polyester fabric.

The private sector has limited itself in the field of textiles to knitting activities, producing sweaters, blouses, cardigans, and other types of clothing using mainly synthetic materials. Future private-sector activities in the textile sector will include diapers, towels, and bedding. Similar to the Sana'a mill, the private-sector projects are constrained by a lack of experienced management and skilled workers. In addition, domestically produced goods face strong competition with imports. However, the return of large numbers of expatriate workers since mid-1983 may help to ease labor shortages and slow the upward domestic wage spiral.

The Extraction Industry

The extraction industry in the Yemen Arab Republic includes minerals, salt, construction material, and energy resources. Increasing attention is being directed toward this sector of the economy. Under the Three-Year Program (1973/74-1975/76) the allocation to this sector amounted to 4.325 million rials.[14] During the First Five-Year Plan, the mining and extraction sector showed an annual growth rate of 6.2 percent, falling substantially below the 12 percent targeted.[15] Fixed capital investment for the mining sector is expected to rise to 905 million Yemeni rials during the Second Five-Year Plan.[16] The 1982-1986 plan envisages, over the medium term, that development of its natural resources will expand the production base of the economy and provide the infant industrial sector with its necessary raw material inputs and, over the long term, will contribute towards the improvement of the trade deficit in the balance of payments. Hence, the optimal resource development strategy of the Yemen Arab Republic at this stage is toward the extraction and utilization of available resources.

The Energy Sector: As the prices of crude oil and petroleum products rose during the decade of the 1970s, so North Yemen's consumption of petroleum products increased, from 81,927 tons in 1970 to 161,875 tons in 1973 to 674,535 tons in 1980.[17] Consequently, the Yemen Arab Republic has suffered a severe oil-payments problem since prices for that commodity increased fourfold in 1973 and 1974. The Yemen Arab Republic's fuel bills have escalated from $7 million in 1973 to $132 million in 1979.[18] The value of petroleum products and gas imports has continued to rise, reaching 828.4 million rials ($184.1 million) in 1982 (see table 38). The government, however, had granted a subsidy to the Yemen Petroleum Company to enable it to sell oil products at a reduced price. In order to ease the financial crunch for petroleum imports, various oil-producing countries and multinational organizations extended assistance to the Yemen Arab Republic. In February 1976, Kuwait agreed to supply 250,000 tons of refined petroleum products over a three-year period. The Jeddah-based Islamic Development Bank has also provided aid on various occasions; for example, the YAR received a $15-million credit from that institution to help pay for petroleum imports from Kuwait and another $10 million, under an agreement signed on December 28, 1981, to finance the import of petroleum products from Iraq.[19] In addition, an agreement signed on January 11, 1982, between the Kuwait National Petroleum Company and the Yemen Arab Republic's General Organization for Petroleum and Minerals, provided the country with 460,000 tons of refined products at $222 million.[20] (These examples are not inclusive of all aid received by the Yemen Arab Republic for petroleum imports.)

Table 38: Value of Energy Imports, 1979/80-1982[a] (*in thousand rials*)

SITC Revision 2 Group	1979/80	1980	1981	1982
Petroleum products	359,695	597,394	589,529	815,275
Gas	9,811	11,796	18,461	13,147
Total	369,506	609,190	608,000	828,422

[a]Gasoline imports are underreported because of unrecorded movements of this product across the borders.

Source: Yemen Arab Republic, Central Bank of Yemen, Research Department, *Financial Statistical Bulletin*, January-March 1984, table 26.

It may be helpful to clarify the institutional framework of the energy sector of the Yemen Arab Republic. Established in 1961, the privately owned Yemen Fuels Company was headquartered in Hodeidah with branches in Sana'a and Taiz. Shell Oil Company was the primary supplier of petroleum products out of its Aden refinery. Product imports ran at about 10,000 barrels per month, 10,800 tons per annum, of which more than two-thirds was kerosene—earmarked for lighting—and most of the remainder was gasoline.[21] By 1969 the company's name and ownership changed, becoming the Yemen Oil Company (YOC), with the government's share being 51 percent of the 10 million rials capitalization. The remaining 49 percent is held by the

Yemen Bank for Reconstruction and Development.

In 1978, the government of North Yemen reorganized the activities of the Departments of Petroleum and Mineral Resources, the General Corporation for Salt Manufacturing, and the YOC, whereby the latter became a unit of the newly created Yemen Oil and Minerals Corporation (YOMINCO). YOMINCO's responsibilities include the formulation of an oil and minerals policy that will stimulate the exploitation of these resources within the goals and limitations of YAR economic policy. Development of North Yemen's natural resources is a high priority during the Second Five-Year Plan, with a total investment of 669 million rials ($148.66 million) being directed primarily toward determining the feasibility of exploration and exploitation.

YOMINCO is the government-owned entity having the authority to explore, evaluate, and control exploitation of the country's mineral resources, with specific responsibility for the supervision of: (a) national and foreign companies involved in oil and mineral exploration; (b) refining, manufacturing, and marketing of mineral and petroleum products both domestically and abroad; (c) imports and exports of oil and minerals; (d) collection of rents, royalties, taxes, and oil/minerals-related revenues per contractual agreements; (e) negotiations between investors to assure that national policy guidelines are met; (f) the establishment of a strategic reserve; and (g) the reviewing of oil and mineral prices and production to meet national policy objectives and requirements.

Steady growth of the Yemen Arab Republic's economy implies increased petroleum imports until its own oil resources can be developed in order to meet the demands of rapidly growing cities, industries, motorized transportation, and other energy-intensive development. The Yemen Arab Republic is projected to require 1,033,520 to 1,096,800 tons of petroleum products by 1985 and as much as 1,541,500 tons by 1990 (table 39).

Investment in storage and port handling facilities for large tankers could pay off quickly in the Yemen Arab Republic by enabling the country to take advantage of freight differentials. The Second Five-Year Plan has undertaken to support the building of additional oil storage tanks, at a cost of 400 million rials, as well as funding an oil distribution network (a pipeline from Salif to Sana'a and a second from Mocha to Taiz), at a cost of 25.3 million rials.[22] Rompetrol, Romania's national oil company, is building 250,000-ton-capacity storage tanks at Hodeidah and Mocha ports.

Establishment of a petroleum refinery in the Yemen Arab Repub-

Table 39: Projected Petroleum-Product Consumption, 1982-1990 *(in thousand tons)*

Product	1982	1983	1984	1985	1986	1987	1988	1989	1990
Diesel	358.4	394.2	430.1	466.0	501.8	537.6	573.4	609.3	645.1
Gasoline	251.1	276.6	301.8	326.9	352.1	377.2	402.4	427.5	452.7
Kerosene	33.7	37.1	40.5	43.8	47.2	50.6	53.9	57.3	60.7
Other	252.0	254.7	257.4	369.5	372.2	274.9	578.0	380.3	383.0
Total	895.2	962.6	1,029.8	1,206.2	1,273.3	1,240.3	1,607.4	1,474.4	1,541.5

Source: Yemen Oil and Minerals Corporation, Department of Planning, *1980 Report of Petroleum Products Consumption* (Sana'a, 1980).

lic could enable the country to import crude oil and convert it into needed refined petroleum products such as gasoline, diesel fuel, kerosene, fuel oil, and naphtha. This facility could also process domestically produced crude oil in the future. However, a refinery in the Yemen Arab Republic would confront special problem, such as processing a combination of products appropriate for domestic demand and operational efficiency. The local market requires a large proportion of light distillates; the demand for fuel oil is limited by the country's small industrial base (see table 40). The Second Five-Year Plan has made no other provision for a refinery since Mobil International Petroleum Corporation withdrew from a joint-venture, 100,000-barrels-per-day refinery which was to have been located at Hodeidah. But after the discovery of oil in late 1984, new plans are being made for construction of a refinery in Marib.[23]

Butane gas is imported from Aden and bottled in Hodeidah. Caltex Petroleum Corporation operates and provides technical assistance to the Yemen Oil and Minerals Corporation for this Romanian-built, butane gas-cylinder-filling station, which was idled for two years after its construction. A second gas-filling center at Hodeidah has been allocated 80 million rials in the Second Five-Year Plan.[24] This plant, to be built by Sumitomo Corporation of Japan, was scheduled to begin operations in 1984; the gas cylinders are expected to sell at 20 rials ($4.30) each, compared with the earlier prevailing price of 30 rials ($6.50).

Table 40: Energy Consumption by Type of Fuel, 1979

Type of Fuel	Thousand Tons of Oil Equivalent
Thermal electricity[a]	13.0
Liquefied petroleum gas (LPG)	5.7
Fuel oil	10.3
Middle distillates (gas oil and diesel oil)	303.0
Jet fuel	17.0
Kerosene	93.0
Gasoline	222.0

[a]For 1978.

Source: I. Ibrahim, H. Abdulla, and A. Iweis, "Energy Demand Forecasts for the Arab Countries," *Middle East Economic Survey*, April 19, 1982, p. i.

Paradoxically, given its location in the region where 370 billion barrels or 55 percent of the world's proven oil reserves are located, oil has only recently been discovered in the Yemen Arab Republic. The government is confident that there are respectable reserves of this resource within its borders, reserves that could be a catalyst to further economic development of the country.

The lack of effort made by international petroleum companies to undertake exploration in oil-importing countries (such as North Yemen) during the 1970s has been attributed to the often exaggerated perception of the increased political and economic risk of doing business in many of these nations; it can also be attributed to the hardening of terms offered by such countries in petroleum exploration and production contracts.[25] However, the economic rate of return on domestic oil production given present and future projected international oil prices is likely to be reasonably high. As regards the Yemen Arab Republic, before a foreign petroleum company will invest in this country it will measure its prospects in relation to opportunities in other nations as well as to the YAR's fiscal, political, and operating risks. Hence, the investment terms of the Yemen Arab Republic must be competitive with those offered by other nations.

The government of the Yemen Arab Republic is open to direct

foreign investment in this area. The International Development Association, an affiliate of the World Bank, extended a $2 million loan to the Yemen Arab Republic, part of which financed a detailed report on the petroleum geology of the Red Sea basin.26 This project is aimed at stimulating foreign oil industry interest in North Yemen's petroleum and geothermal energy potential.

In 1984 the International Development Association made an additional $13-million loan to the YAR to assist in financing a $15.35-million geothermal-exploration program that includes drilling upwards of four exploratory wells, technical assistance, consultancy services, on-the-job and overseas training, and the initiation of a study for expanded exploration and/or development should the results of this first project justify continued activity in geothermal energy resources.27

During the five-year span of the second development plan, the YAR hopes to undertake oil exploration in the north of the country at a projected cost of 61.5 million rials and plans to evaluate oil explorations in the western areas at a cost of 14 million rials.28

Since 1974 a number of companies have been searching for oil along the Yemen Arab Republic's Red Sea coast and offshore. In 1974 Deutsche Shell was granted a 19,000-square kilometer concession offshore, covering an area from the Saudi Arabian border to the port of Hodeidah. In May of 1976 this concession was extended to include the entire southern part of the North Yemeni coastline and the area offshore south of Hodeidah. Eventually, Deutsche Shell ceased offshore drilling operations in its concession in the Red Sea. Yemen Shell Exploration, registered in the Federal Republic of Germany, was established in early 1976 to carry out exploration along the country's Red Sea coast north of Hodeidah. The first well drilled by this company proved unsuccessful since drilling could not go beyond a depth of 8,200 feet because of high temperatures. A second well reported a noncommercial quantity of natural gas.29 Toyo Menka Kaisha (Tomen) of Japan, sharing exploration costs with Santa Fe International of the United States, was also granted a 2,500 square kilometer concession off the country's southern coast. Unfortunately, the product of these concessions was little exploration and inconclusive results.

When the Shell concession for the Salif area of the central Tihama was relinquished, British Petroleum (BP) began negotiations that in January 1984 resulted in signing an onshore 22,000-square kilometer exploration concession covering most of the Tihama coastal plain (from the Saudi border to 10 kilometers south of Hodeidah). The terms of the $4-million agreement required BP to effect the seismic survey of at least 800 kilometers within 18 months (with seismic shooting begun in April 1984). After the 18-month period and requisite activities, BP was to either commence drilling or abandon the concession.[30] In 1984 Hunt Oil Company won a second concession in North Yemen, offshore in the Red Sea next to that of British Petroleum. It is, however, the first area explored by Hunt Oil that has produced definite results.

On September 4, 1981, Yemen Hunt Oil Company, a subsidiary of Hunt Oil Company of the United States, signed a six-year oil exploration and production-sharing agreement with the Yemen Oil and Minerals Organization, covering 12,600 square kilometers in the Marib and Al Jawf areas. Yemen Hunt Oil was to spend at least $4.2 million on an initial two-year seismic research phase (including geological surveys and surface geological studies). Thereafter, spending—and multi-well drilling—was to depend on results. Drilling had never before been undertaken in either the Marib or Al Jawf regions. To date, Yemen Hunt Oil has located several potential oil-bearing structures at different depths during seismic and gravity surveys.

Late in 1984 and early 1985, a flurry of reports appeared just a few months after the July 1984 announcement by Yemen Hunt Oil that its first exploration well—Alef 1—had been successful.[31] The find, located in the Marib-Jawf basin about 70 kilometers east of the town of Marib and some 250 kilometers northeast of Sana'a, lies near the Yemen Arab Republic's undemarcated border with Saudi Arabia. Alef 1 tested 4,162 barrels per day (b/d) of 39.8°API crude from 5,750-5,765 feet and 3,669 b/d of the lighter gravity crude (40.4°API) from between 5,701-5,724 feet. Later flows were testing at 13,000 b/d. Production from the second and third wells in the field is 12,000 to 15,000 b/d.[32] A more exact appraisal of the Marib-Jawf field was scheduled for the spring of 1985, when seven additional wells will have been drilled by Westburne Drilling (Canada). A second rig capable of drilling to 9,000 feet has been brought into the Alef 1 area. Estimates early in 1985, based on drilling data then available, put minimum initial output at 75,000 to 100,000 b/d and projected potential production of about 400,000 b/d. Aside from associated natural gas, the discovery of nonassociated gas was announced in 1986 in the Alef field as well as Lam and Meem fields. First indications are that the nonassociated gas reserves may be substantial.

South Korea's Ministry of Energy and Resources has estimated the Marib-Jawf field's reserves at perhaps 200 million barrels with a possible output of between 100,000 and 200,000 b/d. This attention of South Korea resulted from the 24.5 percent interest in the concession purchased from Hunt Oil by a South Korean consortium of four companies (Yukong, Korean Petroleum Development Corporation, Hyundai Corporation, and Samwhan Corporation). The production-sharing agreement between YOMINCO and Hunt Oil requires that the capital development of the field itself be provided by the concessionaire. Such investment may require as much as $1 billion. Yukong, Hyundai, and Samwhan along with Hunt Oil are forming a group to bid on infrastructure projects related to the Marib-Jawf field costing upwards of $2 billion. Among these projects would be a crude oil pipeline from the northeastern discovery area to Salif port on the Red Sea. The exact route of the 400- to 450-kilometer pipeline (running either to the north or south of Sana'a) will depend upon the feasibility studies undertaken by Hunt Oil and, of course, on the mid-1985 estimates of the field's reserves.

Commercialization of the Alef field is currently under way in a $50.3 million project. Just over half the investment will be earmarked for the drilling of wells and early development facilities, with the remainder divided between the Marib domestic refinery ($22.9 million) and the crude-oil gathering and separation facilities ($1.4 million). The project is financed by equity (25 percent) and long-term loans (75 percent). The equity portion is provided by Yemen Hunt Oil Company ($3.8 million) and the newly established Yemen Refining and Marketing Company ($8.8 million).[33] The long-term loans are provided by a guarantee from the Overseas Private Investment Corporation covering $20.7 million, repayable in 10 years of which the first year is a grace period. The International Finance Corporation is the source of a second credit of $9 million to be repaid over 10 years with Hunt Oil Company providing $8 million, repayable over five years (with one year's grace period).[34]

The government of North Yemen has commissioned Hunt Oil to undertake a feasibility study for the construction of a domestic refinery; in early 1985 two options were under review. The first would entail building a plant near the Marib-Jawf fields, with distribution of the products by truck throughout the country. This plant would be temporary in nature. The second alternative would involve construction of a permanent refinery in the central portion of the country to the south of Sana'a between Dhamar and Yarim. Such a refinery would tap into the crude-oil export pipeline to a Red Sea terminal also under consideration and study.

The first refinery option has been chosen and that facility will be located 56 kilometers east of Marib. It will draw oil from five of the

Alef field wells, with a throughput of 10,000 b/d. The facility will produce 3,600 b/d of diesel oil, 3,045 b/d of gasoline, and 3,000 b/d fuel oil. In addition, almost 61 million British thermal units per hour of fuel gas will be produced. As a domestic refinery, the Marib plant will meet well over a third of the YAR's product demand. Although the refinery will not produce liquefied petroleum (LPG) or kerosene initially, the capacity for their production can be added later. Construction of the facility began in May 1985 by Petrofac Incorporated of Texas and was completed in April 1986.[35]

In November 1984 North Yemen agreed to expand the size of the Hunt Oil concession in the Marib-Jawf area to 14,600 square kilometers. Exxon Corporation reached an agreement in early 1985 with YOMINCO for an onshore concession to explore in the northeastern part of the country; in that same year Exxon purchased 49 percent of Hunt Oil's interests in the YAR. Finally, Soviet drillers report the discovery of oil traces in the Shabwa basin in the border area near South Yemen.

The level of oil exploration activities and the successes reported in 1984 and 1985 are encouraging. Nonetheless, the government of North Yemen is not moving to scrap its multi-front development program in an all-out push to rapidly expand the oil sector. Nonetheless, the timing of the oil discoveries and their location is exceptional because the Yemen Arab Republic needs such energy resources for domestic development and as a foreign-exchange earner. The YAR is a poor country and an oil importer. Its record in the development fields has been positive, that is, achieving good results from limited resources; the same attitude which brought this achievement should facilitate the careful application and utilization of oil-generated revenues. Recent changes in the world oil market and a downward pressure on oil prices have offered a strong lesson in the economic vulnerability of countries that are heavily dependent on the production and export of oil. Many nations in the Arabian Peninsula reflect the problems of the single-product economy. In this respect, the YAR is more fortunate than some of its richer neighbors; North Yemen has the potential for a diversified economy, including a sizeable labor pool. Indeed, the financial problems of the oil-exporting countries during the first half of the 1980s have offered North Yemen a salutary example of pitfalls to avoid in oil-sector development.

Despite the press coverage of the Marib-Jawf discoveries, the oil sector in the YAR is modest at present and will remain so for some time to come, even though its output and reserves may surpass some of the lower-volume producers in the Organization of Petroleum Exporting Countries (OPEC). The time frame, however, before substantial oil exports could be produced is at least five years. Thus, North Yemen will need to encourage foreign investment and seek loans and foreign financing also for some time to come to continue its development path in all the sectors of its economy.

While increased economic activities at home, including those in the oil-related fields, will expand employment opportunities, North Yemen will retain its position as a manpower pool for the region. The oil sector, even with the most manpower-demanding stages of exploration and early production, is characterized by capital intensity, not labor intensity. Yemeni emigrant workers can and should continue to seek employment outside the YAR: the reciprocity between capital (workers' remittances and foreign investment/loans) and labor (Yemeni expatriates) has been a positive and mutually beneficial element in the region. The North Yemen government's handling of the Marib-Jawf finds has been low key, in part to avoid a premature "boom" mentality that would bring nationals home in numbers that would exceed job opportunities.

Within the oil sector itself, the YAR is likely to be able to secure the requisite investment and financing because its overall performance record in development planning and the relative efficiency of implementation have added to the attractive investment atmosphere. Moreover, North Yemen has a locational advantage in that its oil exports would be available at a Red Sea terminal, offering relatively greater supply security than from the volatile Arabian/Persian Gulf. An important issue to keep in mind is the lead time needed before exports can begin on a substantial scale. Domestic petroleum requirements are likely to rise rapidly, above the 20,000 b/d local consumption level of 1984, and internal needs will have to be balanced with the benefits of export revenues. Moreover, the oil has been discovered 400 to 500 kilometers inland from the Red Sea coast, a distance made more formidable by the ruggedness of the terrain. While quantities justify the construction of a pipeline, the distance and difficulty make building such a line time consuming. Finally, the production estimates for the discoveries vary from output of 100,000 b/d to over 400,000 b/d, and even as high as 600,000 b/d or more, which could make North Yemen the major petroleum discovery of the 1980s.[36] Decisions on major projects may have to be delayed until reserves can be more precisely estimated.

Oil can be a boon to the development of the Yemen Arab Republic but, as with many factors, it can prove to be a double-edged sword—just as the Yemeni emigrant workers are. Exaggerated euphoria over the Marib-Jawf discoveries could lead to a massive return of Yemenis from neighboring countries at a time when their remittances are still needed. Overblown reports of oil potential could lead international lending institutions and national assistance agencies to harden loan terms (higher interest, shorter repayment periods) or even decrease the funding. This would be short-sighted and damaging, putting at risk some of the hard-won achievements in the development of the country. In short, for the present and, indeed, for the next two to three years, the discovery of oil may be most important for its political and diplomatic impact on strengthening North Yemen's status as a potential member of the petroleum-producers club. By 1989 or so, after exports commence on a sufficient scale, the YAR could start reaping direct economic benefits from this resource, such as facilitaing new loans as a result of actual and expected oil-generated revenues.

Mining: Basic institution building in the mining sector was initiated with the creation of two organizations. The Mineral Wealth and Petroleum Corporation was established under the Three-Year Program as the authority responsible for planning, executing, and supervising exploration programs and the development of mineral resources as well as formulating policy. By 1982 the first geological laboratory commenced operation. Financing for the construction of this facility was provided by Yemen Oil and Minerals Corporation. The Federal Republic of Germany, long active in this sector of the Yemen Arab Republic, provided $550,000 worth of equipment as well as technical advice. This laboratory will handle wet chemistry analysis, spectrophotometry and automatic absorption, as well as mineral analysis, which heretofore had to be performed abroad.

The Yemen Arab Republic is known to have substantial mineral wealth such as copper ore, iron ore, cobalt, lead, silver, and zinc. Yet there is virtually no production of minerals and there will probably be very little production during the period of the Second Five-Year Plan, with the exception of the copper extraction project at Al Hamoorah which is anticipated to begin production in fiscal year 1983/84.[37] The scope of the Second Five-Year Plan encompasses various surveys and the mapping of areas which contain minerals, evaluation of potential reserves, and the economic and technical feasibility of exploitation. Already involved in this activity is France's state-owned Bureau de Recherches Geologiques et Minieres which has undertaken a contract to continue studying the economic and technical feasibility of exploiting mineral resources in the Nihm area, northeast of Sana'a.

Salt: The unusual and fortunate combination of high-grade salt deposits, proximity to deep-water loading facilities, and the accessibility of open pit mining makes the Salif salt dome a very competitive source of this mineral to be used for chemical purposes. Development of the salt extraction industry at Salif, however, has been beset with problems over the years. In the late nineteenth century the Turkish government built a stone quay at the Salif salt dome, cut a road to the central pit, and set up a state-owned mining and export operation under its Public Debts Administration.[38] By 1900 commercial salt exports to India were profitable. Soon after, English-subsidized salt pans in Aden undercut this trade. Later, the town was left nearly deserted by the political events of World War I and remained so until the establishment of the present government.

The workings of the Yemen Salt Mining Corporation were considered almost nil between 1972 and 1977 as its production hardly exceeded an insignificant quantity extracted for domestic use. Until the summer of 1972 rock salt from Salif was shipped to Japan at an average rate of nearly 80,000 tons a year, with a peak of 107,836 tons in 1966.[39] Because of the sharp fall in world demand, and because of Japanese allegations that the use of Salif salt for industrial purposes caused pollution, Salif production virtually ceased.

The Three-Year Program aimed at raising the capacity of the Salif salt mines from 400,000 tons per year to 1 million tons per year. The First Five-Year Plan carried through on this objective with an allocation of 9.5 million rials.[40] However, the completion date of the project coincided with the period of marketing difficulties experienced by the Yemen Salt Mining Corporation.

To help rectify the marketing problems, a market survey commissioned in March of 1977 by the United States Development Program for the Yemen Salt Mining Corporation was undertaken by O. W. Roskill Industrial Consultants of the United Kingdom. By 1977 Salif salt was once again making inroads in the international market in the face of competition from Australia and Mexico, which together supplied about 1 million tons per year at $8 a ton (f.o.b.). In September of that year salt exports from Salif totaled 10,000 tons per day, with shipments going to North Korea and Bangladesh. By 1980 export customers included: Excem-Madrid of Spain which paid $8 a ton and re-exported the salt to the United States; Japan's Marubeni Corporation which paid $7.50 a ton and then distributed the salt in South Korea; a Kuwaiti company which placed an order for 40,000 tons at $8 a ton; and a Taiwanese firm which entered into a long-term contract for 500,000 tons at $10 a ton.[41]

The First Five-Year Plan envisioned the development of salt-based industries, with 40.7 million rials allocated for the refining and packaging of rock salt for table consumption. Another goal was the establishment of a chemical industry based on salt by-products such as caustic soda and chloride. A second-priority project, with an estimated investment requirement of 6 million rials, was the extraction of chlor gas (by manufacturing salt) for use in local industries.[42]

The Yemen Company for Salt Packing and Marketing was established in Sana'a in 1981 as a 25 million rial ($5.4 million) joint venture with the Industrial Bank of Yemen, the Yemen Company for Investment and Financing, and the Yemen Oil and Minerals Corporation as the shareholders. A factory to process and pack rock salt, with a planned output of 50 tons per day, was built at Salif port. The Yemen Company for Salt Packing and Marketing had obtained a contract with Japan's Marubeni Corporation in 1983/84 and was continuing to pursue negotiations for contracts for salt sales to Gulf states and African nations. (The values of salt exports from 1978/79 through 1982 were given earlier in table 28 of chapter three.)

Production of salt at Salif is projected to grow rapidly over the period of the Second Five-Year Plan; output is planned to double during the first year of the plan through the utilization of existing capacity and will reach the full installed plant capacity of 1 million tons in 1986, the fifth year of the second plan. The second plan aims at achieving self-sufficiency in table salt and towards this goal 11.5 million rials have been earmarked for investment in the expansion and improvement of the Salif salt mines.[43]

Building Materials Industry: The Yemen Arab Republic is endowed with abundant deposits of nonmetallic minerals normally used to produce construction materials. Although only a few of these mineral resources have been investigated in detail, it is well known that the country has substantial deposits of stone: basalt, volcanic stone, sandstone and tuffite, limestone, marble, sand and aggregates (crushed stone), gypsum, clay, and kaolin. Further geological surveys of the most important deposits (limestone, silica sand, gypsum, clay, and kaolin) must be commissioned to determine the quality of the material and the amount of reserves necessary to operate plants for a reasonable number of years.

Parallel with the remittance-financed construction boom of the second half of the 1970s there has been a significant expansion in the nonmetallic building-materials subsector. Under the Second Five-Year Plan fixed capital investment for building materials in the mining sector are expected to total 95.0 million rials to be channelled into the extraction of stones and rocks for building purposes, gypsum production, and marble production.[44]

The building-materials industry is now the Yemen Arab Republic's principal domestic-resource-based industry and consists of 527 enterprises producing cement, red bricks, ready-mix concrete, concrete blocks, gypsum plaster, floor tiles, terrazo, and various stones in blocks and slabs.[45] With the exception of companies manufacturing red bricks and cement concrete, and those conducting integrated quarrying and crushing operations, the building-materials industry is dominated by small- to medium-size establishments, some of which operate with traditional artisan-type methods. Overall, this sector grew at an annual rate of 3.7 percent during the 1981-1984 period, against the second plan's target rate of 4.5 percent.[46]

In the area of marble extraction, the First Five-Year Plan allocated 1.5 million rials for a 6,500-ton capacity project to extract marble and cut it into blocks and small pieces.[47] The Yemen Arab Republic's first marble factory is the Yemen Marble Industries Company, a Yemeni-West German partnership established in the latter part of 1981. The expected price for marble at that time was 120 rials ($27.27) per square meter. The National Company for Construction Materials and Industry has begun work on a 20 million tons per year marble factory.

In the early 1980s domestic production of cement at the Bajil cement factory—built by the U.S.S.R. in 1973 and located 60 kilometers north of Hodeidah—supplied about 10 percent of domestic demand. About 1 million tons of cement are imported annually into the Yemen Arab Republic at a cost of approximately $60 million.[48] The cement industry in the Yemen Arab Republic is based on local raw materials and is an example of the type of industry the government intends to emphasize. Additionally, cement production in the YAR is competitive with imports, provided it is accompanied by a solid distribution and marketing plan comprising the whole country.

The First Five-Year Plan proposed that the Bajil cement plant be expanded from the initial capacity of 50,000 tons per year to 250,000 tons per year at an estimated cost of 120 million rials and an additional expansion to raise capacity to 500,000 tons per year is under consideration in the mid-1980s. Plans for a second cement plant with a production capacity of 500,000 tons per year to be located in Amran, about 50 kilometers north of Sana'a, were also announced in the first plan.[49] Fixed capital investment over the period of the Second Five-Year Plan for the Bajil plant is estimated to total 96.321 million rials; for the Amran cement plant expected investment is to total 237.7 million rials.[50] Funds for investment in the cement plants are allocated in the plan under the industrial sector.

The Amran cement factory involves a joint-venture relationship in which Kuwaiti interests hold 50 percent, the Yemen Arab Republic government holds 40 percent, and the private sector holds 10 percent of the shares. Ishikawajima-Harima Heavy Industries and Nissho-Iwai Company, both of Japan, built the 500,000 ton-per-year facility in Amran. The construction was partially financed by a $40 million Japanese loan. Ishikawajima-Harima Heavy Industries, which received the long-term maintenance and management contract valued at $120 million, is also engaged in training part of the Amran work force; some Yemeni technicians and engineers were trained in Japan while others were trained at the Bajil plant.[51]

Full operations of the Amran cement factory were initiated in September of 1982 but there were occasional closures due to distribution bottlenecks. Apparently private contractors arrived at the plant on an ad hoc basis to purchase cement. To rectify this problem, the government ordered a fleet of cement trucks and set up distribution centers away from the factory. The government is also considering the improvement of access roads to the plant.

A feasibility study for a third 500,000 ton-per-year cement plant to be located at Mafraq, 60 kilometers south of Taiz, was completed in June of 1979 by the Bureau Central d'Etudes pour les Equipments d'outre Mer. The Second Five-Year Plan estimates the fixed capital investment in this facility to reach 724.1ll million rials by fiscal year 1985/86.[52] It has been reported that the North Yemen government was considering Japan's Ishikawajima-Harima Heavy Industries for the Mafraq project and that they have filed application for an $80-million Japanese loan.[53]

Once the three cement plants become fully operational the Yemen Arab Republic is expected to be self-sufficient in cement. Such a development is anticipated to lead to a 20 percent improvement in the balance-of-payments deficit. The National Company for Construction Materials and Industry has established a 150 ton capacity gypsum plant which should meet 50 percent of local requirements; the Industrial

Bank of Yemen partially financed the factory at Raada to cut and polish granite. The bank is also coordinating another resource-based industrial project. And the Yemen Company for Glass Manufacture plans to produce bottles, tableware, and flat glass in the coming years.

Financing Industry

Private-sector industrial development in the Yemen Arab Republic has been financed in part through one of the country's specialized banks, the Yemen Industrial Bank (YIB). Created in 1976 by the government of North Yemen, the YIB's authorized capital of 100 million rials was 70 percent government subscription and the remaining 30 percent open to the private sector, including commercial banks. Operations by the YIB began in early 1978.

The bank's stated objectives are to promote the development of new industrial projects and facilitate the expansion of existing enterprises. The major qualification for borrowers is that ownership of the company or project must be at least 51 percent YAR public or private sector. The bank's functions are characterized by four activities. First, loans are medium to long term (up to 10 years). Second, the bank's equity contributions are not to exceed one-quarter of the capital of any one company receiving a loan. Third, the YIB is empowered to extend technical assistance to borrowers. And, fourth, the bank can provide guarantees and thus assist in securing financing from other sources. In its first year of operations, the YIB made 20 loans totaling 64 million rials (about two-thirds of its paid-in capital). While the bank charges a 1 percent study fee on financed projects, its interest rates are moderate, being set since March 1978 at 6 and 7 percent, respectively, for medium- and long-term loans.[54]

By 1984, the YIB had made loans to nearly 100 projects with cumulative disbursements of 135 million rials. Because of a restriction that no more than 10 percent of the bank's capital may be lent to any one project, most of the borrowers have been small- to medium-sized industrial enterprises. This restriction was being reviewed in 1984, with the possibility of raising the ceiling on YIB's share to 15 percent. It is believed that such a move would allow the bank to become involved in financing larger-scale undertakings.

Of the approximately 100 projects which have successfully borrowed from the YIB, some 7 percent are in default. This figure is not higher than expected, given domestic and world economic conditions of the early 1970s and the fact that a number of the entrepreneurs are still relatively new to industrial management and that manpower training has had to be instituted in many of the projects. In fact, a number of companies have brought in foreign labor to work on production lines until the local work force can be upgraded and integrated into the industrial activities. In part, the use of foreign labor can be traced to the relatively high cost of Yemeni manpower due to scarcity caused by emigration to neighboring countries.

The Industrial Bank of Yemen has received credits and assistance from a number of international/national aid-investment-lending agencies such as the International Development Association, the United Nations Capital Development Fund, and the Kuwait Fund for Arab Economic Development. Should further funding from such sources materialize, the lending capacity of the YIB could be expanded to 600 million rials. As of 1984, the bank had about 150 projects under consideration and study.[55]

Another specialized bank in the Yemen Arab Republic which, strictly speaking, is not directed toward industry but the activities of which, nonetheless, spill over significantly into the construction sector, is the Housing Credit Bank. Set up in 1977 with a capital of 100 million rials (30 percent privately subscribed and 70 percent from the government), this institution extends loans to individuals and institutions. Initial lending rates were from 5 to 7 percent with maturities between 7 and 15 years, respectively, for institutions and individuals. Loans to individuals tend to be extended for actual construction purposes, that is, to persons already owning a building plot. The impact of the Housing Credit Bank's activities and of government-supported housing projects is considerable on those industries, such as cement, with products used in the construction sector. Private housing activities have been fueled by emigrant workers' remittances and by the government projects to upgrade urban infrastructure services. In this vein, the YAR obtained a credit from the International Development Association in early 1984 for $12 million to partially finance a $17.89-million urban infrastructure development project in Hodeidah and, as part of the same program, to upgrade the capacity of the Ministry of Municipalities and Housing to plan and implement local-level development schemes.[56]

Finally, the YAR's tax structure is a factor in industrial-sector investment. Companies, corporations, and enterprises (excluding cooperative associations and nonprofit organizations), including those in agricultural activities and public and mixed corporations, are taxed on profits with capital gains or losses treated as ordinary income or losses.

Capital asset depreciation is allowed according to rates determined by appropriate ministries. The rate of taxation depends on whether a corporation is concessionary or not. Concessionary enterprises are taxed at a graduated rate beginning at 20 percent of taxable profits up to 7,500 rials then going to 35 percent of taxable profits of 22,501 rials and above. For nonconcessionary corporations, the rates range from 7 percent of 7,500 rials taxable profits to 25 percent of 30,001 rials or more.

However, local industry has been extended a rebate of 25 percent on duties of all imported raw materials as well as a tax holiday for the first five years of operations. If a company expands its operations, it can apply for an extension of the five-year holiday, a move aimed at encouraging industrial growth.[57]

Manpower Constraint to Industrial Development

The labor market in the Yemen Arab Republic is anomalous in terms of that market's characteristics as commonly observed in less-developed countries. Whereas most developing nations normally are confronted with low wage costs and a surplus labor situation, the Yemen Arab Republic has been faced with high wage costs and a relative shortage of labor. A brief exposition of the Yemeni labor market as it affects industrial development may be helpful.

Between 1975 and 1981 the total labor force increased from 1,100,400 participants to 1,201,600 participants, an annual growth rate of 1.8 percent. Projections by the Central Planning Organization suggest that the annual growth rate of the labor force will be 2.4 percent over the five years (1982-1986) of the second plan, to be partially absorbed by the creation of new jobs.[58] Table 41 highlights changes in the Yemeni labor force by linking occupational categories to the presumed educational and training requirements of the employed Yemenis in the private and public sectors. Implicit in the table is the fact that the public sector currently employs and will continue to employ the majority of those who have obtained at least an intermediate level of education. On the other side of the employment picture, it is evident that the majority of semi-skilled and unskilled workers are employed in the private sector. However, a World Bank study takes issue with the 1975 public-sector employment figures noting that nearly eight of every ten government employees did not have the education or training necessary for the job held.[59] Some improvement in this situation had undoubtedly occurred by 1981 as students entered the labor force and as em-

Table 41: Changes in Employment by Occupation/Skill Level and Sector, 1975 and 1981

Occupation/ Skill Level[a]	1975 Public[b]	1975 Private	1975 Total	1981 Public	1981 Private	1981 Total
A1	515	226	741	1,230	540	1,770
A2	4,986	268	5,254	6,932	372	7,304
B1	1,314	753	2,067	2,667	1,520	4,187
B2	70	1,258	1,328	2,276	2,516	4,792
C1	10,972	24,116	35,088	33,863	52,377	86,240
C2	12,934	6,169	19,103	2,091	8,972	11,063
D	2,180	49,965	52,145	3,511	80,084	83,595
E	4,500	939,748	944,248	11,238	1,001,419	1,012,657
Total	37,461	1,022,503	1,059,974	63,808	1,147,800	1,211,608

[a]A1 refers to professional occupations presumably requiring a science/math-based university degree; A2 refers to professional occupations presumably requiring an arts-based university degree; B1 refers to subprofessional and technical occupations presumably requiring one to three years post-secondary science/math education; B2 refers to subprofessional occupations presumably requiring one to three years post-secondary arts-based education; C1 refers to skilled and intermediate-skilled office occupations presumably requiring nine to twelve years of general education plus job training; C2 refers to skilled and intermediate-skilled manual occupations presumably requiring five to ten years of general education plus vocational and/or technical education; D refers to semi-skilled occupations presumably requiring functional literacy plus job training; E refers to unskilled occupations presumably requiring no special education.

[b]Public-sector employment figures include expatriates and civilian security forces.

Sources: C. A. Sinclair and J. Socknat, "An Assessment of Manpower Development and Policy and Program Suggestions for YAR," May 1976, tables 4.24 and 4.25, cited in World Bank, *Manpower Development in the Yemen Arab Republic* (Washington, D.C.: World Bank, 1981), p. 191, and Yemen Arab Republic, Central Planning Organization, *Second Five-Year Plan (1982-1986)*, March 1982, chapter 3, p. 38.

ployees completed training programs. However, there is still a critical shortage of trained personnel as evidenced by vacant positions and an estimated expatriate workforce of 17,000 in 1979/80.[60] Such a human capital constraint in skilled labor is not endemic to the Yemen Arab

Republic, but rather it is common to all developing countries and takes time to ameliorate.

To compound the labor situation in the Yemen Arab Republic, the public and private sectors and neighboring oil-producing countries have been competing with each other for some time to employ the scarce stock of qualified Yemeni labor. An individual's decision to work in either the public or the private sector based upon salary considerations will not represent a net loss to the domestic economy as would the decision of an individual to utilize his talent in a foreign country.

Although comprehensive information on wages in the private sector is lacking, it appears that wages are dependent upon both the skill attainment and the origin of the worker. Within the total labor force, there is evidence of an inverse relationship between skill level and wages received by Yemeni workers relative to non-Yemeni workers. An unskilled Yemeni generally earns twice as much as his expatriate counterpart, while at higher skill levels the relationship is reversed—the expatriate receives a higher wage for his greater level of training and experience. Table 42 compares wage rates for workers in selected occupations.

As a consequence of Yemenis migrating to neighboring oil-producing countries for employment and of the subsequent remittance-financed construction boom in the mid-1970s, wages for an unskilled national working in the Yemen Arab Republic had escalated from a meager 5 Yemeni rials per day to 60 or 80 rials per day.[61] The wage differential between a Yemeni working in Saudi Arabia and one working in the Yemen Arab Republic, however, has been reduced substantially as has the shortage of unskilled labor.

Opportunities for Yemeni men to work abroad declined in the early 1980s. Contracts in the Gulf states are more frequently being awarded to the private sector, with project monitoring undertaken by the government, or contracts are offered as an integrated package which is usually too complex for small firms to undertake. In addition, contracts have been going to Indian subcontinent and Far East companies, contracts which include the provision that labor will be supplied by the contractor. Furthermore, capital-intensive technology is replacing some of the demand for laborers. As a consequence of these factors, the quantity and quality of labor available in the Yemen Arab Republic will increase which, in turn, will pressure the prevailing high price of labor downward.

Investments in industrial enterprises in the Yemen Arab Republic

Table 42: Wages in Selected Occupations in the Modern Sector, 1980
(in Yemeni rials)

Occupation	Wage Rate
Professional and highly skilled	YR 7,000/month
Technician (experienced lineman)	YR 5,500/month
Skilled (carpenters, steel fixers)	YR 100-200/day
Skilled (bulldozer operator)	YR 2,500/month for Yemeni
	YR 3,375/month for non-Yemeni
Semi-skilled (electrician)	YR 50 per spot (outlet, etc.)
Unskilled (ordinary laborer)	YR 60-80/day for Yemeni
	YR 30-40/day for non-Yemeni
Unskilled (loader at port)	YR 200-250/day for Yemeni
	YR 117/day for non-Yemeni

Source: World Bank, *Yemen Arab Republic—Manufacturing Industries: Performance, Policies, and Prospects* (Washington, D.C.: World Bank, 1981), p. 152.

have also reflected the mid- to late-1970s labor-market condition of a scarce factor commanding a premium rate of return. A survey of 10 major manufacturing firms undertaken by the World Bank noted that labor costs for the firms sampled were relatively low in relation to total costs, reflecting the high capital intensity of Yemeni industries. If the above scenario is indeed realized, then the reduced cost of one factor in the production process—labor—will lower production costs and, other things remaining constant, will increase the profitability of certain firms (e.g., building materials, construction). Offsetting this, however, is the possibility that the economy may not be able to absorb the returning unskilled Yemeni migrants.

Not all returning expatriates will fall into the unskilled category, however. A number of these have had on-the-job upgrading of skills or exposure to differing levels of skills required over a broad range of work experiences. This factor, combined with the results of the expanded YAR vocational-technical education efforts, should create an opportunity for that country's economy to diversify into completely new areas. For example, some forms of assembly plants could be established to utilize the labor pool, take advantage of the expanding size and purchasing power of the domestic market, and produce a potential export item. One suggestion would be an assembly plant for four-wheel drive vehicles and small delivery trucks suitable for North Yemen's rugged terrain and often unpaved roads which, for similar reasons, could be exported to the Middle East and East Africa.

Notes

1. Yemen Arab Republic, Central Planning Organization, *Second Five-Year Plan (1982-1986)*, March 1982, chapter 3, p. 11, and World Bank, *Yemen Arab Republic—Manufacturing Industries: Performance, Policies, and Prospects* (Washington, D.C.: World Bank, 1981), p. 1.

2. *The Financial Times* (London), November 26, 1984.

3. Yemen Arab Republic, Central Planning Organization,"Fourth Year Annual Report of the Second Five-Year Plan" (February 1985), p. 1 (mimeographed, in Arabic).

4. World Bank, *Yemen Arab Republic—Manufacturing Industries: Performance, Policies, and Prospects*, p. 3.

5. Ibid., p. 4.

6. Yemen Arab Republic, Central Planning Organization, *Second Five-Year Plan (1982-1986)*, chapter 2, p. 29.

7. Ibid.

8. World Bank, *Yemen Arab Republic—Manufacturing Industries: Performance, Policies, and Prospects*, p. 89.

9. Yemen Arab Republic, Central Planning Organization, *First Five-Year Plan (1976/77-1980/81)*, p. 117.

10. Yemen Arab Republic, Central Planning Organization, *Second Five-Year Plan (1982-1986)*, chapter 1, p. 9.

11. World Bank, *Yemen Arab Republic—Manufacturing Industries: Performance, Policies, and Prospects*, p. 8.

12. Yemen Arab Republic, Central Planning Organization, *First Five-Year Plan (1976/77-1980/81)*, p. 117; and Consortium for International Development, *Agricultural Sector Analysis, Yemen Arab Republic* (Sana'a: Consortium for International Development, 1981), table IV.4.

13. World Bank, *Yemen Arab Republic—Manufacturing Industries: Performance, Policies, and Prospects*, p. 28.

14. Yemen Arab Republic, Central Planning Organization, *First Five-Year Plan (1976/77-1980/81)*, p. 59.

15. Based on 1981 prices. Yemen Arab Republic, Central Planning Organization,"Fourth Year Annual Report of the Second Five-Year Plan," table 1, p. 2.

16. Yemen Arab Republic, Central Planning Organization, *Second Five-Year Plan (1982-1986)*, chapter 4, p. 8.

17. Country report presented to the Second Arab Energy Conference, Doha, Qatar, March 6-11, 1982, cited in *OAPEC Bulletin*, January 1983, p. 17.

18. United States, Department of Commerce, *Marketing in the Yemen Arab Republic*, October 1981, p. 7.

19. *Middle East Economic Digest*, May 28, 1976, p. 28, July 18, 1980, p. 46, and March 27, 1981, p. 54.

20. *Middle East Economic Survey*, January 18, 1982, p. 10.

21. Country report, *OAPEC Bulletin*, January 1983, p. 17.

22. Yemen Arab Republic, Central Planning Organization, *Second Five-Year Plan (1982-1986)*, chapter 43, p. 24.

23. *Middle East Economic Digest*, December 7, 1979, p. 58, January 27, 1980, p. 44, March 20, 1981, p. 49, and January 4, 1985, p. 30.

24. Yemen Arab Republic, Central Planning Organization, *Second Five-Year Plan (1982-1986)*, chapter 4, p. 24.

25. National Petroleum Council,"Third World Petroleum Development: A Statement of Principles," October 18, 1982 cited in"U.S. Oil Industry and the Third World: A New Era?" *Energy Detente*, November 11, 1982, p. 3.

26. *Mideast Business Exchange*, April 1982, p. 25, and *Middle East Economic Digest*, April 2, 1982, p. 46.

27. World Bank, *Annual Report 1984* (Washington, D.C.: World Bank, 1984), p. 129.

28. Yemen Arab Republic, Central Planning Organization, *Second Five-Year Plan (1982-1986)*, chapter 4, p. 10.

29. United States, Department of the Interior, *Minerals Yearbook, 1978-1979*, vol. 3, Area Reports: International (Washington, D.C.: Government Printing Office, 1981), p. 1226.

30. *Middle East Economic Survey*, December 3, 1984, p. A6.

31. *New York Times*, December 21 and December 27, 1984; *Christian Science Monitor*, October 4, 1984; *Middle East Economic Survey*, December 3, 1984, pp. A5-6; and *Middle East Economic Digest*, January 4, 1984, p. 30 offer a sampling.

32. *Middle East Economic Digest*, January 4, 1985, p. 30, and *Middle East Economic Survey*, December 3, 1984, p. A5.

33. The Yemen Refining and Marketing Company (YRMC) is owned by Yemen Hunt Oil Company (74.5 percent) and by the South Korean consortium (24.5 percent), the same ownership pattern as the Alef field.

34. Abdulaziz Saqqaf,"Energy Production and Consumption in the Yemen Arab Republic," a paper prepared for the Sixth International Area Conference of the International Research Center for Energy and Economic Development on"The Middle East, Pacific Basin, and United States: Refining and Petrochemicals," University of Colorado, Boulder, October 14-15, 1985, p. 16.

35. Ibid., p. 17.

36. World Bank,"Yemen Arab Republic Country Economic Memorandum Current Position and Prospects," Report no. 5621-YAR (Washington, D.C., June 25, 1985), pp. 39-42 (mimeographed).

37. Yemen Arab Republic, working paper on the extraction industry, 1982, p. 2.

38. Jon Mandaville,"Impressions From a Writer's Notebook—At Work in Yemen," *Aramco World Magazine*, May-June 1981, p. 13.

39. *Middle East Economic Digest*, June 11, 1977, p. 36.

40. Yemen Arab Republic, Central Planning Organization, *First Five-Year Plan (1976/77-1980/81)*, pp. 59 and 318.

41. *Middle East Economic Digest*, June 1, 1977, p. 36, December 2, 1977, p. 42, and May 23, 1980, p. 44.

42. Yemen Arab Republic, Central Planning Organization, *First Five-Year Plan (1976/77-1980/81)*, p. 318.

43. Yemen Arab Republic, working paper on the extracting industry, 1982, pp. 1-2.

44. Yemen Arab Republic, Central Planning Organization, *Second Five-Year Plan (1982-1986)*, chapter 4, p. 10.

45. Yemen Arab Republic,"Industrial Survey of 1975," cited in World Bank, *Yemen Arab Republic—Manufacturing Industries: Performance, Policies, and Prospects*, p. 17.

46. Yemen Arab Republic,"Fourth Year Annual Report of the Second Five-Year Plan," table 2, p. 3.

47. Yemen Arab Republic, Central Planning Organization, *First Five-Year Plan (1976/77-1980/81)*, p. 319.

48. *Middle East Economic Digest*, October 9, 1981, p. 70. Through 1983 the 1 million ton level of demand for cement has remained unchanged although imports have dropped as domestic output has risen. *The Financial Times*, November 26, 1984.

49. Yemen Arab Republic, Central Planning Organization, *First Five-Year Plan (1976/77-1981/82)*, p. 319.

50. Yemen Arab Republic, Central Planning Organization, *Second Five-Year Plan (1982-1986)*, chapter 4, p. 15.

51. *Middle East Economic Digest*, October 12, 1979, p. 60 and October 15, 1982, p. 73.

52. Yemen Arab Republic, Central Planning Organization, *Second Five-Year Plan (1982-1986)*, chapter 4, p. 15.

53. *Middle East Economic Digest*, October 29, 1982, p. 85.

54. World Bank, *Yemen Arab Republic: Development of a Traditional Economy* (Washington, D.C.: World Bank, 1979), p. 188.

55. *The Financial Times*, November 26, 1984.

56. World Bank, *Annual Report 1984*, p. 137.

57. World Bank, *Yemen Arab Republic: Development of a Traditional Economy*, p. 191.

58. Yemen Arab Republic, Central Planning Organization, *Second Five-Year Plan (1982-1986)*, chapter 3, pp. 28, 30, and 35.

59. World Bank, *Manpower Development in the Yemen Arab Republic* (Washington, D.C.: World Bank, 1981), p. 32.

60. Ibid., p. 86.

61. Ibid., p. 55.

7 INTERNATIONAL LINKAGES: TRADE AND INVESTMENT

The rapid rate of development of the oil-rich countries of the Arabian Peninsula during the 1970s did not occur without effect on the economy of the Yemen Arab Republic. The growth in wage remittances from emigrant workers acted to dramatically increase the overall level of economic activity in the country. By 1981 an estimated 800,000 to 1 million Yemenis, or 40 to 50 percent of the labor force, were employed abroad throughout the peninsula, primarily in Saudi Arabia. Private transfers emanating from these emigrant workers grew steadily from 1970/71 to 1977/78, then stabilized at an annual average level of approximately 6 billion rials through the end of the decade, fell in 1981, and recovered to about 5.6 billion rials in 1983 (see table 16 of chapter three).

The flow of private transfers into the country had a major impact on domestic consumption and investment. At the peak level of 6,351 million rials in 1977/78, private transfers amounted to 46 percent of national disposable income (table 15, chapter three). In 1977/78 private transfers alone represented more than three times the total national income in 1970/71.[1] Increased private transfers contributed to substantially increased domestic incomes, particularly in rural areas. Official per-capita income is estimated to have risen from 628 rials ($125) in 1970/71 to an estimated 1,081 rials ($215) in 1979/80 then to about $500 in 1983/84, although average income in the latter year was actually $1,500 due to remittances.[2]

Rising incomes, especially in rural areas, created substantial growth in the demand for both consumer and investment goods. Private final consumption expenditures (at current prices) rose from 1,477 million rials in 1970/71 to 4,902 million rials in 1975/76 and to 12,707 million rials in 1980/81.[3] During the First Five-Year Plan (1975/76-1980/81), private final consumption grew at an annual rate of 21 percent. Gross final capital formation also increased rapidly during the decade, rising from 220 million rials in 1970/71 to 849 million rials in 1975/76 and to 5,600 million rials in 1980/81. At current prices, gross fixed capital formation grew at an annual average rate of 46 percent during the first plan. Total gross fixed capital formation during that five-year period was 19,396 million rials. Of this amount, 17,839 million rials or 88 percent of total gross fixed capital formation during the first plan was financed by remittances from Yemeni workers abroad.4

Elsewhere it has been pointed out that the impact of emigrant North Yemeni workers, despite—and, in some instances, because of—their remittances, has not been an unmixed blessing to the YAR's economy. In a very real sense, the Yemen Arab Republic has exported one factor of production—labor—and imported another—capital. Thus, the role of North Yemen's labor force has been an example of regional mutuality of benefits.

Through its workers, the YAR has contributed to the economic development of neighboring labor-deficit, oil-rich countries. Through its development plans, the Yemen Arab Republic has also been involved in the region's overall development process. The upgrading of North Yemen's agricultural sector can help to assure a greater degree of regional food security. Moreover, given the YAR's still-substantial infrastructure needs, Middle Eastern consulting and construction firms—many established in the 1970s in the major oil-exporting countries—have a new regional outlet for their activities as their own domestic economies reach the end of massive basic infrastructure programs.

And while the Yemen Arab Republic has been able to maximize its ability to secure foreign financing for its development, from an array of agencies and countries in a wide variety of packages ranging from loans to a few outright grants and the provision of technical support, such financial and assistance activities contain a significant investment element. Even soft loans (low interest, long maturity) from such entities as the United States Agency for International Development have stipulations tied to the procurement of U. S. goods and services. National assistance institutions, such as the Kuwait Fund for Arab Economic Development and the Abu Dhabi Fund for Arab Economic Development, reflect an investment component in their lending: they offer an outlet for capital-surplus funds and their respective countries and economies benefit from the greater regional stability that arises from development progress made throughout the Middle East and a lessening of the gap between rich and poor nations in the Arabian Peninsula. Finally, credits from lending agencies frequently pave the way for private-sector or mixed public-private enterprise investment by the provision of guarantees or underwriting of basic infrastructure or services. This is important for broadening regional outlets for such investment firms as the Kuwait Foreign Trading, Contracting and Investment Company, Kuwait Investment Company, and Kuwait International Investment Company. In short, foreign assistance—particularly project

Imports

The rapid increase in demand for consumer goods and capital goods during the 1970s far exceeded the capacity of domestic production and was therefore translated into a massive surge in the growth of imports to the Yemen Arab Republic. The value of imports rose from a level of 175 million rials in 1970/71 to 1,707 million rials in 1975/76, from 7,705 million rials in 1979/80 to a peak of 8,454 million rials in 1980, followed by a decline to 6,940 million rials in 1982 as the government's austerity program took effect.[5] This trend continued through the first three years (1982-1984) of the second plan period, when imports fell by 8 percent compared to the 1982 level.[6]

Import expansion occurred in all SITC (standard industrial trade classification) commodity categories. However, the composition of imports, presented in tables 43 and 44, has shown a significant change over the period of 1973/74 to 1982. The relative share of consumer goods fell from 77 percent to 57 percent of total nongovernment imports between 1973/74 and 1979/80; it dropped during the 1981-1984 span to 47 percent in the latter year, which was still above the second plan's target of 43.5 percent for the fourth year.[7] The share of intermediate goods in imports has remained fairly constant, though in absolute terms the import fuel bill has increased due to the development process. The share of machinery and equipment imports showed the greatest gain during the period of 1973/74 to 1979/80, rising from 12 percent to 32 percent of imports and still accounting for just under 20 percent in 1982.

The fact that the relative share of consumer goods in imports has fallen and leveled off should not distract from the point that imports of consumer goods continue to grow rapidly in absolute terms. Between 1975/76 and 1979/80, the value of imports of consumer goods rose from 1,247 million rials to 4,353 million rials, an increase of 350 percent at current prices.[8] Consumer goods imports grew at an annual average rate of 37 percent during the period of 1975/76 to 1979/80; however, imports of machinery and equipment grew even more rapidly during the First Five-Year Plan, at an annual average rate of 70 percent, leading to the observed shift in the composition of imports. It should be noted that although the share of consumer goods in total imports has

Table 43: Composition of Imports, 1973/74-1979/80 *(in million rials)*

	1973/74		1976/77		1979/80	
	Value	%	Value	%	Value	%
Consumer goods	576.5	77	1,842.7	61	4,352.5	57
Foodstuffs and live animals	380.3	51	928.6	31	2,051.8	27
Manufactured consumer goods	196.2	26	914.1	30	2,300.7	30
Intermediate goods	85.3	11	226.9	7	878.3	11
Fuel	32.6	4	58.9	2	369.5	5
Raw materials	4.2	–a	12.7	–a	35.2	–a
Chemicals	48.5	7	155.3	5	473.6	6
Machinery and equipment	85.9	12	965.7	32	2,474.6	32
Total	747.7	100	3,035.3	100	7,705.4	100

aLess than 1 percent.

Sources: International Monetary Fund, *First Five-Year Plan, Progress Report* (Washington, D.C.: International Monetary Fund, 1979), p. 67, and World Bank, *Mobilization of Domestic Financial Resources in the Yemen Arab Republic* (Washington, D.C.: World Bank, 1982), p. 106.

declined, consumer goods still represent more than half of all nongovernment imports which, in 1979/80, was equal to 37 percent of gross domestic product. The Second Five-Year Plan seeks to reduce the share of consumer goods imports to 40 percent by 1986, to a value equal to 18 percent of gross domestic product.[9]

Emigration has had a substantial effect on domestic consumption patterns, both through rising domestic incomes and the effects of the emigrant experience on Yemeni tastes and preferences. The share of foodstuffs in consumer goods imports fell steadily from 66 percent in 1973/74 to 47 percent in 1979/80.[10] With rising incomes and a tendency to display wealth in conspicuous consumption, Yemeni consum-

Table 44: Imports by Group to Yemen Arab Republic, 1979/80-1982[a]
(in million rials)

SITC Group	1979/80	1980	1981	1982
Food/live animals	1,894.6	2,212.6	2,864.3	2,033.1
	(24.6)	(26.2)	(35.7)	(29.3)
Beverages/tobacco	114.6	103.6	103.9	120.5
	(1.5)	(1.2)	(1.2)	(1.7)
Inedible raw materials	35.3	43.2	39.9	34.2
	(0.5)	(0.5)	(0.5)	(0.5)
Mineral fuel/lubricants	369.5	609.2	608.0	828.4
	(4.8)	(7.2)	(7.6)	(11.9)
Animal/vegetable oil/fat	24.5	65.9	45.0	55.8
	(0.3)	(0.8)	(0.6)	(0.8)
Chemicals	473.6	432.2	412.6	454.5
	(6.1)	(5.1)	(5.1)	(6.5)
Manufactured materials	1,780.4	2,140.0	1,632.8	1,499.2
	(23.1)	(25.3)	(20.4)	(21.6)
Leather manufactures	4.4	2.6	7.2	3.9
Rubber manufactures	109.3	133.4	68.5	129.7
Wood/cork	307.3	400.4	382.2	359.3
Paper manufactures	27.8	58.3	63.1	78.0
Textiles	242.3	269.3	155.5	145.3
Nonmetal mineral products	430.9	417.5	297.4	183.1
Iron and steel	315.4	521.1	306.9	271.5
Nonferrous metals	44.1	28.0	34.3	27.5
Manufactures of metal	298.9	309.4	317.7	300.9
Machinery/transport equipment	2,474.5	2,348.0	1,865.5	1,341.6
	(32.1)	(27.8)	(23.3)	(19.3)
Miscellaneous manufactures	465.9	456.8	389.6	504.6
	(6.0)	(5.4)	(4.9)	(7.3)
Nonclassified commodities	54.3	42.7	60.8	67.9
	(0.7)	(0.5)	(0.8)	(1.0)
Total[b]	7,687.2	8,454.2	8,022.4	6,939.8

[a]Figures in ( ) indicate percentage of total.
[b]May not total due to rounding.

Sources: Yemen Arab Republic, Central Bank of Yemen, Research Department, *Financial Statistical Bulletin*, January-March 1984, table 26, and World Bank, "Yemen Arab Republic Country Economic Memorandum Current Position and Prospects," Report no. 5621-YAR. (Washington, D.C., June 25, 1985), p. 78.

er goods imports have included increasing quantities of automobiles, consumer durables, and luxury items. This prompted a 1979 report that "the shops are simply not big enough to stock all the refrigerators, radios, television sets, videos, and stereos which spill out into the streets."[11] In all, the value of manufactured consumer goods imports increased from 196 million rials in 1973/74 to 2.3 billion rials in 1979/80, and was still over 2 billion rials in 1982.[12]

Rising incomes and changing tastes have had a significant effect in changing the composition of the foodstuffs imported. The general trend during the 1970s was towards increased consumption of animal products, fruits and vegetables, and away from traditional cereals. Consumption of domestic cereals has been further eroded by increased importation of wheat which has a price advantage due to relatively higher domestic production costs resulting from agricultural labor scarcity. In fiscal year 1979/80, 240 million tons of wheat and 82 million tons of wheat flour were imported to North Yemen.

The share of meat and meat products in foodstuff imports increased from less than 1 percent at the beginning of the First Five-Year Plan to 12 percent by 1979/80. The value of meat and meat product imports reached 342 million rials in 1979/80 and was almost 360 million rials in 1981.[13] This increase was due largely to increased poultry consumption which was satisfied by imports and occurred despite substantial increases in domestic production during the First Five-Year Plan. In 1980, 910,000 live chickens and 48,000 tons of poultry were imported to North Yemen. Domestic production of poultry reached 3,400 tons in 1979/80 and is expected to increase to 15,730 tons by 1986. The government's austerity program to reduce budget deficits has had an impact on the importation of meat and meat products, which in 1982 amounted to almost 260 million rials.[14]

Fruit and vegetable consumption in North Yemen increased substantially as a result of rising incomes from expatriate remittances. In response, domestic fruit production increased 33 percent, to 144,000 tons, and domestic vegetable production increased 285, percent to 261,000 tons, during the First Five-Year Plan.[15] Increased domestic production was insufficient to satisfy the substantially increased domestic demand. As a result, the value of fruit and vegetable imports increased 616 percent between fiscal years 1975/76 and 1979/80, reaching a level of 400 million rials and continuing to rise to 570 million rials in 1982.[16] The government's restriction on fruit imports instituted in 1983 was designed to have an impact on 1984 trade.

Labor scarcity, rising wages, low productivity of labor, and competition from imports have depressed overall domestic agricultural production. Traditional cereal production, being both land and labor intensive as well as subject to competition from imported wheat, has been dramatically affected. Production in 1976 exceeded the subsistence needs of the agricultural population, yielding a marketable surplus of 119,222 tons of cereals. Between 1976 and 1980, domestic cereal production fell 17 percent, transforming the marketable surplus of the agricultural sector to a deficit of 53,500 tons in 1980. In 1980 domestic output was 679 million tons while domestic requirements were 1,130 million tons, necessitating the importation of 451 million tons of cereals. The value of cereal imports—70 to 90 percent wheat—increased from 235 million rials in 1975/76 to 400 million rials in 1979/80. The forecasted easing of the unskilled labor shortage during the Second Five-Year Plan and the consequential depressing effect on wages should encourage the return to cereal cultivation and improve its competitiveness with cereal imports. Domestic cereal production is targeted to increase at an annual rate of 17 percent during the Second Five-Year Plan.[17]

The growth in machinery and equipment imports can be traced to the massive increase in public and private investment arising from the increased level of development projects and emigrant labor remittances to North Yemen during the 1970s. Gross investment rose from 577 million rials to 5,237 million rials between 1973/74 and 1979/80. As a share of gross domestic product, gross investment increased from 20.3 to 43.9 percent between 1973/74 and 1979/80.[18]

During the First Five-Year Plan, gross fixed capital formation increased from 849 million rials in 1975/76 to 5,413 million rials in 1980/81, with a total gross fixed capital formation during the five-year span of 19,396 million rials. Housing and construction accounted for the majority (63 percent) of gross fixed capital formation during the first plan. The share of machinery and equipment in annual gross fixed capital formation increased substantially during the plan period, from 30 percent in 1975/76 to 42 percent in 1980/81. Given a rising level of national gross investment and an increasing share of machinery and equipment in gross fixed capital formation, the value of machinery and equipment imports increased dramatically during the First Five-Year Plan—from 289.6 million rials in 1975/76 to 2,474.6 million rials in 1979/80.[19]

The share of intermediate goods in total nongovernment imports remained fairly constant, at between 9 and 11 percent from 1973/74 to 1979/80; however, there has been substantial growth in absolute terms.

Imports of fuel, raw materials, and chemicals have increased from 117 million rials in 1973/74 to 878 million rials in 1979/80, an increase of 754 percent.[20]

Chemical imports accounted for 42 percent of intermediate goods imported in 1979/80. Medicine and fertilizer imports in particular showed significant gains during the First Five-Year Plan, increasing 530 percent and 307 percent, respectively, between 1975/76 and 1979/80.[21]

As in most developing countries, the development-associated increasing demand for energy coupled with increasing fuel prices has added tremendously to North Yemen's import fuel bill during the 1970s. Imports of petroleum products rose from 161,875 tons in 1973 to 584,644 tons in 1979, an annual increase of 24 percent.[22] At the same time, the import fuel bill rose from $7 million in 1973 to $132 million in 1979, growing at an annual rate of 63 percent.[23] Regardless of price movements and the recent discoveries of oil in the Marib-Jawf region of the country, the bill for imported fuel will continue to grow during the Second Five-Year Plan due to the substantially increased demand for energy—forecasted to reach 1,033,520 tons by 1985 and 1,594,920 tons by 1990.[24]

As seen in table 45, North Yemen's overall imports in the 1980-1982 period have come from a diversity of countries, primarily from the Arab world (21 to 24 percent), Western Europe (26 to 30 percent), and Asia. Trade with the United States has been increasing, with imports rising from $4.4 million in 1974 to about $53 million in 1983 and over $31 million in 1982.[25]

Arab countries supplied almost one-fourth of all imported goods to North Yemen in 1980 and just over one-fifth in 1982, of which approximately 80 percent and 50 percent, respectively, came from Saudi Arabia. It should be noted that substantial transiting of goods through Saudi Arabia to the YAR takes place. The amount of goods exported from Saudi Arabia to North Yemen is therefore overestimated to the extent that goods transported through Saudi Arabia are treated as originating in Saudi Arabia.

A substantial portion of North Yemen's trade is with Asia and the European Economic Community; the Community accounted for 30 percent and 28 percent of all imports to the Yemen Arab Republic in 1980 and 1982, respectively. Japan and France have emerged as major trading partners with North Yemen, is as clear in table 45.

Trade with Asian countries is substantial. Imports from Japan grew at an annual rate of over 40 percent between 1974 and 1980, ris-

Table 45: Imports by Major Supplying Countries, 1980-1982 *(in million rials)*

Country	1980 Value	%	1981 Value	%	1982 Value	%
Japan	1,074.9	12.7	1,297.3	16.2	924.3	13.3
France	667.2	7.9	646.1	8.1	498.3	7.2
Saudi Arabia	1,632.6	19.3	1,594.2	19.9	718.3	10.4
United Kingdom	443.2	5.2	291.7	2.7	328.1	4.7
United States	238.2	2.8	207.1	2.6	140.2	2.0
West Germany	496.1	5.9	388.4	4.8	350.7	5.1
China, People's Republic	408.7	4.8	331.0	4.1	283.2	4.1
Italy	425.6	5.0	405.9	5.1	343.1	4.9
Australia	190.9	2.3	115.7	1.4	286.2	4.1
Netherlands	403.7	4.8	298.0	4.7	321.4	4.6
India	231.9	2.7	104.3	1.3	97.4	1.4
Korea (South)	246.2	2.9	183.7	2.3	162.3	2.3
Malaysia	32.3	0.4	55.5	0.7	79.4	1.1
Singapore	329.5	3.9	329.9	4.1	269.7	3.9
Other	1,633.3	19.3	1,773.6	22.1	2,137.2	30.8
Total[a]	8,454.3	100.0	8,022.4	100.0	6,939.8	100.0

[a]May not total due to rounding.

Source: Yemen Arab Republic, Central Bank of Yemen, Research Department, *Financial Statistical Bulletin*, January-March 1984, table 27.

ing from $29.4 million to almost $240 million.[26] Trade has also been increasing with other countries in the region, including India, Malaysia, Singapore, South Korea, and the People's Republic of China.

Due to the impact of the worldwide recession in the early 1980s, the government of North Yemen moved to curtail spending. The Second Five-Year Plan was launched in 1982 and since then imports have been held at a fairly even level—around 8 million rials in 1983 and 1.6 million rials for the first quarter of 1984. For the 1980 to 1984 period, the private-sector share of the value of total imports in those years was consistently around 75 percent.[27]

Exports

The primary export of the Yemen Arab Republic is the labor and services of the Yemeni worker. Up to 1 million Yemenis, or between 30 and 50 percent of the national labor force in 1981, were estimated to be engaged in short-term emigration for employment throughout the Arabian Peninsula. As noted, private transfers from these emigrant workers served as a major stimulus to growth and development during the 1970s and have acted in the trade sector primarily to increase the level of imports to North Yemen. By comparison, the level of commodity exports from North Yemen remains fairly insignificant, reaching a level of approximately 180 million rials in 1982. Nonetheless, this reflects more than a tripling in the value of exports and reexports from 1974/75 to 1982.

The great majority of the commodity exports of the Yemen Arab Republic originate in the agricultural sector. Hides and skins, coffee, biscuits, and confections comprised 96 percent of total identified exports in 1978/79.[28] The 1970s witnessed a substantial decline in the importance of the traditional labor-intensive, cash crops of coffee and cotton due largely to the impact of emigration in creating both labor scarcity and sharply increased wages in the agricultural sector.

Coffee has long been an export of the Yemen Arab Republic, with production reaching as high as 12,000 tons in the 1930s.[29] In 1969/70, coffee accounted for 50 percent of the exports from North Yemen.[30] However, production declined sharply during the early 1970s because of the prolonged drought from 1967 to 1973. Since that time, growth in coffee production has been constrained by labor scarcity and competition from other cash crops for the farmer's investment. (The rate of return to coffee is estimated to be 39 Yemeni rials per man-day.)[31]

Coffee production remained stagnant during the First Five-Year Plan, fluctuating at an annual level between 3,400 and 3,900 tons.[32] (See table 28, chapter five for coffee export figures to 1982.) Yields in coffee production have fallen off sharply with labor scarcity, from 0.78 tons per hectare in 1973/74 to 0.50 tons per hectare in 1979/80.[33] With an easing of labor scarcity, total coffee production is expected to increase 21 percent during the Second Five-Year Plan, reaching, 4,600 tons in 1986.[34]

Cotton production grew sharply at the beginning of the 1970s, with production tripling between 1971/72 and 1973/74.[35] In 1973/74 cotton exports were valued at 35.2 million rials, which represented 64 percent of total exports.[36] Under the dual impact of labor scarcity and rising wages in the agricultural sector, cotton output fell from 20,000 tons in 1973/74 to 2,800 tons in 1979/80. During the same period, the acreage devoted to cotton production decreased from 20,000 hectares to 3,000 hectares. With an easing of labor scarcity and the corresponding downward pressure on wages, there has been some recovery of cotton output. Acreage devoted to cotton production increased from 3,000 to 5,300 hectares in 1981. This increase in acreage along with improved yields led to a 180 percent increase in output, to 5,000 tons.[37] The Second Five-Year Plan forecasts the continued recovery of cotton production and the resumption of its position as a major export, with output forecast to increase 316 percent during the plan period to reach 20,800 tons in 1986.[38]

Hides and skins continued to be major export items through the 1970s. Exports more than doubled during the first half of the decade, reaching a peak level of 8 million rials in 1975/76. Exports ranged between 4 and 8 million rials during the First Five-Year Plan.[39] The potential for production is significantly greater than its current level. It was estimated in 1981 that only 25 to 35 percent of the hides from slaughtered animals were utilized due to inefficient production and the lack of a well-developed market.[40] The advent of programs for government-owned slaughterhouses during the Second Five-Year Plan should significantly reduce waste and increase output.

Biscuits and confections have emerged as major exports in the processed food category during the 1970s. Such exports did not exist at the beginning of the decade but developed rapidly during the First Five-Year Plan, with value growing from 2.9 million rials in 1975/76 to 21.8 million rials in 1979.[41] Saudi Arabia and the People's Democratic Republic of Yemen have developed as significant markets for these products.

.Given the production capacity of the Salif salt mines, salt offers significant potential for export expansion. Exports of this commodity accounted for one-sixth of total exports in 1971/72.[42] Almost all of the 85,000 tons produced in 1971 was exported to Japan. However, as previously noted, exports to Japan ceased in 1972. Marketing problems in the face of the loss of the Japanese market plus international competition caused salt exports to fall off sharply in the mid-decade period. Increased worldwide demand for salt contributed to some recovery in export levels in the later part of the decade, with 62,000 tons being exported in 1979.[43] Established in 1981, the Yemeni Company for Salt Packing and Marketing successfully negotiated a contract to sell an unspecified quantity of salt to Japan's Marubeni Corporation in 1983/84. Further contracts are expected to be negotiated throughout the Gulf states and Africa. As discussed previously, the production capacity of the Salif salt mines was increased to 1 million tons during the First Five-Year Plan.[44] This output is expected to allow for both domestic self-sufficiency in table salt as well as increased exports.

Both Kuwait and the Soviet Union have extended aid to the fishing industry in North Yemen. Exports, in particular, have been promoted by the establishment of a drying station at Hodeidah.[45] Export markets have been established for dried fish in Singapore and for fresh and frozen fish in Saudi Arabia and the Gulf states. Estimates of annual fishing production during the First Five-Year Plan range between 12,675 and 21,200 tons. The potential harvest from fishing operations is tentatively estimated to be as high as 30,000 tons. The Second Five-Year Plan forecasts an annual growth rate of 10 percent for the fisheries subsector between 1981 and 1986. There have been warnings, however, that a significant likelihood of overfishing exists if further studies of harvest potential are not pursued in light of both increased domestic production and discussion of possible foreign fishing agreements.[46]

Table 46 gives the distribution of exports from North Yemen by country. The People's Democratic Republic of Yemen (P.D.R.Y.) emerged as the major market for North Yemen's exports during the 1970s, rising from 12 percent in 1974/75 to close to 50 percent by 1982. The development of North Yemen as an exporter of processed food, primarily biscuits and confections, has been a key factor in the growth of this trade. Together, Saudi Arabia and South Yemen accounted for over half of North Yemen's exports in 1980 and two-thirds of exports in 1982. Saudi Arabia has become an important market for live animals, vegetables, fresh and frozen fish, and processed foods from North Yemen.

China and Japan were important export markets for cotton and salt, respectively, in the early 1970s. Recovery of export levels for these commodities in the 1980s should increase the importance of the Chinese and Japanese markets during the course of the Second Five-Year Plan.

While trade with Asia (primarily China and Japan) dominated North Yemen's export trade in the early 1970s, the European Economic

Table 46: Exports to Selected Countries, 1974/75-1982a *(in thousand rials)*

Country	1974/75	1975/76	1976/77	1977/78	1978/79
People's Republic of China	22,092	24,625	24,953	40	0
	(41.7)	(49.2)	(49.4)	(0.1)	(0.0)
People's Democratic Republic of Yemen (P.D.R.Y.)	6,349	8,423	12,592	20,067	14,016
	(12.0)	(16.8)	(24.9)	(60.1)	(49.1)
Italy	4,340	8,693	5,988	2,866	2,527
	(8.2)	(17.4)	(11.8)	(8.6)	(8.9)
Saudi Arabia	2,542	4,592	4,510	4,998	9,208
	(4.8)	(9.2)	(8.9)	(15.0)	(32.3)
Djibouti	434	534	846	2,898	116
	(0.8)	(1.1)	(1.7)	(8.7)	(0.4)
Netherlands	853	370	595	38	0
	(1.6)	(0.7)	(1.2)	(0.1)	(0.0)
West Germany	1,260	332	432	163	517
	(2.4)	(0.7)	(0.9)	(0.5)	(1.8)
United States	263	635	218	0	981
	(0.5)	(1.3)	(0.4)	(0.0)	(3.4)
Japan	7,258	150	200	91	168
	(13.7)	(0.3)	(0.4)	(0.3)	(0.6)
Others	7,575	1,709	200	2,257	1,008
	(14.3)	(3.4)	(0.4)	(6.8)	(3.5)
Totalb	52,966	50,063	50,534	33,418	28,541
	(100.0)	(100.0)	(100.0)	(100.0)	(100.0)

aFigures in ( ) indicate percentage of total.

bMay not total due to rounding.

(continued)

Table 46 (continued): Exports to Selected Countries, 1974/75-1982[a] *(in thousand rials)*

Country	1979	1980	1981	1982
People's Republic of China	217	9,552	384	288
	(0.4)	(9.3)	(0.2)	(0.2)
People's Democratic Republic of Yemen (P.D.R.Y.)	30,054	43,749	50,309	89,555
	(48.7)	(42.4)	(23.2)	(49.8)
Italy	4,173	6,690	5,044	18,937
	(6.8)	(6.5)	(2.3)	(10.5)
Saudi Arabia	14,047	5,603	16,953	29,606
	(22.8)	(5.4)	(7.8)	(16.5)
Djibouti	617	1,901	700	837
	(1.0)	(1.8)	(0.3)	(0.5)
Netherlands	2,601	617	5,273	21
	(4.2)	(0.6)	(2.4)	(0.0)
West Germany	2,365	3,416	9,904	583
	(3.8)	(3.3)	(4.6)	(0.3)
United States	187	9,100	6,472	88
	(0.3)	(8.8)	(3.0)	(0.0)
Japan	2,189	1,451	175	1,112
	(3.5)	(1.4)	(0.1)	(0.6)
Others	5,230	21,054	121,375	38,936
	(8.5)	(20.4)	(56.0)	(21.6)
Total[b]	61,680	103,133	216,589	179,963
	(100.0)	(100.0)	(100.0)	(100.0)

[a]Figures in ( ) indicate percentage of total.

[b]May not total due to rounding.

Sources: Yemen Arab Republic, Central Planning Organization, Statistics Department, *Statistical Year Book, 1981*, p. 161, and Central Bank of Yemen, Research Department, *Financial Statistical Bulletin, January-March 1984*, table 25.

Community (EEC) and the United States have emerged as important trading partners in the latter part of the decade. North Yemen's exports to the United States show considerable fluctuation, with a peak in 1980 of 9 percent as compared to less than 1 percent in 1974/75. The EEC countries received approximately 25 percent of North Yemen's exports in 1980.

Balance of Payments

Throughout much of the 1970s North Yemen had a small but persistent deficit in the balance-of-payments current account. In 1973/74 the current-account deficit stood at a level of 83.7 million rials. The quadrupling of oil prices at that point in the decade had the indirect effect of substantially increasing the level of official aid from the Arab oil-exporting countries as well as raising the level of private transfers received from a growing number of Yemeni workers employed in those nations.

As table 47 shows, the initial impact of increased emigration of Yemeni workers was a near doubling of private transfers between 1973/74 and 1974/75. In the same period, official transfers to North Yemen increased from 139.2 million rials to 418.9 million rials. The result of the increased flow of private transfers and foreign aid to North Yemen was the emergence of a current-account surplus of 306.7 million rials in 1974/75.

North Yemen maintained a current account surplus through the middle years of the decade. During these years the growth of private transfers more than offset the worsening balance-of-trade deficit which was due to increased commodity imports. In this respect the flow of workers' remittances into the country grew more rapidly than the demand for imports arising from increased domestic incomes. The value of imports grew at an annual rate of 53 percent between 1974/75 and 1977/78. The level of private transfers during the same period, however, increased at an annual rate of 84 percent, rising from 1,013 million rials in 1974/75 to a peak level of 6,351 million rials in 1977/78. Imports in 1977/78 equaled only 65 percent of private transfers, leading to a current-account surplus of 1,473 million rials in that year.

A 1979 World Bank study estimated that official loan commitments roughly totaled $560 million by 1976/77, with more than half of those monies disbursed. Annual disbursements rose from $32 million in 1973/74 to an average level of $47 million in 1975/76 and 1976/77 due to increased utilization of development loans.47 With higher levels of foreign aid, substantially increased private transfers, and limited absorptive capacity, convertible foreign-exchange reserves grew rapidly in the mid-decade period, reaching a level of $1,447 million in 1978.48 This level of reserves was sufficient for approximately 15 month of imports at the 1978 rate. Table 48 offers a breakdown of capital flows during the first plan.

During the final three years of the First Five-Year Plan private transfers stabilized and then declined but the value of imports continued to grow. The decline of private transfers from peak 1977/78 levels can be attributed to: (1) moderation in the growth of expatriate labor demand in the Gulf oil economies; (2) shifts in the composition of expatriate labor demand in the oil countries; (3) a 1979 compulsory military service law in the Yemen Arab Republic; and (4) inflation in the YAR leading to increased purchases and investment of worker remittances outside the country. The decline in the level of private transfers was not accompanied by restraint in the growth of imports. Imports grew at an annual rate of 24 percent in 1979/80 and 10 percent in 1980/81, reaching a level of 7,652.2 million rials in 1980/81. As a result, the current-account surplus of 1,473 million rials in 1977/78 was transformed into a current-account deficit of 2,983 million rials in 1980/81. The deficit continued thereafter but with a diminishing pattern, reaching 2,556.5 million rials by 1983. Convertible foreign-exchange reserves fell from $1,447 million in 1978 to $947 million by 1981.49

The Second Five-Year Plan's Balance of Payments: In 1981, the base year of the Second Five-Year Plan, the Yemen Arab Republic experienced a balance-of-trade deficit of 7,820 million rials (table 47). Since 1977/78 private transfers have been insufficient to meet this trade deficit; consequently, there was a current-account deficit of approximately 2,990 million rials in 1981. This deficit was financed in part by approximately 2.7 billion Yemeni rials in official loans and grants and by reducing foreign-exchange reserves of the Central Bank by 1,499 million rials.50 The Second Five-Year Plan aims at reducing the current-account deficit to 2,558 million rials by 1986, primarily by restricting the growth of imports and improving the balance of services.51 The need to finance a cumulative current-account deficit of 15,457 million rials during the second plan, however, reveals the continued dependence of the Yemen Arab Republic on external economic relations. The Central Planning Organization's forecast for the balance

168 *International Linkages*

Table 47: **Summary Balance of Payments, 1973/74-1984**[a] *(in million rials)*

Items	1973/ 1974	1974/ 1975	1975/ 1976	1976/ 1977	1977/ 1978	1978/ 1979	1979/ 1980
Trade balance[b]	-811.4	-1,105.4	-1,666.0	-3,199.9	-4,102.7	-5,613.2	-6,925.5
Exports/ f.o.b.	61.9	58.0	55.3	83.9	31.8	13.2	32.1
Imports/ c.i.f.	873.3	1,163.4	1,721.3	3,283.8	4,134.5	5,626.4	6,957.6
Net services	84.7	134.6	195.9	196.6	218.7	-160.8	-1.5
Net private transfers	503.8	858.6	2,057.3	3,790.8	4,904.4	3,750.1	4,943.5
Receipts	594.6	1,013.0	2,363.3	4,561.2	6,350.7	5,595.0	6,118.4
Payments	90.8	154.4	306.0	770.4	1,446.3	1,844.9	1,174.9
Net official transfers	139.2	418.9	513.2	469.9	452.3	1,402.6	503.1
Balance on current acct.	-83.7	306.7	1,100.4	1,257.4	1,472.7	-621.3	-1,480.4
Net official capital	129.3	147.4	199.0	188.2	340.4	932.5	1,301.8
Errors and omissions	71.2	-36.7	122.0	53.5	199.5	452.8	169.4
Balance of payments	116.8	417.4	1,421.4	1,499.1	2,012.6	764.0	-9.2

[a]Fiscal years ending June 30 for 1973/74 through 1980/81 used, based upon Central Planning Organization reporting procedure, while calendar years are used 1980 through 1984, based upon Central Bank of Yemen reporting procedure.

[b]Estimates compiled by the Central Bank from banking data. A discrepancy may be noted between these figures and the figures utilized in the previous sections, depending on the source of reporting, i.e., Central Planning Organization or Central Bank of Yemen.

(continued)

Table 47 (continued): **Summary Balance of Payments, 1973/74-1984**[a] *(in millions of rials)*

Items	1980/81	1980	1981	1982	1983	1984
Trade balance[b]	-7,580.1	-8,562.0	-7,820.4	-8,764.1	-8,038.0	-4,974.8
Exports/ f.o.b.	72.1	57.5	47.4	21.6	44.0	18.6
Imports/ c.i.f.	7,652.2	8,619.5	7,867.8	8,785.7	8,082.0	4,993.4
Net services	-118.2	-93.3	-231.8	-168.5	-217.5	-240.5
Net private transfers	4,047.5	4,879.6	3,547.0	4,158.4	4,967.6	4,091.0
Receipts	4,935.8	6,034.1	4,444.2	5,360.6	5,600.7	4,417.1
Payments	888.3	1,154.5	897.2	1,202.2	633.1	326.1
Net official transfers	668.2	665.2	1,515.8	2,002.9	731.4	665.9
Balance on current acct.	-2,982.6	-3,110.5	-2,989.4	-2,771.3	-2,556.5	-458.4
Net official capital	1,217.9	2,678.7	1,390.1	972.0	1,328.6	232.8
Errors and omissions	-230.8	109.0	104.1	207.8	288.9	153.6
Balance of payments	-1,995.5	-322.8	1,495.2	-1,591.5	-939.0	-72.0

[a]Fiscal years ending June 30 for 1973/74 through 1980/81 used, based upon Central Planning Organization reporting procedure, while calendar years are used 1980 through 1984, based upon Central Bank of Yemen reporting procedure.

[b]Estimates compiled by the Central Bank from banking data. A discrepancy may be noted between these figures and the figures utilized in the previous sections, depending on the source of reporting, i.e., Central Planning Organization or Central Bank of Yemen.

Sources: Yemen Arab Republic, Central Planning Organization, Statistics Department, *Statistical Year Book, 1981*, pp. 184-185, and Central Bank of Yemen, Research Department, *Financial Statistical Bulletin*, January-March 1984, table 16; and World Bank, "Yemen Arab Republic Country Economic Memorandum Current Position and Prospects," Report no. 5621-YAR (Washington, D.C., June 25, 1985), p. 77.

Table 48: Capital Flows, First Five-Year Plan *(in million rials)*

	1976/ 1977	1977/ 1978	1978/ 1979	1979/ 1980	1980/ 1981	Cumulative Total 1975-1976/ 1980-1981
Official transfers	469.9	461.3	1,402.6	503.1	670.5	3,507.4
In cash	417.9	409.3	1,350.6	451.1	609.3	3,238.2
In kind	52.0	52.0	52.0	52.0	61.2	269.2
Official loans (net)	188.2	340.4	467.4	525.3	1,162.1	2,683.4
Disbursements	207.6	366.5	511.7	558.8	1,449.3	3,093.9
Repayments	-19.4	-26.1	-44.3	-33.5	-287.2	-410.5
Total official capital	658.1	801.7	1,870.0	1,028.4	1,832.6	6,190.8

Source: Yemen Arab Republic, Central Planning Organization, Statistics Department, *Statistical Year Book, 1981*, pp. 184-185.

of payments during the Second Five-Year Plan is presented in table 49.

Let us turn first to examine the current account as outlined in the second plan and table 49. The balance-of-trade deficit in 1981 was equal to 60 percent of gross domestic product. The Second Five-Year Plan seeks to reduce this percentage to 44 percent of GDP by 1986. With this goal in mind, the balance-of- trade deficit is targeted to increase by less than 1 percent annually, from 7,821 million rials in 1981 to 8,015 million rials in 1986.[52] At the same time, gross domestic product is expected to increase at an annual rate of 7 percent, from 12,949 million rials in 1981 to 18,162 million rials in 1986.[53]

To achieve the goal of increased self-reliance, the focus of attention in the current account during the Second Five-Year Plan will be on lessening the importance of imports in the domestic economy while increasing their contribution to the development process. Specifically, the plan aims to achieve a 1 percent rate of growth in imports and to restructure the composition of imports. [54] Reduction of imports and a greater degree of self-reliance are to be achieved through emphasis on the following: (a) limitation of nonessential imports through the development and production of import substitutes, especially of foodstuffs and intermediate goods; (b) provision of new opportunities for Yemenis working abroad to channel their earnings into investments in productive projects; (c) the judicious use of commercial policies to rationalize imports and rectify the deficit in the balance of trade; and (d) intensification of efforts in the search for oil and use of alternative sources of energy, such as geothermal and solar energy.

Thus, the second plan clearly places emphasis on increased domestic production, specifically in those areas which contribute to import substitution or expansion of exports. In the agricultural sector, increased output is seen as a means of reducing foodstuff imports, expanding agricultural exports (particularly of cotton and coffee), and providing the requisite agricultural raw materials for the growth of domestic industry. In the industrial sector, industries with cost-competitive, import-substitution potential, are promoted. Particular attention is being paid to the development of industries that have a comparative advantage regarding transportation costs, e.g., domestic production of building materials. Finally, the increasing demand for energy in the development process, and the rising level of the import fuel bill, has focused attention on the need for greater exploration and evaluation of North Yemen's energy resources as a possible means of reducing this aspect of the balance-of-trade deficit. The discoveries in the Marib-Jawf basin will contribute to the realization of this objective.

Along with a reduction in the overall rate of growth of imports, the second plan seeks to restructure the composition of imports in a manner favorable to the development process. The objective is to reduce the share of consumer goods in imports while increasing the share of capital and intermediate goods. The desired shift in the composition of imports is outlined in table 50. Customs policies and incentive measures undertaken by the government will largely determine the success of the Second Five-Year Plan in achieving the desired shift in the composition of imports. The reduction of the balance-of-trade deficit will also depend, to some degree, on the policies and incentives which apply to exports. The following measures are outlined in the Second Five-Year Plan.[55]

1. The customs tariff system will be reviewed carefully, inconsistencies will be eliminated, and exemptions will be limited to those promoting domestic industrial projects.

Table 49: Balance of Payments in the Second Five-Year Plan (1982-1986)
(in million rials at 1981 prices)

Item	1982	1983	1984
Current-account trade balance	-7,872	-7,927	-7,958
Exports	75	100	150
Imports	-7,947	-8,027	-8,108
Balance of services	-571	-434	-277
Exports	1,215	1,370	1,545
Imports	-1,786	-1,804	-1,822
Current transfer and income factors	4,955	4,950	5,120
Received private transfers	4,450	4,475	4,500
Received official cash transfers	850	850	1,000
Received official materials transfers	75	75	100
Paid returns on investment	500	540	400
Total of received transfers/returns	5,875	5,850	6,000
Paid private transfers	-850	-825	-800
Paid returns on investments	-70	-75	-80
Total of paid returns/transfers	-920	-900	-880
Balance of current account	-3,488	-3,411	-3,115
Capital-account balance	3,000	3,025	3,100
Received capital transfers	50	75	100
Drawings on loans	2,700	2,700	2,700
Direct private investment	250	250	300
Changes in stock	488	386	15

(continued)

2. The tariff rates and customs collections will be used to change the import structure in favor of intermediate and capital goods.

3. The promotion of exportable commodities will be realized through the efficient use of export credits, insurance, tax rebates, and tax exemptions.

Table 49 (continued): Balance of Payments in the Second Five-Year Plan (1982-1986) *(in million rials at 1981 prices)*

Item	1985	1986	Total[a]
Current-account trade balance	-7,990	-8,015	-39,762
Exports	200	250	775
Imports	-8,190	-8,265	-40,537
Balance of services	-105	92	-1,295
Exports	1,735	1,950	7,815
Imports	-1,840	-1,858	-9,110
Current transfer and income factors	5,240	5,320	25,600
Received private transfers	4,525	4,550	22,500
Received official cash transfers	1,100	1,200	5,000
Received official materials transfers	125	125	500
Paid returns on investment	350	300	2,000
Total of received transfers/returns	6,100	6,175	30,000
Paid private transfers	-775	-730	4,000
Paid returns on investments	-85	-90	-400
Total of paid returns/transfers	-860	-840	-4,400
Balance of current account	-2,855	-2,588	-15,457
Capital-account balance	3,175	3,200	15,500
Received capital transfers	125	150	500
Drawings on loans	2,700	2,700	13,500
Direct private investment	350	350	1,500
Changes in stock	-320	-612	-43

[a]May not total due to rounding.

Source: Yemen Arab Republic, Central Planning Organization, *Second Five-Year Plan (1982-1986)*, table VIII.

4. Public agencies will help potential exporters in their export-oriented activities, in project preparations, in project evaluations, and in choice and transfers of technology, etc.

Table 50: Target Change in the Composition of Imports During the Second Five-Year Plan *(at 1981 constant prices)*

Categories	Base Year 1981	%	Final Year 1986	%
Consumer goods	3,973	50.5	3,306	40.0
Intermediate goods	2,337	29.7	3,223	39.0
Capital goods	1,558	19.8	1,736	21.0
Total imports	7,868	100.0	8,265	100.0

Source: Yemen Arab Republic, Central Planning Organization, *Second Five-Year Plan (1982-1986)*, chapter 3, p. 24.

Net current transfers and factor income from abroad are forecast to increase at a 1.8 percent annual rate, providing a cumulative total of 25,600 million rials during the Second Five-Year Plan (table 49). Private transfers are forecast to contribute 75 percent of these current transfers to North Yemen.[56] Despite the decline in private transfers between 1979/80 and 1980/81, private transfers are forecast to increase slightly during the period 1982-1986. As table 47 indicates, the level of these transfers has actually picked up somewhat in the 1982-1984 span. The Second Five-Year Plan acknowledges the unreliability of this source of financing for domestic consumption and investment given its reliance on labor market conditions in Saudi Arabia and other Gulf states. Official transfers (in cash and kind) are expected to provide a cumulative total of 5,500 million rials during the second plan period.

As noted earlier, the expected cumulative deficit in the current account during the 1982-1986 program is 15,477 million rials. This deficit will be financed by capital transfers of 500 million rials, drawings on foreign loans of 13,500 million rials and direct private foreign investments of 1,500 million rials. External financing will provide a cumulative total of 15,500 million rials, allowing the accumulation of 43 million rials in convertible foreign-exchange reserves during the Second Five-Year Plan.

The schedule of amortization payments for existing debts calls for 64 million rials in 1982, 109 million rials in 1983, 151 million rials in 1984, 185 million rials in 1985, and some 194 million rials in the last year of the plan (1986).[57] Allowing for amortization payments on existing debts, approximately 2,660 million rials in net loans and grants will be available annually during the Second Five-Year Plan.

Foreign Aid

Information gaps make a comprehensive examination of foreign aid to North Yemen a difficult prospect. However, a broad outline of aid flows since independence can be attempted. It should be remembered that not only must the Yemen Arab Republic meet the demands of development, but the nation also was faced with reconstruction costs after the civil war of the 1960s. A 1979 World Bank study estimated that the cumulative level of foreign aid to North Yemen from independence through the Three- Year Program, the period of 1962 through 1975/76, amounted to roughly $600 million. Over half of this total, $356 million in foreign assistance, was received during the Three-Year Program (1973/74-1975/76).[58] Aid continued to increase during the First Five-Year Plan (1976/77-1980/81), with cumulative foreign assistance during that period of approximately $1,350 million (table 48).[59] The major donors of foreign aid to the Yemen Arab Republic have been Saudi Arabia, Iraq, the Gulf states, the People's Republic of China, the U.S.S.R., the Federal Republic of Germany, the United States, the World Bank's International Development Association, and the Arab Fund for Economic and Social Development.

It was further estimated that roughly $316 million in nonreimbursable grants had been extended to the Yemen Arab Republic by 1975/76. Of this amount, $240 million in grants had been received by North Yemen during the Three-Year Program.[60] The level of grants received by the YAR increased substantially during the First Five-Year Plan, with the cumulative total of official aid to the Yemen Arab Republic during this period reaching about $770 million.[61] Table 48 gave the distribution of grants as official transfers in cash and official transfers in kind.

Overall, roughly one-half of foreign aid to North Yemen by the end of 1980/81 had taken the form of grants largely for budget support, commodities, and technical assistance. In the early years of independence, budget support was undertaken by Egypt but it was discontinued when relations were disrupted in 1967. In the 1970s, budget support was provided by Saudi Arabia. Official transfers in cash increased from 57 million rials in 1971/72 to 458 million rials in 1975/76.[62] The cumulative total of cash grants during the First Five-Year Plan was 3,238 million rials (table 48).

Commodity aid to North Yemen has largely taken the form of petroleum products and food, the major suppliers being Saudi Arabia, the Gulf states, the United States, and the World Food Program. Food aid under the World Food Program amounted to $45 million between 1966 and 1976/77.[63] Assistance from the United States Agency for International Development to North Yemen was disrupted in 1967 with the severing of diplomatic relations but resumed in 1972 when diplomatic relations were restored. Food aid under U. S. Public Law 480 (Food for Peace) totaled $29 million in the first three years of restored relations between the United States and North Yemen.[64] Grants from the United States to North Yemen totaled $12.7 million in 1980.[65]

A substantial portion of foreign aid has taken the form of technical assistance. Unfortunately, a complete rendering of technical assistance provided by various donors is made impossible by a lack of information. The 1979 World Bank study estimated that technical assistance reached a level of $30 million in 1975/76, just prior to the First Five-Year Plan.[66] Technical assistance has been given in almost every sector of the economy but is largely centered on education, public health, and agriculture and, to a lesser extent, on industry, construction, and public administration.

In terms of technical assistance, the United Nations Development Program has one of its largest operations in North Yemen. With the start of the First Five-Year Plan, it was committed to a $30.2 million program involving 65 projects in 11 sectors of the economy.[67] Moreover, the Arab countries which provide substantial technical aid to the YAR were involved in a triangular assistance program. Under this arrangement, the financial cost of such a program is met by the wealthier Arab oil-exporting nations while the skilled labor is supplied by those Arab countries with surplus manpower. Other important sources of technical assistance include the Western industrialized countries and the Soviet Union.

During the 1970s the YAR received an increased flow of aid in the form of official loans on concessional terms because of its classification by the United Nations as a "least-developed country." With a heightening of the development effort, international borrowing increased rapidly in the later part of the decade. In 1976/77 total commitments were estimated to be roughly $560 million, of which $330 million had been disbursed.[68] By September 30, 1980 total official borrowing was estimated to have grown to $1,208 million with disbursements of $638 million. A 1983 report by the Central Bank of Yemen placed total international borrowing by the Yemen Arab Republic between 1962 and 1982 at $2,325 million, of which about $110 million had been repaid.[69] Disbursements rose steadily through the decade of the 1970s as development loans were increasingly utilized. Drawings on official loans increased from 144.4 million rials in 1973/74 to 366.5 million rials in 1977/78, and to some 1,449.3 million rials in 1980/81 (the final year of the First Five-Year Plan).[70]

Prior to 1970, the Soviet Union and the People's Republic of China were the principal lenders to North Yemen. This early lending concentrated primarily on the development of infrastructure, industry, and the urban sector.

The triangular trunk road system linking Sana'a, Hodeidah, and Taiz was completed with foreign aid in the 1960s. The Sana'a-Hodeidah road was built by the People's Republic of China, the Sana'a-Taiz highway was financed by the United States, and the Hodeidah-Taiz road was built by the Soviet Union. This is indicative of the YAR's ability to diversify its development financing and assistance sources and thus avoid excessive dependence on one lender/donor. Some of the major industries of North Yemen received foreign aid in this early period: the Sana'a textile factory was financed by China; the cement plant at Bajil and the aluminum plant in Taiz were financed by the Soviet Union. Other major projects included Sana'a airport construction (financed by Germany), modernization of port facilities at Hodeidah (financed by the Soviet Union), improvements at the Salif salt mine and port (financed by Kuwait), and various urban-sector water and sewerage systems.

During the Three-Year Program, increased emphasis was placed on development of the rural and agricultural sectors. Table 51 gives the distribution of government external loan drawings, by sector, during the 1973/74-1975/76 period. Actual expenditures in the agricultural sector during the program were 73 million rials, most of which came from foreign aid.[71] The largest project in the agricultural sector was the Tihama Agricultural Development Program financed by the International Development Association and the Kuwait Fund for Arab Economic Development. Loan drawings for this undertaking during the Three-Year Program amounted to about 50 million rials, largely for irrigation projects and rural water-resource evaluation. Infrastructural development and maintenance and urban-sector development continued

Table 51: Government External Loan Drawings by Sector, Three-Year Program (1973/74-1975/76) *(in millions of U.S. dollars)*

Fiscal Years Ending June 30	1973/74	1974/75	1975/76
Project loans	26.7	25.1	39.2
Education	—	0.2	0.7
Water supply	—	0.8	3.5
Agriculture (including livestock)	0.7	4.1	6.5
Mining	4.3	2.4	1.5
Roads	18.5	16.0	11.8
Airport	0.9	0.1	1.4
Telecommunications	—	—	—
Industry	—	—	0.2
Electric power	—	—	11.7
Other projects	2.3	1.5	1.9
Other loans	5.4	11.5	14.8
Commodity loans	0.4	0.6	8.1
Cash loans	4.2	10.9	6.7
Others	0.8	—	—
Total	32.1	36.6	54.0

Source: International Monetary Fund, "International Monetary Fund Report on the Yemen Arab Republic (Article IV Consultation)," (Washington, D.C.: International Monetary Fund, 1980), p. 69.

during the program with financing from the International Development Association, the Arab Fund for Economic and Social Development, Kuwait, the People's Republic of China, the U.S.S.R., and the Federal Republic of Germany. Oil subsidies in the form of cash loans in the amount of 48.9 million rials in 1974/75 and 30.4 million rials in 1975/76 were provided by the Arab Fund for Economic and Social Development.[72]

Total drawings from official loans during the First Five-Year Plan amounted to 3,093 million rials. Emphasis in project financing continued to be on water resource development, agriculture and livestock, roads, electricity, and other areas of infrastructural development. Major project donors during the plan were Saudi Arabia, Iraq, the People's Republic of China, the U.S.S.R., the Federal Republic of Germany, the Netherlands, the International Development Association, the Kuwait Fund for Arab Economic Development, the Abu Dhabi Fund for Arab Economic Development, and the Arab Fund for Economic and Social Development. Of the $2,325 million in international borrowing between 1962 and 1982, Soviet lending totaled $819 million and Arab lending totaled $744 million. Saudi Arabia was the major Arab lender, followed by Iraq.[73] Table 52 offers the position of foreign loans as of the first quarter of 1984.

Several points should be made about the Yemen Arab Republic's position as an aid recipient and borrower. First, North Yemen has emphasized that its development comes first, i.e., foreign assistance and investment are welcomed from a wide diversity of sources without undue weight ascribed to the political-ideological-economic persuasion of the donor or investor. Second, because of its willingness to utilize multinational agencies to assist in formulating its projects and plans, the Yemen Arab Republic has established a solid reputation in its planning procedures. Third, implementation of programs by the YAR has been among the most efficient of the less-developed nations. Finally, North Yemen has restrained its borrowing, particularly in capital markets, so that its debt burden is small by developing-country standards.

Summing-Up

Despite the impact of the worldwide recession, the Yemen Arab Republic appears to have moved to minimize the downturn of its economy. The foreign-exchange pinch in the 1982-1984 span reflects lower income but not a higher debt burden. In October 1984 the YAR's external debt was $2.5 billion in aid borrowing at concessionary (nonmarket) rates.[74] Moreover, by devaluing the rial in 1984, the North Yemen government has moved to bring the official rate and free-market rate of exchange closer together. By restricting the Central Bank in its supply of foreign exchange to other banks on demand, privately held dollar remittances were lured into financing a portion of imports. In both 1982 and 1983, the foreign-exchange reserves would

Table 52: Foreign Loans Position as of March 31, 1984 *(in million rials)*

	Current Value of Loan	Utilization 1st Q 1984	Repayment 1st Q 1984
International/regional			
organizations	3,146.5	48.2	18.2
I.D.A.[a]	1,603.4	17.1	0.8
AFESD[a]	903.0	2.3	2.8
OPEC Fund[a]	196.5	25.2	—
I.D.B.[a]	40.8	—	—
KFAED[a]	133.9	3.6	—
Arab Monetary Fund	269.1	—	14.7
Arab countries	4,090.8	13.2	33.0
Kuwait	672.5	1.8	1.8
Algeria	5.0	—	—
Iraq	1,399.4	—	17.8
Abu Dhabi	243.7	5.8	2.6
Saudi Arabia	1,770.2	5.6	10.9
Western Europe/U.S.	277.1	38.5	—
France	79.5	—	—
Italy	150.0	38.5	—
United States	31.8	—	—
Denmark	15.9	—	—
East Europe/China	4,430.9	-2.1	—
U.S.S.R.[a]	3,849.2	0.3	—
P.R.C.[a]	530.5	-2.4	—
D.R. of Germany[a]	25.0	—	—
Czechoslovakia	26.2	—	—
Asian countries	451.9	4.2	—
Japan	451.9	4.2	—
Bank facilities	41.0	11.3	4.1
National Westminister	41.0	11.3	4.1
Total[b]	12,437.9	113.3	55.2

[a]I.D.A.=International Development Association (a World Bank affiliate); AFESD = Arab Fund for Economic and Social Development; OPEC Fund=Organization of the Petroleum Exporting Countries Fund; I.D.B.=Islamic Development Bank; KFAED=Kuwait Fund for Arab Economic Development; U.S.S.R.=Union of Soviet Socialist Republics; P.R.C.=People's Republic of China; D.R. of Germany = Democratic Republic of Germany.

(continued)

Table 52 (continued): Foreign Loans Position as of March 31, 1984 *(in million rials)*

	Cumulative Repayment	Debt Outstanding	Undisbursed Balance
International/regional organizations	97.7	1,622.3	1,426.4
I.D.A.[a]	2.2	798.5	802.7
AFESD[a]	64.1	513.2	325.7
OPEC Fund[a]	1.4	75.2	119.9
I.D.B.[a]	0.8	27.8	12.2
KFAED[a]	—	30.2	103.7
Arab Monetary Fund	29.4	177.5	62.2
Arab countries	113.3	2,504.3	1,473.3
Kuwait	14.7	303.5	354.4
Algeria	0.2	1.0	3.8
Iraq	48.5	879.7	471.2
Abu Dhabi	10.7	156.7	76.4
Saudi Arabia	39.2	1,163.5	567.5
Western Europe/U.S.	21.0	122.7	133.4
France	21.0	58.2	0.3
Italy	—	38.5	111.6
United States	—	24.8	7.0
Denmark	—	1.3	14.6
East Europe/China	399.2	3,178.4	853.4
U.S.S.R.[a]	334.0	2,790.0	725.2
P.R.C.[a]	60.0	348.1	122.4
D.R. of Germany[a]	1.6	17.7	5.8
Czechoslovakia	3.6	22.6	—
Asian countries	—	249.9	202.0
Japan	—	249.9	202.0
Bank facilities	4.1	26.5	10.4
National Westminister	4.1	26.5	10.4
Total[b]	635.2	7,704.1	4,098.6

[b]Regional and total figures may not total due to rounding.

Source: Yemen Arab Republic, Central Bank of Yemen, Research Department, *Financial Statistical Bulletin*, January-March 1984, table 17.

have covered imports for three and a half months.75 Table 53 offers a brief review of North Yemen's public finances.

The discovery of oil in the Marib-Jawf area in 1984 holds pluses and minuses for North Yemen. Expansion of oil exploration activities will be reflected in increased employment, support services, and anticipatory investment, both indigenous and foreign. Such activity can stimulate the economy as it fights to recover from the worldwide recession. But a premature and sizeable return of emigrant workers—buoyed by the hope for oil-related work at home—would slash remittances and could flood the labor market. The bidding up of scarce support services can fuel inflation as can anticipatory (sometimes speculative) investment.

The second set of pluses and minuses of North Yemen's oil discovery involves a longer time frame. Before production and export of petroleum can begin, there are costly and time-consuming infrastructure and field development requirements. Thus, oil-generated revenues lie some years in the future. It would be a problem for North Yemen's development progress were the country unable to secure continued foreign-assistance lending and, instead, were forced to borrow in the capital markets. The attitude of the YAR government has been to restrain excessive euphoria and/or claims for its petroleum potential since reserves have not yet been evaluated; it is a realistic attitude premised upon lead times. This approach is also evidenced in the initial draft of the Third Five-Year Plan (1987-1991) where close to half of the plan's expenditures are estimated to be covered from existing domestic revenues (i.e., taxes, user charges, the governmental share in profits of public corporations), a fifth from the government's share of oil revenues, over a quarter (about 28 percent) from foreign grants and borrowing, and with the remainder coming from local borrowing.76

A positive aspect of the heightened interest in North Yemen caused by the oil discoveries is possible expansion of foreign investment. The YAR outlined its policies and incentives in Law 12 of 1970 on the investment of foreign and national capital. All sectors are open to investment—industry, agriculture, mining, tourism, or any other activity that would strengthen the national economy and increase the national income. Enterprises likely to be approved would utilize domestic primary materials, function as import substitutes, or expand exports. A minimum of invested capital is required. During the first five years there is complete exemption from all customs duties and taxes on imports of capital equipment, machinery, and spare parts as well as a reduction in duties and taxes on required raw-materials imports. Finally,

Table 53: Summary of Public Finances, 1976-1984 *(in million rials)*

Item	1976-1977	1978-1979	1982	1983	1984
Revenues/grants	1,716.4	3,525.3	5,455.6	5,562.6	6,195.9
Revenues	1,298.5	2,174.7	3,451.6	4,816.0	5,335.0
Grants	417.9	1,350.6	2,004.0	746.6	860.9
Expenditures	1,444.4	4,464.9	9,119.3	9,276.9	11,729.2
Current	841.0	1,847.2	5,936.8	7,269.5	7,453.4
Capital	603.4	2,617.7	3,182.5	2,007.4	4,275.8
Overall surplus or deficit (-)	272.0	-939.6	-3,663.7	-3,714.3	-5,533.3
Financing of surplus or deficit	-272.0	939.6	3,663.7	3,714.3	5,533.3
Net external financing	188.2	553.8	844.9	900.4	725.3
Net domestic bank financing	-532.1	380.7	4,415.1	3,799.0	4,808.0
Statistical adjustment	71.9	5.1	-1,596.3	-985.1	—

Sources: Yemen Arab Republic, Central Bank of Yemen, Research Department, *Financial Statistical Bulletin*, January-March 1985, tables 20, 21, and 22, and *The Financial Times* (London), November 26, 1984.

a five-year tax holiday is extended and, if the company's investment is in excess of 2 million rials, a 50-percent reduction in taxes on its profits can be granted for an additional five years. Profits are transferable in the original currency at the prevailing exchange rate and expatriates in the employ of approved firms may transfer up to half of their wages and salaries.[77] These concepts were more recently reaffirmed in the National Charter of 1983. Such an atmosphere, when coupled with on-

184 *International Linkages*

going development programs and efforts, and stimulated by the prospect of an expanding natural-resource base, should attract foreign financing and investment as well as mobilize domestic private investment.

Notes

1. Yemen Arab Republic, Central Planning Organization, Statistics Department, *Statistical Year Book, 1981*, pp. 184 and 340, and *Statistical Year Book, 1979-1980*, p. 350.
2. Yemen Arab Republic, Central Planning Organization, Statistics Department, *Statistical Year Book, 1979-1980*, p. 350, and *The Financial Times* (London), November 26, 1984.
3. Yemen Arab Republic, Central Planning Organization, Statistics Department, *Statistical Year Book, 1981*, p. 359, and *Statistical Year Book, 1981*, p. 351.
4. Ibid.
5. Yemen Arab Republic, Central Planning Organization, Statistics Department, *Statistical Year Book, 1979-1980*, p. 218, and *Statistical Year Book, 1981*, p. 184; and Central Bank of Yemen, Research Department, *Financial Statistical Bulletin*, January-March 1984, table 23.
6. Yemen Arab Republic, Central Planning Organization, "Fourth Year Annual Report of the Second Five-Year Plan," (February 1985), p. 12 (mimeographed, in Arabic).
7. Ibid., p. 22.
8. Consortium for International Development, *Agriculture Sector Analysis, Yemen Arab Republic* (Sana'a: Consortium for International Development, 1981), table II.12.
9. Yemen Arab Republic, Central Planning Organization, *Second Five-Year Plan (1982-1986)*, March 1982, chapter 3, p. 24.
10. World Bank, *Mobilization of Domestic Financial Resources in the Yemen Arab Republic* (Washington, D.C.: World Bank, 1982), p. 106.
11. Chris Kutschera, "North Yemen: The Gilt Peels Off," *The Middle East*, February 1981, p. 57.
12. World Bank, *Mobilization of Domestic Financial Resources in the Yemen Arab Republic*, p. 106, and Yemen Arab Republic, Central Bank of Yemen, Research Department, *Financial Statistical Bulletin*, January-March 1984, table 26.
13. Consortium for International Development, *Agriculture Sector Analysis, Yemen Arab Republic*, and Yemen Arab Republic, Central Bank of Yemen, Research Department, *Financial Statistical Bulletin*, January-March 1984, table 26.
14. Ibid., p. 77 and table IV.3, and ibid.
15. Yemen Arab Republic, Central Planning Organization, *Second Five-Year Plan (1982-1986)*, chapter 1, p. 9.
16. Consortium for International Development, *Agriculture Sector Analysis, Yemen Arab Republic*, p. 20, and Yemen Arab Republic, Central Bank of Yemen, Research Department, *Financial Statistical Bulletin*, January-March 1984, table 26.
17. Consortium for International Development, *Agriculture Sector Analysis, Yemen Arab Republic*, pp. 20, 69, 90, and table IV.2.
18. Yemen Arab Republic, Central Planning Organization, Statistics Department, *Statistical Year Book, 1981*, pp. 333-344.
19. Ibid., p. 348, and Consortium for International Development, *Agriculture Sector Analysis, Yemen Arab Republic*, p. 20.
20. Consortium for International Development, *Agriculture Sector Analysis, Yemen Arab Republic*, p. 20.
21. Ibid.

22. Country report presented to the Second Arab Conference, Doha, Qatar, March 6-11, 1981, cited in *OAPEC Bulletin*, January 1983, p. 17.
23. United States, Department of Commerce, *Marketing in the Yemen Arab Republic*, October 1981, p. 7.
24. Country report presented to the Second Arab Energy Conference, in *OAPEC Bulletin*, January 1983, p. 17.
25. International Monetary Fund, *Direction of Trade Statistical Year Book, 1981* (Washington, D.C.: International Monetary Fund, 1981), and Yemen Arab Republic, Central Bank of Yemen, Research Department, *Financial Statistical Bulletin*, January-March 1984, table 27.
26. Ibid.
27. Yemen Arab Republic, Central Bank of Yemen, Research Department, *Financial Statistical Bulletin*, January-March 1984, table 16.
28. Consortium for International Development, *Agriculture Sector Analysis, Yemen Arab Republic*, p. 21.
29. John M. Cohen and David B. Lewis, *Rural Development in the Yemen Arab Republic: Strategy Issues in a Capital-Surplus Labor-Short Economy* (Cambridge, Massachusetts: Harvard Institute for International Development, 1979), p. 15.
30. World Bank, *Yemen Arab Republic: Development of a Traditional Economy* (Washington, D.C.: World Bank, 1979), p. 62.
31. Consortium for International Development, *Agriculture Sector Analysis, Yemen Arab Republic*, p. 65.
32. Yemen Arab Republic, Central Planning Organization, Statistics Department, *Statistical Year Book, 1981*, p. 87.
33. Yemen Arab Republic, Central Planning Organization, Statistics Department, *Statistical Year Book, 1979-1980*, p. 87.
34. Consortium for International Development, *Agriculture Sector Analysis, Yemen Arab Republic*, table IV.2.
35. World Bank, *Yemen Arab Republic: Development of a Traditional Economy*, p. 62.
36. International Monetary Fund, "International Monetary Fund Report on the Yemen Arab Republic (Article IV Consultation)," (Washington, D.C.: International Monetary Fund, 1980), p. 65.
37. Yemen Arab Republic, Central Planning Organization, Statistics Department, *Statistical Year Book, 1981*, p. 88.
38. Consortium for International Development, *Agriculture Sector Analysis, Yemen Arab Republic*, table IV.2.
39. International Monetary Fund, "International Monetary Fund Report on the Yemen Arab Republic (Article IV Consultation)," p. 65.
40. Consortium for International Development, *Agriculture Sector Analysis, Yemen Arab Republic*, p. 73.
41. United Nations, *Year Book of International Trade Statistics 1980* (New York: United Nations, 1981).
42. World Bank, *Yemen Arab Republic: Development of a Traditional Economy*, p. 62.
43. United States, Department of Commerce, *Foreign Economic Trends and Their Implications for the United States: Yemen Arab Republic* (Washington D.C.: Government Printing Office, 1981), p. 7.
44. Yemen Arab Republic, Central Planning Organization, *First Five-Year Plan (1976/77-1980/81)*, p. 36.
45. John M. Cohen and David B. Lewis, *Rural Development in the Yemen Arab Republic: Strategic Issues in a Capital-Surplus Labor-Short Economy*, p. 21.
46. Consortium for International Development, *Agriculture Sector Analysis, Yemen Arab Republic*, p. 79.
47. World Bank, *Yemen Arab Republic: Development of a Traditional Economy*, p. 68.
48. International Monetary Fund, *International Financial Statistics*, (Washington,

D.C.: International Monetary Fund, 1983).

49. Ibid.

50. Yemen Arab Republic, Central Planning Organization, Statistics Department, *Statistical Year Book, 1981*, p. 184.

51. Yemen Arab Republic, Central Planning Organization, *Second Five-Year Plan (1982-1986)*, chapter 3, p. 24.

52. Ibid.

53. Ibid., chapter 3, table II.

54. Ibid., chapter 2, p. 13.

55. World Bank, *Yemen Arab Republic: Macroeconomic Framework and Investment Priorities of the Second Development Plan (1982-86)*, p. 32.

56. Yemen Arab Republic, Central Planning Organization, *Second Five-Year Plan (1982-1986)*, chapter 3, table V and p. 24.

57. World Bank, *Yemen Arab Republic: Macroeconomic Framework and Investmest Priorities of the Second Development Plan (1982-86)*, p. 32.

58. World Bank, *Yemen Arab Republic: Development of a Traditional Economy*, p. 68.

59. Yemen Arab Republic, Central Planning Organization, Statistics Department, *Statistical Year Book, 1981*, p. 184.

60. World Bank, *Yemen Arab Republic: Development of a Traditional Economy*, p. 68.

61. Yemen Arab Republic, Central Planning Organization, Statistics Department, *Statistical Year Book, 1981*, p. 184.

62. World Bank, *Yemen Arab Republic: Development of a Traditional Economy*, pp. 227 and 232.

63. Ibid., p. 67.

64. Ibid.

65. United States, Department of Commerce, *Foreign Economic Trends and Their Implications for the United States: Yemen Arab Republic*, p. 4.

66. World Bank, *Yemen Arab Republic: Development of a Traditional Economy*, p. 67.

67. Ibid.

68. Ibid., p. 68.

69. *Middle East Economic Digest*, April 10, 1982, p. 58 and June 3, 1983, p. 70.

70. Yemen Arab Republic, Central Planning Organization, Statistics Department, *Statistical Year Book, 1981*, p. 185.

71. World Bank, *Yemen Arab Republic: Development of a Traditional Economy*, p. 94.

72. International Monetary Fund, "International Monetary Fund Report on the Yemen Arab Republic (Article IV Consultation)," table 39.

73. *Middle East Economic Digest*, June 3, 1983, p. 70.

74. *The Financial Times*, November 26, 1984.

75. Ibid.

76. Estimates of Dr. Abdulaziz Saqqaf, Department of Economics, Sana'a University, April 1986.

77. World Bank, *Yemen Arab Republic: Development of a Traditional Economy*, p. 194.

SELECTED BIBLIOGRAPHY

Arab News (Jeddah). December 6, 1981.
Birks, J. S. and Sinclair, C. A. *Arab Manpower: The Crisis of Development.* New York: St. Martin's Press, 1980.
Birks, J. S. and Sinclair, C. A. *International Migration and Development in the Arab Region.* Geneva: International Labor Organization, 1980.
Christian Science Monitor. Various issues.
Cohen, John M. and Lewis, David B. *Rural Development in the Yemen Arab Republic: Strategy Issues in a Capital-Surplus Labor-Short Economy.* Cambridge, Massachusetts: Harvard Institute for International Development, 1979.
Consortium for International Development. *Agriculture Sector Analysis, Yemen Arab Republic.* Sana'a, Yemen Arab Republic: Consortium for International Development, 1981.
The Financial Times (London). Various issues.
International Monetary Fund. *Direction of Trade Statistics, 1981.* Washington, D.C.: International Monetary Fund, 1981.
International Monetary Fund. *International Financial Statistics.* Washington, D.C.: International Monetary Fund, 1983.
International Monetary Fund. "International Monetary Fund Report on the Yemen Arab Republic (Article IV Consultation)." Washington, D.C.: International Monetary Fund, 1980.
Kutschera, Chris. "North Yemen: The Gilt Peels Off." *The Middle East.* February 1981.
Kuwait Fund for Arab Economic Development. *Annual Report 1977-78.*
Mandaville, Jon. "Impressions from a Writer's Notebook—At Work in Yemen." *Aramco World Magazine.* May-June 1981.
Mideast Business Exchange. April 1982.
Middle East Economic Digest. Various issues.
Middle East Economic Survey. Various issues.
National Petroleum Council. "Third World Petroleum Development: A Statement of Principles." October 18, 1982. In "U. S. Oil Industry and the Third World." *Energy Detente.* November 11, 1982.

New York Times. Various issues.
OAPEC Bulletin. January 1983.
Sherbiny, N. A. and Sirageldin, Ismail. "Expatriate Labor and Economic Growth: Saudi Demand for Egyptian Labor," in *Rich and Poor States in the Middle East: Egypt in the New Arab Order,* eds. Malcolm H. Kerr and El Sayed Yassin. Boulder, Colorado: Westview Press, 1982.
Siragledin, Ismail. "Labor Adoption in the Oil Exporting Countries," in *Manpower Planning in the Oil Countries,* ed. N. A. Sherbiny. Greenwich, Connecticut: JAI Press Inc., 1981.
Swanson, Jon. *Emigration and Economic Development: The Case of the Yemen Arab Republic.* Boulder, Colorado: Westview Press, 1979.
United Nations. *Year Book of International Trade Statistics 1980.* New York: United Nations, 1981.
United States. Department of Commerce. *Foreign Economic Trends and Their Implications for the United States: Yemen Arab Republic.* Washington, D.C.: United States Government Printing Office, 1981.
United States. Department of Commerce. *Marketing in the Yemen Arab Republic.* Washington, D.C.: United States Government Printing Office, 1981.
United States. Department of the Interior. *Minerals Yearbook, 1978-79.* Vol. 3. Area Reports: International. Washington, D.C.: United States Government Printing Office, 1981.
Universal Postal Union. International Bureau. *Yemen Arab Republic: Situation of Postal Services and Technical Assistance Needs.* Bern: International Postal Union, 1981. (Translation from French.)
World Bank. *Manpower Development in the Yemen Arab Republic.* Report no. 3181a-YAR. Washington, D.C.: World Bank, March 26, 1981.
World Bank. "Yemen Arab Republic Country Economic Memorandum Current Position and Projects." Report no. 5621-YAR. Washington, D.C., June 25, 1985. Mimeographed.
World Bank. *Yemen Arab Republic: Development of a Traditional Economy.* Washington, D.C.: World Bank, 1981.
World Bank. *Yemen Arab Republic: Macroeconomic Framework and Investment Priorities of the Second Development Plan (1982-1986).* Washington, D.C.: World Bank, 1981. Mimeographed.
World Bank. *Yemen Arab Republic—Manufacturing Industries: Performance, Policies, and Prospects.* Washington, D.C.: World Bank, 1981.
World Bank. *Yemen Arab Republic: Urban Sector Report.* Washington,

D.C.: World Bank, 1981.

Yemen Arab Republic. Central Bank of Yemen. Research Department. *Financial Statistical Bulletin.* January-March 1984 and 1985. Mimeographed.

Yemen Arab Republic. Central Planning Organization. Statistics Department. *Statistical Year Book 1979-1980, 1981, 1982, 1983.*

Yemen Arab Republic. Central Planning Organization. "Fourth Year Annual Report of the Second Five-Year Plan." February 1985. Mimeographed. In Arabic.

Yemen Arab Republic. Central Planning Organization. *First Five-Year Plan (1976/77-1980/81).*

Yemen Arab Republic. Central Planning Organization. *Second Five-Year Plan (1982-1986).* March 1982.

Yemen Arab Republic. The Confederation of Yemeni Development Associations. Central Planning Organization. Statistics Department. *Summary, Final Results of the Cooperative Population Census.* February 1981.

Yemen Arab Republic. Ministry of Agriculture. Working paper. 1982. Mimeographed.

Yemen Arab Republic. Ministry of Education. Working paper. 1982. Mimeographed.

Yemen Arab Republic. Ministry of Electricity and Water. Working paper. 1982. Mimeographed.

Yemen Arab Republic. Ministry of Public Works. Working paper. 1982. Mimeographed.

Yemen Arab Republic. Working paper on the extraction industry. 1982. Mimeographed.

Zabarah, Mohammed Ahmed. *Yemen: Traditionalism versus Modernity.* New York: Praeger, 1982.

INDEX

Abdul-Ghani, Abdul Aziz (Prime Minister) 10
Abu Dhabi 180; *see also* foreign aid, Abu Dhabi Fund for Economic Development
Aden (capital of P.D.R.Y.), Gulf of, port of, 6-7, 9, 11, 40, 70, 72, 75-76, 79, 81, 129, 131, 139
Afghanistan 2
Africa 5, 40, 81, 118, 126, 140, 149, 163
Agency for International Development *see* foreign aid
agriculture 1, 4, 10, 11, 26, 32-33, 36, 47, 50, 52, 70, 74, 82, 85-87, 90, 92-118, 126, 144, 153, 157-158, 161, 176-179, 182; Agricultural Credit Bank 106, 109-110; Agricultural Credit Fund 106; Center for Scientific Agricultural Research 92; animal husbandry 93, 96, 97, 99, 102- 103, 106, 108, 110-112, 114; cereals 97-100, 101, 105-106, 108, 111-113, 116, 118, 157-158; coffee 3, 6, 8, 12, 92, 99-100, 105-106, 108-109, 111, 113, 126, 161, 171; Cooperative Agricultural Credit Bank 109; Cooperative Credit Bank 109; cotton 92, 99-100, 105-106, 108-113, 116, 126-127, 161-162, 171; economic output 55, 93, 102, 118, 121; exports of agricultural products 3, 6, 8, 12, 92, 97-102, 106, 108, 111, 113-114, 157, 171; fishing 24, 26, 53, 93-95, 97, 103, 106, 110-112, 114, 163; food processing 103, 122-126, 163; forestry 24, 26, 53, 93-95, 97, 102, 110, 112, 114, 127; labor force in 18-19, 22, 24-25, 41-42, 46, 52-54, 92- 93, 97, 99-100, 102, 104, 109, 111-112, 116; land for 92-93, 96-99, 101, 106-107, 109, 112, 115, 127; modernization of 96-97, 102-104, 106-107, 109-111; *see also* First Five-Year Plan, foreign aid, Ministry of Agriculture, Second Five-Year Plan, Southern Uplands Rural Development Project, Third Five-Year Plan, Three-Year Program, Tihama Agricultural Development Program, water
Ahmad, Imam 7-8
Al Arashi, Abdul Karim 10

Al Badr, Crown Prince Muhammad 7-8
Al Din, Hamid, family of 6
Alef field, Alef 1, 134-136
Al Ghashmi, Lt. Col. Ahmed Hussein 10
Al Hamdi, Col. Ibrahim Mohammed 10
Al Hamoorah 138
Al Husayn, Al Hadi Yahya 5
Ali, Mohammad 6
'Ali 5
Al Iryani, Qadi Abdul Rahman 9; regime of 9-10
Al Jawf *see* Jawf
Al Sallal, Col. Abdullah 8; regime of 9; *see also* Revolution of 1962
Al Yaman 4
Amey Roadstone Construction 78
Arab Fund for Economic and Social Development *see* foreign aid
Arabian Empire 5
Arabian Peninsula 1, 3-4, 11, 15, 40-41, 43, 55, 59, 62, 81, 92-93, 96, 99, 127, 132, 136, 152-153, 161
Arabian/Persian Gulf 4, 137
Arab League *see* League of Arab States
Arabsat 81
Asia, trade with, 40, 159-160
Asian labor 43, 60, 62, 147
austerity program *see* Second Five-Year Plan
Australia 139, 160
aviation *see* civil aviation

Bab El Mandeb, strait of, 1, 75
Bahrain 2, 15, 17, 41, 62
Bakil tribe 8
balance of payments *see* trade
Bangladesh 139
Beida 71-73, 75, 88
Berger, Louis, International 77
Birks and Sinclair study 61-62
Boeing 78-79
Britian *see* United Kingdom
British Petroleum (BP) 83, 133-134
budgets *see* First-Five Year Plan, Ministry of Finance, Second Five-Year Plan, Third Five-Year Plan, Three-Year Program

Bureau Central d'Etudes pour les Equipments d'outre Mer 142
Bureau de Recherches Geologiques et Minieres 138

Cable and Wireless 80
Cairo 9
Caltex Petroleum Corporation 131
Canada 134
canals 106, 113
census *see* population
central administration 23-24
Central Bank 10, 45, 167, 177, 179
Central Planning Organization (CPO) 10, 15, 17, 22, 40, 74, 145, 167
China, *see* People's Republic of China
CIT-Alcatel 80
civil aviation 71, 77-80; *see also* International Civil Aviation Organization, Yemen Airways, Yemeni Civil Aviation and Meteorology Authority
civil courts 3
civil war 9, 175
climate 1, 92, 93, 98, 101 *see also* meteorology
Command Council 10
communications 10, 26, 53, 54, 71, 76, 80-82, 94, 95; telecommunications 78, 80, 178; telephone system 74, 81; television 81; *see also* Ministry of Communications
Confederation of Yemeni Development Associations (CYDA) 15, 17, 40, 47
Constain International 78
Constituent People's Assembly 11
constitution 3, 9, 11
construction 22, 24, 26, 29, 41, 43, 48, 49, 52-54, 62, 73, 94-95, 117, 128, 141, 144, 147-148, 158, 176
Consultative Council 9
Cooperative Agricultural Credit Bank *see* agriculture
Cooperative Credit Bank *see* agriculture
copper *see* mining and quarrying
"Corrective Movement" 10
Coup, of June 1974, 10
Crown Prince Badr *see* Al Badr

Departments of Petroleum and Mineral Resources *see* Ministry of Petroleum and Mineral Resources
Deutsche Shell 133
Dhamar 71, 73, 75, 84, 86, 88, 90, 93, 97, 111, 135

Dhofar 6
Djibouti 2, 40, 72, 75, 79, 81, 164-165
Dorsch 89
drought, of 1983 and 1984, 87, 111, 116, 118, 121, 161

earthquake, of 1982, 86, 111, 121
East Africa *see* Africa
economy, economic development *see* First Five-Year Plan, gross domestic product, Second Five-Year Plan, Third Five-Year Plan, Three-Year Program
education 10, 18, 21, 28, 40, 48, 51, 54, 55, 57, 58, 64, 65, 69, 145, 176, 178; and work 18, 22, 145, 147; literacy 18, 21, 22, 28, 31, 51, 64, 65, 69; manpower training 29, 34, 35, 46, 50, 59, 64, 65, 106, 107, 146, 148; of women 18, 21, 29, 31, 32 *see also* Ministry of Education
Egypt, Arab Republic of, 2, 4, 6, 7, 9, 63, 79, 126, 175
elections, general, 9
electricity 26, 46, 49, 53, 54, 71, 74, 82, 87, 89, 90, 94, 95, 122, 132, 178-179; *see also* Ministry of Electricity and Water, Yemen General Electric Corporation
emigration 3, 8, 12, 13, 15, 25, 40, 51, 57, 59, 62, 63, 66, 103, 107, 116, 117, 137, 138, 144, 147, 148, 152, 155, 158, 161, 166, 182; long-term 16, 17, 66; short-term 15, 17, 19, 20, 40, 59, 66, 70, 104, 161; Yemeni workers *in* Saudi Arabia 15-17, 31, 42, 46, 59, 61, 63, 64, 147, 152
employment *see* labor force, emigration
energy sector 128-138, 159, 171; natural gas 133, 134; *see also* electricity, Ministry of Petroleum and Mineral Resources, oil
England *see* United Kingdom
Eritrea 4
Ethiopia 12, 45, 12, 72, 75, 79, 99, 100
Europe 40, 159
European Economic Community (EEC) 159, 163, 166
Excem-Madrid 139
expatriate laborers in the Yemen Arab Republic 32, 38, 39, 41, 42, 52, 55, 57, 144, 147
exports *see* trade
Exxon 83, 136

farming *see* agriculture
Federal Republic of Germany 73, 78, 79,

Federal Republic of Germany *cont'd* 133, 138, 141, 160, 164-165, 175, 177-181; *see also* Yemen Shell Oil
Fifth Highway Project 74, 75
First Five-Year Plan (1976/77-1980/81) 13, 18, 22, 24, 25, 28, 30, 36, 48, 50, 53, 88, 93, 97, 101, 106, 109, 116, 128, 139, 142, 152-154, 157-159, 161-163, 167, 175-177, 179
fishing *see* agriculture
Food for Peace 176
foreign aid 11, 12, 73, 87, 89, 113, 114, 129, 137, 138, 141, 142, 144, 153, 166-167, 170, 172-182, 184; Abu Dhabi Fund for Economic Development 73, 89, 153, 179; Agency for International Development, U. S. (A.I.D.) 88, 89, 153, 176; Arab Fund for Economic and Social Development 73, 81, 90, 175, 178-181; International Development Association (I.D.A.) (World Bank affiliate) 39, 73, 74, 76, 88, 90, 105, 114, 133, 144, 175, 177-181; International Finance Corporation 135; International Fund for Agricultural Development 114; Iraqi Fund for External Development 78; Islamic Development Bank 129, 180-181; Kuwait Fund for Arab Economic Development 73, 76, 105, 144, 153, 177, 179-181; Overseas Development Administration, U. K., 114; Overseas Economic Cooperation Fund, Japan, 77; Overseas Private Investment Corporation 135; Saudi Development Fund 89; United Nations Capital Development Fund 144; United Nations Development Program 79, 82, 176; United States Development Program 139; World Food Program 176
foreign trade *see* trade
forestry, products *see* agriculture
Fourth Highway Project 74
France 40, 78, 81, 159-160, 180-181; *see also* Bureau Central d'Etudes pour les Equipments d'outre Mer, Bureau de Recherches Geologiques et Minieres, CIT-Alcatel, Sofreavia, Thomson-CSF
Free Yemenis, organization of, 8, 9

gas *see* energy sector
General Corporation for Salt Manufacturing 130
General Organization for Petroleum and Minerals 129
General People's Congress 11

geography 1-3, 47
Germany *see* Federal Republic of Germany
Gibb, Sir Alexander and Partners 76
Gitec 89
governorates (*liwa*) 3, 70-72, 93
Great Britian *see* United Kingdom
gross domestic product (GDP) 55, 59, 93-95, 116-118, 121, 155, 158, 170
Gulf of Oman 12
Gulf states 19, 20, 40, 50, 66, 79, 140, 147, 163, 174-176

Hadramut Kingdom 4
Hajjah 71-72, 75, 84, 88, 93, 97
Halcrow, Sir William and Partners 77
Hanab Stevin Pipelines Middle East 89
Hashed confederation 7, 9
Hashed tribe 8-9
Hashemite 5, 6
Hassan, Prince 8
Hazen and Sawyer 89
health, health care 10, 17, 29, 42, 48, 50, 53-54, 57, 65, 69, 113, 176; disease 88; qat use 99-100; *see also* Ministry of Health
High Council for Water Resources 90
Highway Authority 34, 73-74, 76
Himyarites, Himyarite Kingdom 4-5
Hodeidah 3, 7-8, 35, 70-75, 77-80, 82-85, 87-89, 93, 97, 106, 129-131, 133, 141, 144, 163, 177; port of 70, 76, 133
housing 48-49, 122, 158; Housing Credit Bank 144; real estate sector 122; urban 25, 48; *see also* Ministry of Municipalities and Housing
Hunt Oil Company 83, 98, 134-136; *see also* Alef field, Yemen Hunt Oil Company
Hyundai Corporation 135

Ibb 70-72, 75, 82, 84-89, 93, 97-98, 106
Imam, Imamate 5-10, 70
imports *see* trade
India 41, 79, 139, 147, 160
Indian Ocean 1, 6
industry 43, 50, 52, 62-63, 82, 87, 90, 92, 103, 111, 121-149, 171, 176, 178, 182; building materials 122, 140-143, 148, 171; cement 49, 83, 141-142, 144, 151; chemicals 122-124, 139-140, 159; energy for 130; financing of 48, 143-145, 147, 177, 182-184; manpower for 24, 50, 52-55, 122, 127, 145-149; manufacturing 22,

Index 193

industry *continued*
24-26, 55, 94-95, 117, 122-123, 141, 144; textiles 8, 122-123, 125-128; *see also* agriculture, food processing; construction; First Five-Year Plan; foreign aid; mining and quarrying; Second Five-Year Plan; Third Five-Year Plan; Three-Year Program; Yemen Industrial Bank
inflation 41, 43, 46, 49, 50, 167, 182
International Civil Aviation Organization (Geneva) 78
International Development Association *see* foreign aid
International Finance Corporation *see* foreign aid
International Fund for Agricultural Development *see* foreign aid
investment *see* foreign aid; industry, financing of; Yemen Bank for Resconstruction and Development; Yemen Company for Investment and Financing; Yemen Reconstruction and Development Bank
Iran 2, 103
Iraq 2, 7, 129, 175, 179-181; *see also* foreign aid, Iraqi Fund for External Development
Ishikawajima-Harima Heavy Industries 142
Islam 3, 5, 8; Islamic courts 3; Prophet Mohammed 5; Shari'a 3, 8, 35; Shi'a 5; *sunna* 5; Sunni 5; Waqf 93
Islamic Development Bank *see* foreign aid
Italy 7, 81, 160, 164-165, 180-181 ; *see also* Telettra

Japan 139, 159-160, 162-165, 180-181; *see also* foreign aid, Ishikawajima-Harima Heavy Industries, Marubeni Corporation, Mitsubishi Corporation, Nissho-Iwai Company, Sumitomo Corporation, Toyo Menka Kaisha
Jawf 71-72, 87, 98, 115
Jordan 2
judicial system 3

kadas 3
Korea *see* North Korea, South Korea
Kreditanstalt fuer Wiederaufbau 89
Kuwait 2, 15, 17, 41, 62, 79, 128-129, 140, 142, 153, 163, 177-178, 180-181; *see* foreign aid, Kuwait Fund for Arab Economic Development
Kuwait National Petroleum Company 129

labor force 19-28, 31, 41, 43, 55, 122, 136-137, 145, 148-149, 152-153, 157, 161, 182; and children 19-20, 33, 41, 93; manpower planning 15, 51-65, 145; shortages 40-41, 49-50, 52, 55, 59, 97, 99, 101, 104, 107, 109, 111-112, 116-117, 127, 144-149, 157, 161-162; wages 42-51, 55, 57, 116-117, 144-145, 147-148, 152-153, 157, 161-162; and women 19-20, 41, 52; Yemeni expatriate labor 3, 8, 11, 13, 22-23, 40-42, 60-63, 92, 116, 137-138, 146-147, 152-153, 167, 171, 174, 182-183; *see also* Asian labor, emigration, expatriate laborers *in* YAR
Lam field 134
League of Arab States 81
Lebanon 2
literacy *see* education
liwa see governorates
Local Development Association (LDA) 47-48
long-term emigration *see* emigration, Free Yemenis

Mahweet 71-72, 87, 93, 97
Malaysia 160
Mameluke 6
manufacturing *see* industry
Marib (former capital, dam) 4, 11, 71-73, 75, 87, 92, 98, 115, 131, 134-136
Marib-Jawf basin 98, 134-138, 159, 171, 182
Marubeni Corporation 139-140, 163
McDonnell Douglas 78-79
medical services *see* health
Medina 5
Meem field 134
meteorology 79, 96
Mexico 139
military service 43, 167
Minean Kingdom 4
mineral resources *see* Mineral Wealth and Petroleum Corporation, Ministry of Petroleum and Mineral Resources, Yemen Oil and Minerals Corporation
Mineral Wealth and Petroleum Corporation 138
mining and quarrying 26, 53-54, 92, 94-95, 122, 125, 128, 130, 138-139, 178, 182; building materials 49, 140-143; copper 138
Ministry of Agriculture 34, 104, 107, 109
Ministry of Communications 34, 81
Ministry of Development 74

194 Index

Ministry of Education 28-29, 38, 51
Ministry of Electricity and Water 83, 88, 91; see also Yemen General Electric Corporation
Ministry of Finance 10
Ministry of the Interior 22, 24
Ministry of Municipalities and Housing 144
Ministry of Petroleum and Mineral Resources 130
Ministry of Planning 126
Ministry of Public Works 74, 88
Mitsubishi Corporation 76-77
Mobil International Petroleum Corporation 131
Mocha 70, 72, 75, 86, 130; port of 73, 76-77

nahayas 3
National Assembly 9
National Charter 11, 183
National Company for Construction Materials and Industry 141-142
national disposable income (NDI) 43-44, 152
National Institute of Public Administration (NIPA) 34-35
National Water Supply Authority (National Water and Sewage Authority) 34, 37, 88
National Yemeni Union 9
natural gas *see* energy sector
Near East 5
Netherlands 77, 79, 89-90, 160, 164-165, 179; *see also* Deutsche Shell, Hanab Stevin Pipelines Middle East, Dirk Verstoep, Volker Stevin Pipelines
Nissho-Iwai Company 142
nonalignment, policy of, 12, 179
North Korea 139
Nouisser, Ameen 90

oil, oil states 11, 12, 15, 26, 60, 62, 98, 116, 128, 130, 135-138, 152-153, 166-167, 176; explorations and discoveries 83, 131-138, 159, 171, 182; imports 129-131, 136, 154, 159, 171, 176; prices 60, 128, 136, 166; revenues 66, 136-138, 182; subsidies for 129, 133, 137, 178; *see also* energy sector, Mineral Wealth and Petroleum Corporation, Ministry of Petroleum and Mineral Resources, Yemen Refining and Marketing Company

Oman 2, 12, 92
Organization of the Petroleum Exporting Countries (OPEC) 137, 180-181
Ottoman Empire 6
Overseas Development Administration *see* foreign aid
Overseas Private Investment Corporation *see* foreign aid

Pakistan 2, 41
parliament *see* Constituent People's Assembly
People's Council 3
People's Democratic Republic of Yemen (P.D.R.Y.) (South Yemen) 1-2, 11-12, 43, 72-73, 75, 81, 136, 162-165
People's Republic of China (P.R.C.) 7, 73, 127, 160, 163-165, 175, 177-181
Permanent Constitution 9, 11
Persian Empire 5
Petrofac Incorporated 136
petroleum *see* oil
Philippines 43, 60
political parties 10; *see also* National Yemeni Union
population 3, 10, 15-21, 25-26, 61, 65, 70-72, 88, 93; rural-to-urban migration 19, 25, 70, 102; *see also* emigration
ports 62, 71, 76-79; *see also* Hodeidah, Mocha
Portugal 6
postal system 81-82; *see also* Universal Postal Union
Preece Cardew and Rider (PCR) 81
principal cities *see* Hodeidah, Sana'a, Taiz

qat (*catha eduli*) 3, 99-100, 105, 111
Qataban Kingdom 4
Qatar 2, 15, 17, 40-41
Queen of Sheba 4; balloon 76

Ras Al Kateeb 76, 85-86
Rassuli Dynasty 6
Red Sea 1-2, 4, 6, 12, 72, 75, 77, 98, 133-135, 137
The Republic 5, 8
Republicans 9
Revolution, of 1962, 7, 9, 65, 70, 175
roads 48, 62, 71, 73-76, 106, 113, 142, 177-179; *see also* Ministry of Public Works
Roman Empire 4
Romania 130-131
Rompetrol 130

Index 195

O. W. Roskill Industrial Consultants 139
Royalists 9
rural-to-urban migration *see* population
Rural Water Department *see* Ministry of Public Works
Russia *see* Union of Soviet Socialist Republics
Saadah 5, 71-73, 75-77, 85, 88, 98
Saba, Sabean Kingdom 4-5
Salif 7, 77, 85, 130, 133, 135, 140; salt mine 139-140, 162-163, 177
Salih, Lt. Col. Ali Abdullah (President) 10-11; regime of 11
Samwhan Corporation 135
Sana'a (capital) 3, 5-8, 35, 49, 70-75, 77-80, 82-85, 87-90, 98, 106, 122, 127, 129-130, 134-135, 139-140, 142, 177; Sana'a basin study 115; *see also* University of Sana'a
Sana'a Higher Technical Institute 33
Sana'a Technical School 33
Sante Fe International 133
Saudi Arabia 1-2, 9, 15, 40, 59-63, 72-73, 75, 78-81, 89, 133-134, 159-160, 162-165, 174-176, 179-181; Asir Province 1; Yemeni Workers in 15-17, 19, 31, 40-42, 46, 59-64; *see also* foreign aid, Saudi Development Fund
Saudi National Commercial Bank 8
Saudi-Yemeni Coordination Council 78-79
schools *see* education
Second Five-Year Plan (1982-1986) 11, 13, 18, 22, 28-29, 31-33, 36, 38, 50-52, 54-59, 61, 63-64, 74, 83, 85-86, 88-89, 93, 100, 102, 109-118, 121-122, 128, 130-131, 133, 138, 140-142, 145, 154-155, 158, 160-163, 167-175; austerity program 45-46, 154, 157, 159
shakla 47, 49
Shari'a *see* Islam
Shell Oil Company 129
Shi'a *see* Islam
short-term emigration *see* emigration
Sinclair and Socknat 22
Singapore 30, 160, 163
Sirageldin, Ismail 62
Sofreavia 78
Solomon, King 4
Somalia 2, 81
Southern Uplands Rural Development Project 10, 73
South Korea 134-135, 140, 160; labor pool 43, 60; *see also* Hyundai Corporation, Korean Petroleum Development Corporation, Samwhan Corporation, Yukong
South Yemen *see* People's Democratic Republic of Yemen
Soviet Union *see* Union of Soviet Socialist Republics
standard of living 42-43, 67, 69, 88, 103, 110, 116, 152, 155, 157, 166
State Electricity Organization 91
states *see* governorates
Strait of Hormouz 12
Strickland and Davis 102
Sudan 2, 79, 126
Suez Canal 12
Sumitomo Corporation 131
sunna see Islam
Sunni *see* Islam
Swanson, Jon, emigration study 42, 46-48
Sweden 81
Swedtel 81
Switzerland 78, 82
Syria 2

Taiwan 140
Taiz (principal city) 3, 6-8, 33, 35, 49, 70-75, 77-80, 82-89, 93, 97-98, 106, 129-130, 142, 177
telecommunications *see* communications
telephone system *see* communications
television *see* communications
Telettra 81
textiles *see* industry
Thailand 43, 60
Third Five-Year Plan (1987-1991) 11, 13, 182
Thomson-CSF 81
Three-Year Program (1973/74-1975/76) 10, 13, 70, 93, 104, 106-107, 128, 138-139, 175, 177-178
Tihama (coastal plain) 1, 3, 6, 93, 97-98, 127, 133
Tihama Agricultural Development Program 177
Tihama Development Authority (TDA) 10, 97, 113-115
Tihama Development Project 73, 106
Toyo Menka Kaisha (Tomen) 133
trade 22, 24, 26, 48, 53-54, 94-95, 117, 121-122, 137, 140, 152-184; balance of payments 8, 10, 41, 43, 45, 50, 92, 101, 104, 106, 111, 166-175; exports 7-8, 102, 105-106, 130, 139, 149, 161-166,

trade *continued*
168-169, 171-173, 182; imports 8, 42-46, 48, 50, 97, 101, 103-107, 117, 121-123, 126, 130, 151, 154-161, 166-174, 179, 182
transportation 10, 26, 46, 48, 53-54, 73-74, 94-95, 110, 123, 130, 135, 142, 149; *see also* civil aviation, Highway Authority, roads
Turkey 139
Turkish Ottoman Empire *see* Ottoman Empire

unemployment 22-23
unification, of North and South Yemen, 11-12
Union of Soviet Socialist Republics (U.S.S.R.) 7, 9, 12-13, 73, 76, 78, 136, 141, 163, 175-181
United Arab Emirates 2, 15, 17, 40-41, 98
United Kingdom 7, 40, 76-81, 160; *see also* Amey Roadstone Construction; British Petroleum; Constain International; foreign aid, Overseas Development Administration; Sir Alexander Gibb and Partners; Peece Cardew and Rider; O. W. Roskill
United Nations (U. N.) 8, 9, 65, 176; *see also* foreign aid, U. N. Capital Development Fund, U. N. Development Program
United States of America (U. S.) 9, 40, 73, 139, 153, 159-160, 164-166, 175-177, 180-181; *see also* Louis Berger International; Boeing; Caltex Petroleum Corporation; Food for Peace; foreign aid, U. S. Agency for International Development, U. S. Development Program; Hazen and Sawyer; Hunt Oil; McDonnell Douglas; Petrofac Incorporated
Universal Postal Union (UPU) 81-82
University of Sana'a 32-37, 92

Verstoep, Dirk, Company 77
Volker Stevin Pipelines 89

wadis (streambed valley) 72, 97-98
Waqf (Islamic religious trust) 93
water and sewerage 26, 47, 49, 53-54, 65, 69-71, 74, 86-90, 94-95, 104, 106, 109-111, 115-116, 122, 177-179; irrigation 3, 11, 46, 48, 86-87, 96-99, 101, 106-107, 109, 111-114, 116, 118, 177; water rights 97, 103; *see also* Ministry of Electricity and Water, Ministry of Public Works, National Water Supply Authority
Westburne Drilling 134
West Germany *see* Federal Republic of Germany
World Bank, studies, 17, 24, 27, 32, 34-36, 40, 42, 46, 49, 51, 54, 57, 59, 60, 62-63, 145, 148, 166, 175-176; *see also* foreign aid
World Food Program *see* foreign aid
World War I 6, 139

Yahya, Imam 6, 7
yaman 4
Yemen Airways (Yemenia) 79-80
Yemen Bank for Reconstruction and Development 129-130
Yemen Company for Glass Manufacturing 143
Yemen Company for Investment and Financing 140
Yemen Company for Salt Packing and Marketing 140, 163
Yemen Fuels Company 129
Yemen General Electric Corporation (YGEC) 34, 83, 90
Yemen Hunt Oil Company 134-135
Yemeni Civil Aviation and Meteorology Authority 79
Yemeni expatriate labor *see* labor
Yemen Industrial Bank (YIB) 140, 143-144
Yemenis abroad *see* emigration, Free Yemenis
Yemen Oil Company (YOC) 129-130
Yemen Oil and Minerals Corporation (YOMINCO) 130-131, 134-136, 138, 140
Yemen Petroleum Company 128
Yemen Reconstruction and Development Bank 9
Yemen Refining and Marketing Company (YRMC) 135
Yemen Salt Mining Corporation 139
Yemen Shell Exploration 133
Yemen Tourism Corporation 11
Yemen Weaving and Textile Corporation 127
Yukong 135
yumn 4

Zabid 72, 106, 115